D1325364

PATTERNS OF RECRUITMENT

AMERICAN POLITICS RESEARCH SERIES

PATTERNS OF RECRUITMENT

A State Chooses Its Lawmakers

LESTER G. SELIGMAN
UNIVERSITY OF ILLINOIS

MICHAEL R. KING
PENNSYLVANIA STATE UNIVERSITY

CHONG LIM KIM
UNIVERSITY OF IOWA

ROLAND E. SMITH
TEXAS TECH UNIVERSITY

RAND McNALLY COLLEGE PUBLISHING COMPANY · CHICAGO

NORTHWEST MISSOURI STATE
UNIVERSITY LIBRARY
MARYVILLE, MISSOURI 64468

AMERICAN POLITICS RESEARCH SERIES
Aaron Wildavsky, Editor

Current Printing (last digit)

15 14 13 12 11 10 9 8 7 6 5 4 3 2 1

Copyright © 1974 by Rand McNally College Publishing Company
All Rights Reserved
Printed in U.S.A.
Library of Congress Catalog Card Number: 74-10405

329
P31p

Table of Contents

List of Figures

List of Tables

Preface

THE EXPERIENCE in conducting this study was as rewarding as the discovery of its findings about patterns of recruitment. The study began at the University of Oregon in Professor Seligman's graduate seminar on the recruitment of political elites. Professors King, Kim and Smith were then graduate students in political science and members of the seminar. The research design of this study was a product of that seminar. Professor King was the first to join the project and his efforts throughout all phases were vital to the fulfillment of the study. For almost three years, the four of us, joined now and then by others, spent many hours in lively and congenial intellectual discussion including those with the "mobility for lunch bunch" which was one of its sectarian offshoots.

This study is a collective effort. Each one of us has worked on various chapters at various times. We had thought we would acknowledge primary authorship of chapters to particular individuals, but when we finished, we realized we had worked collegially throughout. We decided therefore to omit such attributions. Even though the study was completed a few years after we had conducted our interviews in 1966 and published in 1974, the conditions we have described remain substantially the same as they were in 1966.

The study would have been impossible without the cooperation of the many candidates for the State legislature in Oregon who gave generously of their time for our lengthy interviews. We appreciate their assistance.

We wish to thank the following individuals for their generous assistance at various stages of the study: Professor Robert Ziller, now Chairman of the Department of Psychology at the University of Florida, whose NSF grant in part supported this study at a crucial stage; Dr. Ben Bronfman, now of the Urban Research Section, Oak Ridge National

Laboratory, for his enlightening assistance with methodological problems; Peter Shocket, now Assistant Professor at the University of Nebraska; Maurice Foisy, Assistant Professor of Political Science at Western Washington State University; Don Laws, Associate Professor at Southern Oregon College; the late and lamented Charles Garrison, who at the time of his tragic passing was Assistant Professor of Political Science at Colorado State University; Professor Roland Pellegrin, former Director of CASEA and Professor of Sociology at the University of Oregon, now at Penn State University; and Professor Lawrence Pierce, Department of Political Science, University of Oregon.

We are grateful to the following agencies: The Offices of Scholarly Research, the graduate school, and the Wallace Fund of the University of Oregon, and The College of Liberal Arts Central Fund for Research, Pennsylvania State University. We alone are responsible for the errors and shortcomings of this study.

A Selected Bibliography on Political Recruitment appears at the end of the book.

We wish to express our gratitude to Lawrence Malley and our Editor, Kevin Thornton, both of Rand McNally, whose commitment to high standards sustained us throughout the tedious process of getting the manuscript ready for publication.

To our wives, Judith, Karen, Hwa, and Carol, who endured our work with patience and understanding, we dedicate this book with all our love and appreciation.

Lester G. Seligman
Michael R. King
Chong Lim Kim
Roland E. Smith

CHAPTER I

The Democratic Recruitment Process: The Selection of State Legislators

INTRODUCTION

The development of democracy is associated with changes in the process of selection of political leaders and public officials, designed to reduce the social distinction and difference in power between the citizen and elective officials. In various ways and at various rates in democratic countries,[1] legal, social and religious barriers to the participation of all citizens in choosing elective public officials were removed; the proportion of the electorate eligible to compete for public office was steadily enlarged; groups and parties that would sponsor candidates became organized; rules were instituted that opened the selection process to public participation while protecting the privacy of the citizen's choice, and last, but not least, the duties and responsibilities of elective public office were made specific and limited so that, as Madison stated: "The interest of the man would be connected with the constitutional rights of the place."[2] The preceding legal changes thus removed historic barriers to

[1] Stein Rokkan, "The Structuring of Mass Politics in the Smaller European Democracies: A Developmental Typology," in Otto Stammer, ed., *Party Systems, Party Organizations and the Politics of New Masses* (3rd International Conference on Comparative Sociology, Berlin, 1968; Berlin: Institut für Politische Wissenschaft an der Freien Universität Berlin, 1968), pp. 26–65; Robert R. Palmer, *The Age of the Democratic Revolution: A Political History of Europe and America, 1760–1800* (2 vols.; Princeton, N.J.: Princeton University Press, 1969–1970).
[2] *The Federalist Papers*, Mentor Books (New York: New American Library, 1961), No. 51, p. 322.

popular participation and to the accountability and responsibility of elective public officials.

In the United States, in keeping with its federal structure, elective legislators are chosen through electoral systems that vary from state to state. Such systems generally specify the apportionment of seats in the legislatures, the minimum qualifications of candidates and voters, procedures for the nomination of candidates, and the formulae for scoring votes. But the informal relationships which underlie the politics of recruitment are far more varied and complex than the statutory prescriptions of electoral systems. The way political aspirants maneuver for position and prominence, the ingenious tactics and propaganda of rival campaign organizations are peculiarly endemic to the recruitment process. The electoral laws governing recruitment tell us little about the interactions among candidates, their sponsors, opponents and the electorate. This book concerns the interaction patterns in the recruitment of state legislators in Oregon.

Oregon was one of the earliest states (1910) to adopt the direct primary as the prescribed method for nominating candidates for elective office. The primary was adopted together with the initiative, referendum and recall, which became identified as the "Oregon system." The direct primary broke new ground when it provided that all registered voters were allowed to participate in the selection of party nominees for elective public offices. The assumptions that underlie the direct primary were the classic liberal correctives for the evils of monopoly.[3] The Progressives who advocated the primary to restore political competition applied the same logic to the problem of oligarchical control in political parties and elections that they applied to the problem of economic monopoly. Accordingly, under the provisions of the direct primary, party leaders could not bar the candidacy of any registered party voter who wished to seek elective office. The primary ordained that the electorate would choose the candidates, not a caucus of party leaders in a smoke-filled room, nor a party convention of paid party workers. The proponents of the direct primary hoped that the removal of such barriers to candidacy and competition among candidates would enable them to gain influence in parties, prevent oligarchy in political parties, and weaken oligarchical tendencies in state legislatures and Congress.

Such political reforms proved as superficial as the economic reforms of the Progressives. Both political and economic reformers neglected the social preconditions that would make their reforms effective.

[3] Samuel P. Hays, *The Response to Industrialism, 1885–1914* (Chicago: University of Chicago Press, 1957), pp. 154–155.

We will show that despite the influence of the direct primary, the processes of recruitment in some legislative districts remain oligarchical, in others they are dominated by one party, and are competitive only in a few districts. Ironically, in still other legislative districts, the direct primary serves only to reinforce the oligarchical control that the proponents of the direct primary intended to overthrow.[4]

The various patterns of recruitment became discernible to us through interviews with all the candidates for the state legislature, losers as well as winners. Candidates were interviewed in three waves, corresponding to each significant phase in the recruitment process: after filing, after the primary election, and after the general election. In this way we were able to trace the changes in the relationships among the candidates, primary groups, political parties and associations.

We chose to study the recruitment of state legislators for several reasons. The state legislative office is the most common starting point in the political career of elective officials.[5] For many political aspirants, the campaign for this office is their first election experience. As in other elections, the incumbents are difficult, if not impossible, to unseat. Yet many neophyte candidates who are defeated after their first attempt, try again. A smaller percentage of the defeated never make another attempt. Because such a high percentage of first-time losers elect to run again, we sought to determine the perceived net costs and benefits of defeat that might explain such resiliency among candidates.

Legislative seats are frequently vacant because many first term legislators and some veteran legislators do not seek reelection. However, many are eager to replace them. The position of state legislator attracts a variety of political aspirants because the qualifications for office are so ambiguous and the costs of campaigning are moderate. In addition, the state legislature is often a common stepping stone to higher political office. By observing those who campaign for office and the respective methods of both the successful and the unsuccessful, the difficulty of recruitment onto the "first rung" of elective office could be assessed. Thus, election campaigns for the state legislature resemble a turnstile through which pass all who seek admission to public office: the incumbents, the new recruits, and the candidates who were defeated before and wish to try again.

The Oregon state legislator, like his counterpart in most other states, holds a marginal position. The office of state legislator is a part-

[4] Frank J. Sorauf, *Party and Representation* (New York: Atherton, 1963), Chapter V.
[5] Joseph A. Schlesinger, *Ambition and Politics* (Chicago: Rand McNally, 1966).

3

time occupation. The legislature convenes once every two years for six months or a little less. The legislator receives a modest salary, so that he must continue working at his regular occupation. He has but one secretary and no staff. Tenure in office is often insecure because state legislators are especially vulnerable to electoral tides that sweep the state and/or the nation. There are few privileges that the office bestows. At the time of our study, Oregon legislators did not even have private offices. Every two years, for six months, a legislator leaves his home and his constituency and goes to the state capital where he seems to recede from public view. As a rule, the local and state-wide newspapers do not give much coverage to the legislator's activities, except when scandals are discovered or taxes are being discussed. Proceedings of legislative committee meetings or floor debates are not published. It is understandable that legislators have complained that their constituents did not understand their role, and hold them in low regard. When citizens turn to the legislators, it is usually to complain and criticize. Legislators bridle under the excessively moralistic judgments made about their performances and the unreasonable demands made upon them to run errands for their constituents.[6] It is no wonder that after each term some legislators decide not to seek reelection. Thus, neither private citizen nor full-time official—underpaid, overworked and unhonored, the state legislator may receive less public regard as an elective public official than he did as a private citizen.

Yet, in spite of these working conditions, every two years many new political aspirants seek the office of state legislator. One of the reasons they do, we discovered, is that they are naive and ambitious. They are naive about the costs and demands of candidacy and of office holding. Novice candidates tend to minimize the costs and exaggerate both the intrinsic and extrinsic rewards of campaigning and legislative service. The rookie candidate usually entertains high political aspirations. He has his head in the clouds in sharp contrast with the tougher veteran legislator who is more aware of the hazards in public office. Such naive perceptions are functional for the system because they ensure the steady flow of new aspirants, and sustain political competition. Grave realism and greater sophistication at this stage of a budding political career would discourage many potential candidates from running.

The recruitment of candidates for elective office is generally defined as one of the principal functions of political parties. Yet, studies of recruitment in several American states indicate that the role of political parties in the recruitment process varies considerably from state to state.

[6] John C. Wahlke, *et al.*, *The Legislative System* (New York: Wiley, 1962), pp. 300–308.

Party Instigation of Candidacy in Six States[7]

State	% of State Legislators Instigated by Party
New Jersey	69
Pennsylvania	43
California	20
Wisconsin	21
Ohio	31
Tennessee	17

What then accounts for such differences? What agencies or associations play an active part in encouraging individuals to become candidates? Why are some agencies or associations more active than others in the recruitment of candidates? What factors determine who will win a nomination and who will lose?

We began our investigation with the premise that the interactions among those active in the recruitment process are not random. In Chapter II the model we used defines the variables of the recruitment process and spells out their interrelationships. The model will show how the actors are linked together in a chain of influence that selects some office seekers and transforms them into candidates and office holders and rejects the others.

OPPORTUNITY, SELECTION AND RISK

The recruitment process begins with a pool of socially certified activists who are ready or willing or able to seek political office. In the various legislative districts the number and membership in this pool varies with the factors that affect political opportunity. The breadth or narrowness of recruitment opportunity determines which individuals have the best and which the poorest chances should they seek office. The incentives that public office offers the prospective candidate vary as do the individuals who choose to run. What occupations, education, sex, race and religion are conducive to consideration of a person as a potential candidate? The social profile of the candidates identifies those whom the social and political structure favors for consideration as legislative candidates. An examination of such factors will enable us to compare the candidate pool in Oregon with the pool in other states.

[7] Ibid.; Leon Epstein, *Politics in Wisconsin* (Madison: University of Wisconsin Press, 1958), p. 96; and Sorauf, op. cit., pp. 149–150.

Sharing importance with the personal attributes of candidates are public beliefs about the attributes conducive to recruitment. These public expectations, spurious or genuine, that only those individuals who possess a particular set of attributes have the best chances to be elected, can and do become powerfully self-confirming. Many potential candidates do not become candidates or even consider candidacy because they believe that people like themselves have no chance of success. It is evident that underlying the basic recruitment process (that presumably should choose among individuals for what they can do) are ascriptive factors which hold back and discourage many others because of their social backgrounds, ethnic or religious identifications.[8]

But the restrictions in the selection process determine the potential candidates as much as does the social structure. Where one party is able to dominate a legislative district for a long period of time, a small number of king-makers choose the state legislators. Such restricted selection practices at the starting levels of politics serves only to constrict the pool of political talent from which future Congressmen, Senators and Presidents will come. In the United States, the starting level of the political career is nearly always local, a feature which broadens political opportunity in the nation in some respects, but restricts it in others. Because candidates must reside in the districts they represent, each of the many local constituencies may launch individuals into public life, and thus, in the aggregate, expand political opportunity in the nation as a whole. However, the same local residence requirement reinforces parochial biases and stereotypes which bar some capable candidates and thus constrict political opportunity.

A candidate's home district shapes the character of the recruitment process for him. The social and economic structure and the degree of political competition within and between parties distinguish four types of legislative districts: (1) the urban two-party, (2) the urban one-party, (3) the rural two-party, and (4) the rural one-party. The social diversity-homogeneity of a district and the degree of political competition in each district type determines who the principal actors in recruitment will be, whether the political party will be important, and the recruitment phase that will prove decisive (chapter IV).

Each of the four types of legislative district in Oregon has a particular socio-economic and political complexion. In the rural one-party district most of the citizens are farmers, small town merchants, farm

---

[8] Judson Jones, "Expectations of Political Opportunity," (unpublished seminar paper, University of Oregon, n.d.). This paper presents an analysis of our data with regard to candidates' expectations and disclosed significant ascriptive factors that would bar or disadvantage some people from running for the state legislature.

workers, loggers, and some professionals. A handful of leading citizens who identify with the same party control the political life. The rural two-party district resembles its one-party counterpart in style of life, except that social cleavages divide the electorate into two opposing camps. Two religious denominations may divide sharply, or farmers may battle for influence with the Main Street businessmen. The homogeneity of small rural communities magnifies frictions or rigidifies consensus.

The selection process in each district is distinct, because a different phase of the process is decisive. At one extreme, in single-party rural districts, candidates are virtually elected the day they file for office because they are never challenged. At the other extreme, in urban competitive districts, candidates are challenged throughout all phases of recruitment. Such differences in selection diversify the patterns of relationship between candidates and sponsors. Such relationships or mechanisms fall into four types: agency, conscription, cooptation, and self-starting (chapter VI).

Candidates who are agents represent interest groups and serve as their voice in the legislature. Agents are beholden only to their sponsors. Conscripted candidates consent to run only because they are loyal to their party and recognize that the party must have a candidate. They usually represent the minority party in districts where the majority party dominates. Coopted candidates, found in some districts, are prominent individuals (civic leaders, news broadcasters, members of "old" families, famous athletes, etc.) who are persuaded to run in order to strengthen the party list. Coopted candidates become prestigious spokesmen for interest groups or party factions and enhance their standing among the electorate. Self-starters, as the term implies, are individuals who run without any apparent sponsors. Such candidates run in order to advertise themselves, hoping that the publicity will raise their status in the community or bring them clients and customers.

Just as candidates vary, so do their sponsors vary in number and kind among legislative districts. In one district, parties actively seek out individuals and importune them to become candidates, while in another, party leaders sit on the side lines and interest groups actively sponsor and groom candidates. Interest groups are sometimes active and at other times less so. The activity of parties and interest groups does not vary exactly with the degree of party competitiveness.

The relationship between a candidate and his sponsors contributes specific meaning to that elusive concept called representation.[9] In recent

---

[9] Hannah Pitkin, *The Concept of Representation* (Berkeley: University of California Press, 1967), p. 56.

years several trends have added new dimensions to representation. The growth of the executive and the bureaucracy has created agencies that have direct relationships with the public and interest groups. The growth in the scope of government is associated with enlarging the agenda of the legislative and the discretion and initiative of the executive. The increasing complexity of issues has made it more difficult to discover clear public demands.[10] Legislators deny that an active public opinion guides their decisions, except on a few vital issues.[11] For what or whom a legislator represents we must look beyond electoral majorities and coalitions to the role of sponsorship in the recruitment of candidates.

Under the laws governing the Oregon direct primary, a simple declaration or a petition allows any registered voter to run for the state legislature. But, what makes a citizen decide to run? That decision, during the recruitment phase which we call candidate "instigation," brings into play motivations, various groups and the incentives to run. For novice candidates, the decision is often an anguished one. The neophyte may be eager to run, but his family and friends may oppose his wishes. Conversely, those closest to him may urge him to run, but the role may seem onerous. The candidate may have the endorsement of his primary group, but the support he needs from other groups may not be forthcoming. In this decision to run, considerable interplay occurs between primary groups and leaders of interest groups and parties. The recruitment process shows once again the fluid boundaries between primary and secondary associations in American politics.[12]

Every phase of recruitment, from the decision to run through the election, may involve risks. At many points a candidate faces the probabilities of defeat and its costs, material and psychological, which vary with the individual's resources and the availability of cushions that reduce his losses. If defeat brings negligible losses in income or social and political status and the rewards are considerable, the incentives to run will remain strong. But, if defeat devastates the losers, the expected rewards become illusory and only the desperate or driven few will seek public office. Our interviews with the losers in the primary and general elections showed how they perceived the political risk of candidacy and the subjective and objective consequences of defeat.

[10] Marvin G. Weinbaum and Dennis R. Judd, "In Search of a Mandated Congress," *Midwest Journal of Political Science*, XIV (May, 1970), pp. 276–302.
[11] Warren E. Miller and Donald E. Stokes, "Constituency Influence in Congress," *American Political Science Review*, LVII (March, 1963), pp. 45–56.
[12] Richard E. Dawson and Kenneth Prewitt, *Political Socialization* (Boston: Little, Brown, 1969).

RECRUITMENT AND THE ROLE CULTURE OF THE STATE LEGISLATURE

Those who perform a particular political role such as state legislators create a distinct role culture which Almond and Verba define as a "set of values, skills, loyalties and cognitive maps."[13] The legislative role culture may contribute to cohesiveness or fragmentation among the role occupants. Such a role culture also determines how much affinity there will be among the legislature, the public or to members of other specialized elites. The role culture thus expresses itself in the overt and subtle conflicts and understandings which characterize the process of legislation.

Recruitment affects the legislative role culture because the subcultures from which legislators are recruited, the process of their selection, the risks and rewards (both present and future), influence the cohesiveness or fragmentation of the legislative elite. Each candidate-role, i.e., coopted, agents, conscripts, or self-starters, reflects (1) a particular orientation to the legislative role and to the legislature, (2) the degree to which legislators give expression to the values and interests of their constituencies, and (3) the extent to which all legislative districts share a common culture that contributes an underlying consensus to the legislature.

We shall distinguish between two types of legislative role cultures: a citizen legislature and a professional legislature. A citizen legislature achieves consensus because its members derive from a relatively homogeneous culture, whereas a professional legislature is a fellowship of political technicians. The members of citizen legislatures share a common culture and a set of values which foster mutual understanding. A professional legislature is comprised of seasoned politicians who work well together because they share common ways of practicing politics.

The consensus of a citizen legislature derives in good measure from the recruitment of legislators. Roots in the culture of the district, deep historic attachments to the state, a consciousness-of-kind among legislators deriving from a particular wave of immigration, or common ancestry in the state are the sources of solidarity in the citizen legislature. Citizen legislators are Oregonians first and foremost; the professional legislators are primarily legislative technicians who represent a particular subculture or section of the state.[14]

[13] Gabriel A. Almond and Sidney Verba, *The Civic Culture* (Princeton: Princeton University Press, 1963), p. 30.
[14] Daniel Elazar, *American Federalism: A View from the States* (New York: Crowell, 1966), pp. 79–116; Samuel C. Patterson, "The Political Cultures of the American States," *Journal of Politics,* XXX (February, 1968), pp. 187–209.

The Oregon legislature functions within a homogeneous political culture whose cohesion due to "overarching sentiments of solidarity exists despite political divisions."[15] Neither party competition, interest conflict, nor the subcultures from which some legislators derive threaten the cohesion of the Oregon polity.

Sponsors contribute to the role culture because they play a critical and continuous role in recruitment. The most common sponsors are interest groups concerned with gaining legislative support for an economic interest. For this reason, sponsors instigate candidacy, organize political campaigns, pay the bills for the use of the mass media, mobilize the electorate, and lobby in the legislature. Candidates and sponsors act in a continuous partnership in all phases of recruitment, both in the constituency and the legislature.

The sponsors' relationship to candidates influences how the candidate will relate to other candidates, both of his own and of the opposing party, because the sponsors are active as a "third house" of the legislature. The sponsor-candidate relationship will also determine what kind of role the novice legislator will play in the legislature. Will he be a dutiful agent or follow his own conscience? Will he be an innovator or a rubber stamp, a proponent or an opponent, a parochial or a cosmopolite? The part he plays is determined in some measure by those who worked to put him in the legislature and who continue to look over his shoulder when he assumes office.

In the citizen legislature, the candidate is essentially *of* his sponsors; in the professional legislature, the candidate is only *for* his sponsors, but does not necessarily share their culture. In the professional legislature, the sponsors are concerned with the tangible and symbolic policy *outputs*. Whereas, in the citizen legislature, sponsors attach greater weight to their affinity with their candidates and the outputs are taken for granted.

In which legislature is recruitment more congruent with legislative decision making? In the citizen legislature, the norms and experiences in recruitment are historic values of the constituency which give consensual underpinnings to legislative bargaining. In the professional legislature, the recruitment norms are no less important, but are of a different order. The norms are those of a fraternity of skill. Recruitment generates policy obligations which the legislator as a skilled technician tries to fulfill. These two ideal types, the citizen and professional legislature,

[15] Harry Eckstein, *Division and Cohesion in Democracy* (Princeton: Princeton University Press, 1966), p. 194.

are two ends of a continuum. In reality, no legislature fits either type. The tendencies toward citizen and professional legislatures are found, to a greater or lesser degree, in all legislatures. The technician-professionals predominate in urban states; the citizen legislators predominate in agrarian states. The ends of the continuum conceptualize contrasting role cultures.

The historical archetype of the democratic legislator in America was the citizen legislator.[16] It was believed that a successful but ordinary man could serve in elective office if he had common sense and resembled the people he represented in values and background. The model of the citizen legislator stood opposed to the legislator as aristocrat, the patrician steward of the masses. In modern times, as the scope of government has enlarged, increasing the size of the bureaucracy and the complexity of issues, the professionalization of legislative elites has occurred. Limited government, diffuse political parties and decentralized recruitment produce the citizen legislature. The welfare state and a powerful executive that tries to control recruitment produce the professional legislature.

Our analysis of the recruitment of Oregon state legislators stems from research on one election in 1966. It may be called a case study. Yet, this particular case is only one species in a large genus of democracies.[17] We have drawn distinctions between consensual democracies and those characterized by deep cleavages. Such distinctions derive from the way in which social cleavages in a country are given political expression and their effects on political stability. These typologies are drawn because a democratic nation or a political system is always discovering and testing its integration and political effectiveness. Cleavages are distinguished from social differentiations. All cleavages are not the bases of political conflict, nor is the least differentiated society free of social and political friction.

Political recruitment gives expression to various subcultures and interests and translates them into the decision-making process. The politics of recruitment determines the actors in decision-making and shows how they will act in decision-making roles. Whether cleavages will be aggravated or reduced and how policies will be enacted is directly and indirectly determined by the recruitment processes. Diverse patterns

[16] Jackson T. Main, "Government by the People: The American Revolution and the Democratization of the Legislatures," *William and Mary Quarterly,* XXIII (July, 1966), pp. 391–407.
[17] Arend Lijphart, "Typologies of Democratic Systems," *Comparative Political Studies,* I (April, 1968), pp. 3–44.

of recruitment thus act out legitimations of authority and translate how cleavages and consensus will be transmitted among the ranks of the political elite.

In sum, the roots of recruitment run deep in the social and political structure. The selection of leaders and public officials is the stem, and legislative decision-making is the branch. The roots and the stem are the focus of our study. From such perspective, a model of political recruitment was formulated that identified the variables we investigated in this study of legislative candidates in Oregon.

CHAPTER II

A Model of the Recruitment Process

INTRODUCTION

The statutes of the State of Oregon specify in great detail how an eligible voter may become a candidate for the state legislature.[1] These include the filing date, the legitimate activities of the political parties in the nomination of candidates, the dates of the primary and general elections, how the voting will be conducted, the ballots counted and the winner designated. The statutes further identify three phases of nomination and election: (1) filing, (2) the primary and (3) the general election. In summation, the statutes prescribe rules that govern a process that must be followed in each legislative district. But, the statutes are silent about the presupposed social, economic and political conditions and the informal interactions between sponsors and candidates that are necessary if statutory objectives and prescriptions are to be realized.

Therefore, the student of recruitment requires a working model that conceptualizes both the institutionalized and the informal aspects of the recruitment process.[2] As a starting point, the recruitment process includes phases of interactions among a particular group of actors: the candidates, their sponsors, the voters registered in each party, and the total electorate. The term sponsors refers to various associations that

[1] Oregon, Secretary of State, *Election Laws, State of Oregon, 1972–1973* (Salem: Secretary of State, 1972), Chaps. 248, 249, 250.
[2] Lester G. Seligman, *Recruiting Political Elites* (New York: General Learning Press, 1971), pp. 2–4.

encourage and support candidates, such as political parties or factions, primary groups, and interest groups.

Recruitment as a Process of Selecting Individuals

As a selective flow of individuals, the political recruitment process unfolds in three phases: certification, selection and role assignment. The interrelationships among particular variables explain each phase. The first, *certification,* derives from a person's status in the structure of political opportunity, his opportunity costs and political socialization. The second phase, *selection,* involves the interaction among aspirants, candidates, sponsors, and the electorate. The final phase, *role assignment,* chooses the successful candidate and legitimizes his assumption of the office of state legislator as representative of a particular legislative district.

The selection process is the "how" of recruitment, i.e., the sequential phases of interaction. Each phase of the selection process refines the preceding ones until, finally, individuals are elected and assigned to specific political roles. Aspirants and candidates join with sponsors, and together they mobilize political support in behalf of the candidate. The selection process engages all the contestants for power—parties, groups, individuals, and organizations—because the ability to influence recruitment confers influence in decision-making.

The selection process may be schematized in the following way:
1. *From What* (the certified political activists)

    Social and political status as defined by the formal and effective political opportunity structures; opportunity costs and political risk
2. *By Whom* (sponsors)

    Political parties, interest groups, sub-cultures, primary groups, the electorate
3. *What Criteria*

    Ascriptive: age, family, social status, race, nationality, group affiliation

    Achievement: skill in organizing, communication, bargaining, policy expertise
4. *How: Selection Mechanisms*

    Sponsorship: cooptation, conscription, agency, bureaucratic ascent

    Self-recruitment: self-starting candidate
5. *To What* (selection and assignment)

    Specific political roles; the political career

When the selection process is conceptualized this way, we realize that we formalize a dramatic and idiomatic aspect of politics. Usually, nominations and elections are described with the metaphors of military battle or melodramatic theater. Doubtless, the conceptualization of the dramatic events of nominations and elections robs them of their color and tension. Yet, underlying the drama, determinative influences govern the principal actors in the selection of candidates. It is such influences which concern us.

Each phase of recruitment modifies the roles of the candidates and sponsors who pass through it. The first phase sorts out the potential candidates from among those who are formally and effectively eligible. From this pool emerge the candidates, which marks another critical juncture in selection. Particular mechanisms of selection join candidates with sponsors; sponsors and their candidates contest with other sponsors and candidates and elections decide the winners. In each phase, individuals are selected and rejected; some are winners, others are losers. What happens to the losers is as critical to the recruitment process as what happens to the winners, because the consequences for both modify the incentives of political recruitment. Given the uncertainty and probabilities of various outcomes, and the costs of losing may then be called *recruitment risk,* and the extent of such risk influences a person's decision to seek public office.

FROM WHAT: POLITICAL OPPORTUNITY
OPPORTUNITY COSTS AND RISK

Formal and Effective Opportunity

The selection process does not operate randomly; candidates who are prominent emerge from a pool of eligible individuals, politically active, skillful, and motivated. Neither the attributes of the individual nor the character of the selection process alone determine who is chosen; the relationship among candidates, sponsors and selection is a reciprocal one. The same actors, i.e., the primary groups, political parties and associations which first socialize, then sponsor and play a leading part in the campaigns of political candidates, link together each selection phase.

If a candidate wins, his sponsors, whether they are a group or a party, enhance their political influence among the electorate, in the legislature and in the state government. Considering that the legislature passes laws which directly affect various groups, occupations, as well as commercial and industrial interests in the state, a good deal is at stake in the success or failure of a candidacy.

All the registered voters in the state of Oregon are legally qualified to become candidates, but only a small number have the resources, or opportunity, to regard themselves and/or be regarded by others as available for candidacy. Of these only some are highly motivated and have the talents requisite for campaigning and serving in the legislature.

How is it that only a segment of the electorate enjoys such *effective* opportunity?[3] The answers lie in the social structure and the variable opportunities for political socialization that family status, education and occupation furnish. Whether some people will be considered also involves opportunity costs. Can individuals at any particular time afford to give up their private occupations and run for office? We shall examine these factors in turn.

Men are not born politicians; political socialization and opportunities make them so. In all political systems, only a small number of people become politically active, and an even smaller number of people become candidates for office. Almond and Verba concluded from their five-nation survey that "the overwhelming majority of the members of all political systems live out their lives, discover, develop and express their feelings and aspirations in the intimate groups of the community. It is the rare individual who is fully recruited into the political system and becomes a political man."[4]

Some people are given (or achieve) greater opportunity to seek and/or attain public office than others. An exclusive political opportunity structure is synonymous with high social barriers against admission to public office that favors an exclusive elite. And conversely, more egalitarian political opportunity diversifies political elites. Every political view or theory about "who should rule" rests on some value assumptions about the age, background (family, race, nationality), skills, character and experience that public officials should have. Such views and theories thus justify the particular criteria that should be used to restrict political opportunity.

Systems differ according to the criteria they legitimize for restricting recruitment opportunity. Hence, political opportunity may be sub-divided into *formal* or legal political opportunity (designating those who may seek office), *effective* (or practical) political opportunity (indicating those who *can* seek office), and motivational patterns, which define those who will aspire to political office (distinguishing those who are strongly attracted to a political career from the rest). Twin sets of influences expand and contract effective political opportunity. The attrac-

[3] Ibid., p. 3.
[4] Gabriel A. Almond and Sidney Verba, *The Civic Culture* (Princeton: Princeton University Press, 1963), p. 10.

tiveness of political roles relative to alternative roles in private occupations (opportunity cost) determines how many people will be interested in public office, while existing and anticipated changes in the scope of government determine the demand for political aspirants. We may define the boundaries of *effective* political opportunity as coterminous with the characteristics of those nominated and/or elected compared with the characteristics of the excluded. For example, if lawyers are found disproportionately high among legislators compared with their proportions in the electorate, then differential *effective* political opportunities are responsible.

At any particular time those certified to run for public office are synonymous with those termed political activists. Various indices of political activity measure the number of activists. One well-known study of participation in the United States used the following indicators: exposure to stimuli perceived as political; voting; discussion of political issues or subjects; wearing a button or placing a sticker on a car; petitioning political leaders; making a monetary contribution; attending political meetings, and a few others.[5] From such data, the study concluded that one-third of the American adult population is apathetic, and only some five to seven percent are politically involved and participate consistently. Other studies have examined decision-making in particular political issues and have identified a thin political stratum which they label "issue publics" or the "attentive public."[6] In sum, the determinants of effective political opportunity provide the predispositions to political involvement and aspiration, and competition among the leadership of political groups and political parties creates vacancies that attract those predisposed to run. Crossing the threshold from political activity to political candidacy involves more than the sum of a number of factors of equal importance. Thus, one type of candidate chooses to run only when chances are most favorable, while other types are willing to run under less favorable odds because one factor, the enjoyment they derive from using their political skill, or facing the challenge, overrides all others.

The Determinants of Effective Political Opportunity

SOCIAL STATUS. The social and economic structure of a legislative district determines political opportunity. Just as states within the United States vary in their degree of industrialization and urbanization; ethnic,

---

[5] Lester W. Milbrath, *Political Participation* (Chicago: Rand McNally, 1965).
[6] Donald J. Devine, *The Attentive Public: Polyarchical Democracy* (Chicago: Rand McNally, 1970).

religious and racial homogeneity and heterogeneity; and levels of education and differential rates of emigration and immigration, so do the small subunits called legislative districts vary. Whether or not a legislative district was recently settled or is an established area of settlement, with deeply rooted political traditions and stereotypes, also can modify political opportunity. When identifying such influential factors that can shape political opportunity, we wish to point out that influential factors in the Oregon context also differentiate among other states in the U.S.A., and among foreign nations.

The association in other nations between social status and access to political status varies with the type of social and political systems utilized. In simple and traditional political systems, social status and political opportunity are ascribed, more or less fixed and restricted to those with the highest status. In the past in India, for example, membership in a high caste guaranteed high position in government. In France of the Eighteenth Century, the nobility were entitled to hold offices, while the bourgeoise secured positions by patronage or purchase. The church was also an important avenue to political roles.[7] But in modern industrial democratic systems, such as the United States, considerable social mobility and democratic values make political status less exclusive. High social status usually (but not always) confers commensurate political status. Thus, political opportunity depends not only on social position at birth, but education and wealth provide access to avenues of social and political advancement. Historically, the democratization of the United States proceeded hand in hand with the emergence and development of the mass political party. Ambitious members of the middle and lower middle classes used the mass membership party to reduce the power of the aristocracy. As members of the upper class withdrew from politics, the middle class lawyers, businessmen and farmers took their place in political activity and public offices.[8]

Another significant factor in the determination of certification may be called the generational expectations of leadership. Thus, in some areas, seniority and long service are regarded as desirable for political office. Stereotypes about age and generations facilitate the recruitment

---

[7] Bernard Barber and Elinor G. Barber, *European Social Class: Stability and Change* (New York: Macmillan, 1965).
[8] Richard P. McCormick, *The Second American Party System* (Chapel Hill: University of North Carolina Press, 1966), pp. 329–358; Richard Hofstadter, *The Idea of a Party System* (Berkeley: University of California Press, 1969), Ch. VI; Robert Dahl, *Political Oppositions in Western Democracies* (New Haven: Yale University Press, 1966), pp. 11–12; E. Digby Baltzell, *The Protestant Establishment* (New York: Random House, 1964), analyses the alienation of the American upper-middle class from politics.

of some and impede the progress of others. As evidence, we observe that political leaders seem to emerge in "generational sets."[9]

Just as status cleavages divide political opportunity horizontally away from the electorate, so do vertical cleavages among ethnic, linguistic, religious and geographic groups divide the population vertically. Such divisions often coincide with a particular social status, e.g., the low social status of the Blacks in the United States. In Western Europe and England, as the right to participate was extended to the middle and later the lower classes during the 19th and early 20th centuries, ethnic, religious and racial cleavages became more significant barriers to political opportunity.[10]

Within the United States, as legal barriers to political participation were removed, middle class status enhanced opportunities for political status. Most elective and appointive officials in the United States are of middle-middle and lower-middle class origin.[11]

The middle class in the United States predominates among political activists and office holders because it embraces that broad stratum of the highly educated, i.e., the professionals, merchants, and others with intellectual skills, which epitomizes the urbanized, mobile, sophisticated, ambitious, aware, and skilled elements in the population. Political roles require these attributes for their performance.[12] The roles are defined and performed in such a way as to make middle class characteristics prerequisite for prospective office holders.

Social and economic status also determines the level of office of initial recruitment. People of higher social status usually enter roles that are higher up in the pyramid of political roles than do those of lower status. Achieved high social status eases entry into higher levels of the political hierarchy. The fit between social status and points of entry is far from perfect, but this general pattern is found in most political systems.[13] Social status is a major determinant of political opportunity. Among the factors that determine one's *social* status, family background is the *most* important element. Family defines social status by positioning

[9] Samuel P. Huntington, *Political Order in Changing Societies* (New Haven: Yale University Press, 1968), pp. 14–15.
[10] Giovanni Sartori, "The Sociology of Parties: A Critical Review," in Otto Stammer, ed., *Party Systems, Party Organizations and the Politics of New Masses* (3rd International Conference on Comparative Sociology, Berlin, 1968; Berlin: Institut für Politische Wissenschaft an der Freien Universität Berlin, 1968), p. 19.
[11] Donald R. Matthews, *The Social Background of Political Decision-Makers* (New York: Random House, 1954).
[12] Leon D. Epstein, *Political Parties in Western Democracies* (New York: Praeger, 1967), Ch. VII.
[13] Richard E. Dawson and Kenneth Prewitt, *Political Socialization* (Boston: Little, Brown, 1969).

its members in a network of social and economic relationships. Family determines ethnic, linguistic, religious, and social class position; it also influences cultural and educational values and achievements, occupational and economic aspirations and accomplishments, and one's exposure to other groups and individuals. "The social status of the family serves as a reference point for political attachments ... rather than as agents of political socialization. Trade unions, farmer organizations, trade associations often serve as agents of political learning ... and membership in these groups often is established, directly or indirectly, by the family."[14] The son of a middle class father has a better chance to become familiar with the political milieu, meet politically involved people, and emulate their social and political skills than the son of a working class father.

RESOURCES, SOCIALIZATION AND MOTIVATION. When individuals climb the political ladder, particular political resources such as organizational or group sponsorship, financial support and access to mass media enhance their advancement. Yet, political institutions and socioeconomic structure allocate such resources unequally in the population. The high costs of access to mass media and organization place them out of reach of many groups and individuals.[15] For example, a candidate who challenges an incumbent for elective public office has greater difficulty in getting access to the media than does his or her opponent. Because access to and costs of resources are distributed unequally among individuals, they seek the collective resources of party and special interest organizations.

The support of political party organization and interest groups is an important political resource. Political parties enhance effective opportunity by (a) socializing individuals for a political career, (b) legitimizing and sponsoring the nomination of candidates for political office, (c) mobilizing the electorate for election campaigns, and (d) providing political roles that cushion the unsuccessful or defeated, thereby diminishing hazards of political careers.

Political parties socialize potential candidates in various ways. Some parties select candidates only from the ranks of party workers and professionals.[16] Political party branches and auxiliary organizations —youth and adult groups—induct the individual into party and political activity. Party organizations furnish jobs to the defeated candidates and

---

[14] Ibid., p. 55.
[15] Herbert E. Alexander, *Financing the 1968 Election* (Lexington, Mass.: D. C. Heath, 1971), and other studies by the same author.
[16] Leo M. Snowiss, "Congressional Recruitment and Representation," *American Political Science Review*, LX (September, 1966), pp. 627–639.

office holders, and cushion those whose status is declining. Political parties mobilize the electorate, raise money, conduct election campaigns and distribute propaganda, thereby helping to offset the unequal distribution of resources among candidates. In some instances, interest groups and associations are principal sponsors of candidates and provide the organizational resources necessary for effective candidacy. In yet another pattern, transitory organizations sponsor candidates and political aspirants, such as the volunteer organizations set up to promote the candidacy of Eisenhower and later, McGovern.

High social status alone does not ensure recruitment to political elite roles. Although middle class and upper-middle class groups contribute the major share of political officials, only a small proportion of the population in such classes seek or become political office holders. A person's social status is a staging area that conditions and improves his or her chances for recruitment, but an individual's political socialization will determine the individual's political predispositions and skills. How does a person acquire knowledge of politics and political predispositions, beliefs and attitudes? Why do individuals gravitate to a particular political activity? How does one acquire the relevant, needed skills? The answer lies with the *political socialization* of the individual, which determines whether or not a person would be likely to choose a political vocation and also helps us predict their degree of success.

As agencies of political socialization, family, peer groups, associations, schools and political parties play disparate roles in different systems. Within each system, socialization varies throughout the entire social structure. A salient finding is the critical role of primary groups (family, peer groups and neighborhoods) in political socialization. Primary groups impart and nurture political attitudes that may encourage or discourage adult political participation. As the most important primary group, the family may link its members to various political associations or it may make its members apathetic, hostile or cynical toward political involvement. Evidence of family political socialization in different cultures supports this theory. Parents in France communicate less with children about politics than do parents in the United States and as a result the French children develop more hostile attitudes toward politics.[17]

In the United States, autonomous associations play an important part in political life because the boundaries between activity in non-

[17] Laurence W. Wylie, *Village in the Vaucluse* (Cambridge: Harvard University Press, 1957), p. 208; Philip E. Converse and George Dupeux, "Politicization of the Electorate in France and the United States," *Public Opinion Quarterly*, XXVI (Spring, 1962), pp. 1–23.

political and political associations are thin and permeable. The inter-penetration of the social and political associations enlarges opportunities for political experience and expression for some citizens. Political skills and political interest are taught in many ways. A study of state legislators in the United States reported that various agents were responsible for their initial political interest. Political interest develops "at various states in life for different people through a great variety of stimuli—family, friends, associations of one kind, significant political figures, or dramatic public events."[18]

The process of selection is itself an important socialization experience. A candidate must establish rapport with many groups and interests. Nomination and election require the candidate to win the support of party leaders, and to communicate with diverse public audiences. "To succeed in American politics, one must win the acceptance of many people and the approval of some, but compared to other fields the approval needs to be more widespread and need not be as strong."[19]

Political socialization reflects an individual's exposure to political milieus and his or her particular political experiences, but the intensity and style of political activity varies with the *motivation* of political actors, a variable in recruitment which resists easy analysis. Motivational studies that compare political activists and office holders with those less involved, in an attempt to identify kinds and degrees of motivation are not conclusive. "Except for the most gross personality traits, ego strength, ability to compromise and the like, which undoubtedly separates leaders in all spheres, no evidence argues that it is a psychological variable which distinguishes the public official from any random sample of the population."[20] Moreover, among individuals with similar personality structures, some will choose political activities and others will not. The same motivations seem to impel the ambitious in politics, business, and other lines of endeavor. Apparently, the extent or character of political socialization determines the ambitious person's preference for political pursuits. When a person's primary groups provide opportunities for political socialization then he or she might feel emotional gratifications in political activity. Primary groups serve as a meeting ground where personality factors and influences from the broader po-

---

[18] John C. Wahlke, *et al., The Legislative System* (New York: Wiley, 1962).
[19] Stimson Bullitt, *To be a Politician* (Garden City, N.Y.: Doubleday, 1959), p. 8.
[20] Rufus P. Browning and Herbert Jacob, "Power Motivation and the Political Personality," *Public Opinion Quarterly,* XXVIII (Spring, 1964), pp. 75–90; Harold D. Lasswell, "The Selective Effect of Personality on Political Participation," in Richard Christie and Marie Jahoda, eds., *Studies in the Scope and Method of "The Authoritarian Personality"* (Glencoe, Ill.: Free Press of Glencoe, 1954), pp. 197–225.

litical environment come together. Primary groups select and nurture appropriate motivations and skills for political activity. If family and peer groups are permeated by the political parties, political associations and mass media, they make a primary group a political milieu. A newspaper, a magazine holding a particular point of view, a favorite commentator or program help make a family a political family. Whether such political nurture will find adult expressions varies with many factors, including the structure of political opportunity, the incentives for political activity, role models, and the salience of political issues.

In analyzing political socialization and motivation, the cognitive, affective and instrumental influences are not easily separable. The tendency to focus exclusively on the highly motivated, dramatic political leaders, the politically ambitious, the psychologically deviant, and the political extremists overlooks a large number of candidates and officeholders. Ordinary people, motivated in various ways, fill many political roles. For some, politics is the core of their lives, a calling or profession; for others, politics is an avocational interest, and for still others, only specific issues or candidates will activate them. Political activists vary widely in political roles, orientations, intensities of political interest and level of aspiration.[21] Motivational analysis must explain such variations and weigh their significance as determinants of various kinds of political activity. The ordinary politician as well as the exceptional one must be explained. Some problems which beset motivational analysis derive from conflicting theories and evidence in personality theory; others arise from the difficulties in discerning personality variables in various political situations.

When interrelating political contexts with personality factors, there is an omnipresent danger in using personality factors alone to explain the recruitment process, while neglecting opportunity, incentives and risk that may favor some personalities and disadvantage others.[22] Moreover, the motivations of politicians have not been studied in representative samples of the range of political roles, situations, or at *various* levels of political activity. What concerns us is not political motivation and socialization *per se,* but the part they play in recruitment and selection of candidates. Because the state legislator is a common point of entry into a political career, through studying recruitment at this level

---

[21] V. O. Key, Jr., *Public Opinion and American Democracy* (New York: Knopf, 1961); Fred I. Greenstein, *Personality and Politics* (Chicago: Markham, 1969), *passim.*
[22] Nathan Kogan and Michael A. Wallach, "Risk Taking as a Function of the Situation, the Person, and the Group," in *New Directions in Psychology,* III (New York: Holt, Rinehart & Winston, 1967), p. 115.

we can discover why some individuals create their own opportunities for public advancement while others, more passive, respond only when others have prepared the way for them. The research of Browning[23] and Barber[24] shows how a candidate's personality structure is a necessary, but not sufficient explanation of his motivations in recruitment situations. As Greenstein cogently states, personality variables are less relevant in highly structured situations than in those where behavior is less prescribed.[25] Therefore motivation should be studied in *diverse contexts* or situations of recruitment, where cognitive, instrumental and affective factors intermix, comparing the successful with the unsuccessful, as we shall do. In other words, motivation should be studied under various conditions of opportunity, risk and selection.

Summing up, effective political opportunity certifies a social slice drawn chiefly from the educated, appropriately politically socialized and politically involved middle classes. Thus, men become potential candidates through a political upbringing that is customary among families of particular social status. Families, education, peers and occupation, the mass media each contribute to "positioning" a potential candidate who aspires to candidacy or whom others will regard as a potential candidate. The attendant social status, motivation, socialization, resources, and skills are mutually reinforcing factors which determine who the candidates will be.

ON BECOMING A CANDIDATE:—THE DECISION TO FILE, REWARDS AND COSTS. The factors we have discussed only "groom" a person for candidacy. Whether or not he will actually become a candidate involves a mixture of motives and incentives. In this study, we examined incentives more than we examined the motives. The relative advantages and disadvantages to candidacy were considered under the heading of recruitment risk.

Every legislative district structures the rewards and costs of seeking legislative office. In one state legislative district, a candidate can expect political advancement if he gains a state legislative office and the range of policies he will be called upon to deal with will open up avenues to greater political influence. In another district, the state legislature is as far as he can go; the issues are so narrow, the legislators political horizons remain local and do not contribute to advancement. The paths to political advancement are often perilous and at the least, tedious. Disraeli likened the political career to climbing a "greasy pole." Those

[23] Rufus P. Browning, "Businessmen in Politics: Motivation and Circumstance in the Rise to Power" (unpublished Ph.D. dissertation, Yale University, 1960).
[24] James D. Barber, *The Lawmakers* (New Haven: Yale University Press, 1965).
[25] Greenstein, *Personality and Politics,* p. 58, *passim.*

who seek a political career may incur many losses, but it is the variability of the losses and rewards that is significant. Hence, the analysis of recruitment to political roles must include the probabilities of failure, its costs, and political reverses, as well as its rewards. The literature on recruitment has ignored the defeated, even though their political fate and destinies shed much light on the recruitment process. The likelihood and consequences of defeat affect the cognitive assessments of benefits and costs which enter into decisions to seek political roles. Both as motives and disincentives, the fear of losses, especially when the probabilities are not known, may outweigh the rewards of power in the pursuit of political office. The probabilities of both the rewards and costs of candidacy and incumbency are more or less durable in every legislative district.

Recruitment risks involve consideration of three factors: (1) the opportunity costs, e.g., giving up private occupation and income for a period; (2) the probability of winning and losing, and (3) the net costs (over the rewards) of losing either the primary or the general election. These are immediate considerations. But, if the prospective candidate is considering a longer run investment in a political career, then that person must consider what career risks state legislators encounter; that is, what happens when they are defeated.

Uncertainty and the probability of winning and losing are synonymous with competitive election. Uncertainty is endemic in political roles and gives rise to uncertain chances of loss and gain. Assuming then that some roles and careers are more uncertain than others, an overriding consideration, it seems, is what may happen to those who seek political roles and fail. If the costs to them are overwhelming, then, for some, the degree of uncertainty and the probabilities of winning and losing will become secondary. Likewise, if losing is not costly, then the uncertainties will become secondary. Politicians are risk bearers. Some experience greatest risk in candidacy; others in incumbency. In some political systems the costs of losing are insurable or compensated (cushions); in other systems, the losses cannot be recovered or recompensed.

For would-be candidates, the degree of recruitment risk influences the decision to run for office. Let us assume that aspirants to office have a single purpose: to gain public office. Other goals would be secondary. Then the following considerations will influence decisions to run: (1) political objectives and aspirations; (2) costs and rewards that result from the probabilities of various outcomes of winning or losing; (3) the uncertainty of achieving long-run objectives as a result of each possible or probable outcome.

High recruitment risk results when great uncertainty exists about winning or losing and the defeated experience high costs and low rewards. Then candidates have no private occupations to return to, either because they had none to begin with or they lost them when they chose to run for office. There are cases where employees have lost their jobs, lawyers have lost clients, businessmen have been boycotted, and ministers have lost their pulpits, all because they might have espoused an issue or political party scorned by their clients or congregation. In some legislative districts and constituencies, running for office in behalf of an unpopular cause brings social sanctions. Friends become estranged, associations ostracize a member and individuals become pariahs. The availability or non-availability of *cushions* differentiates high risk and low risk recruitment. In high risk recruitment, the net costs of losing are severe and not insurable. Individuals are dismissed without institutionalized protections. Dismissal from office results in severe sanctions—banishment, detention, disgrace, liquidation.[26] Consequently, officials try at all costs to protect themselves against the eventuality of dismissal. The political aspirant threads his way gingerly in this perilous milieu where "betting" on the wrong sponsors or sudden changes in policies and personnel will spell the end to his political career and personal status. In dictatorships, political elites, fearful of the high risks of dismissal, suppress potential opposition. Sponsorship of candidates by groups independent of the governing elites is not permitted and only factions and cliques within the governing elites may assist aspirants up the political ladder. Rival sponsors engage in conflict for available positions, and the losing sponsors may be purged by the winners.

In general, in the United States, the risk of recruitment is moderate for a number of reasons. First, a person becomes a candidate for the first time *after* he has achieved occupational and social status, which supports his aspirations. In the event of political defeat, the candidate may usually return to his private occupation. Competitive selection permits passage back and forth from non-political to political roles at all levels of the political pyramid.[27] Alternative private and/or public roles that uphold their status are available to the defeated.

Second, the norms of political competition insure against losses the defeated or demoted might incur. Such political norms include rules of the game that govern the relationships among incumbents, the opposition, and defeated elite members. Between the representatives of the

---

[26] See John A. Armstrong, *The Soviet Bureaucratic Elite* (New York: Praeger, 1959); Myron Rush, *Political Succession in the U.S.S.R.* (New York: Columbia University Press, 1965).

[27] Geraint Parry, *Political Elites* (New York: Praeger, 1969), p. 69.

party in power and the opposition party, a "live and let live" exchange prevails. Sportsmanship between winners and losers cushion "the fall" in power and self-esteem of the losers, and remind both winner and loser that political defeat need not be devastating. The victors expect that eventually they may lose, and losers expect some chances to return to power. Politics is not a zero sum game. Therefore, both winners and losers share a common interest in preserving and protecting the status of the losers, and thereby uphold the incentives to pursue a political career. Such an outlook is held especially by political "professionals." Such incentives for those in and out of power encourage a stream of candidates for roles with both the government and the opposition.

Common interest with the reduction of recruitment risks, based on "exchange," makes aspirants, candidates and officials maintain a bargaining or exchange style of politics. Each politician depends upon an exchange relationship with other politicians, which is thus collective protection that maintains their status and prestige. Mutual interdependence fosters forbearance and expectations about the limits to which adversaries may or should be driven. A common concern with reducing the losses of political defeat shores up democratic tolerance just as does pluralism and belief in freedom to dissent.

Expectations about the consequence of political status loss affect recruitment in many ways. When the norms and methods of acquiring political roles contradict the norms and practices of losing them, the incentives for a political career are diminished. Criteria and processes of political advancement that are inconsistent with those which determine defeat encourage political aspirants to resort to violence and other anomic methods of recruitment. When men are elected to political office by the public and lose their positions by methods other than public consent, then why bother with winning popular support? Further, when the costs of losing a political position (measured in status, prestige, and income) are great, then the incumbents will zealously protect their positions. Contradictory norms of recruitment and dismissal from office result in corrupt oligarchies. Thus, the processes of upward and downward political mobility are closely interrelated because the norms and practices of the latter can destroy the former. The supply of candidates can balance the demand arising from competition (vacancies in political roles) only when the twin processes of winning and losing in politics are consistent.

Recruitment risk depends also upon non-political factors. The rewards and costs in private occupations may provide alternatives which cushion against political defeat. If political roles receive higher rewards than do private occupations, then presumably many will seek political roles, but private occupations cannot then serve as "cushions," and risk will increase. If the difference in status between political roles and non-political roles is not great, then political defeat won't result in a great loss in status.

The degree of recruitment risk serves also as an indicator of the intensity of political motivation of candidates. The losses a candidate expects if he is defeated test the intensity of a candidate's commitment. When recruitment risk is high, candidacy will attract only the desperately ambitious and/or those who subconsciously enjoy losing. Conversely, when recruitment risk is low, running for office will attract more of the less motivated. Such low risk takers are of a different set of personalities than those who run when the risk is high. Just as secure occupations, e.g., civil service, attract personalities that seek security, so do high risk occupations, e.g., auto racing or business speculation, attract those whose personalities relish the risky challenge and the chance to win high rewards.

The degree of recruitment risk conditions the conduct and intensity of recruitment and selection contests, which also has a selective effect on the types of people who seek office. A high recruitment risk necessitates intense political contests where no holds are barred and attracts those who enjoy such a struggle. High recruitment risk restricts the contest to extreme types, those with high income and status who can afford to lose and those with low status and income and who have nothing to lose. Low recruitment risk opens the door to a broader spectrum of individuals. High risk socializes politicians to a conspiratorial style of career tactics; low risk makes for more open and sportsmanlike contests for public office.

Summing up, political opportunity and its costs are related inversely. When political opportunity is flexible and competitive, then defeat in recruitment does not result in great losses; but, when political opportunity is rigid and exclusive, then both the rewards (prestige, power and status) and the losses are greater. In these respects, the office of state legislator neither promises nor delivers high rewards nor high costs to candidates or incumbents. Thus, lower rewards and costs temper the incentives to compete for public office.

BY WHOM: SPONSORS

The selection process engages a characteristic set of sponsors, primary groups, political parties, party factions, interest groups, associations and subcultures. Three of the most important are political parties, interest groups and primary groups. The variety of ways in which political parties are organized in various legislative districts resists simple classification. It may be enough to say the variance ranges the extremes, from party organizations that resemble simple primary groups to some that resemble bureaucratic organizations.[28] A number of factors determine the character of party organization: (1) the competitive position of a party vis-à-vis its opponent; (A hopeless minority party exhibits a different kind of organization than does one that is dominant.) (2) the degree of intra-party cohesion or division, (3) the relationship of parties to interest groups and associations, and (4) the character of their leadership. Each of these factors determines whether or how parties will act as sponsors of candidates in each and all phases of the selection process. But party organization is also influenced by its recruitment capacity and success in the past.

Primary groups are the core of the candidacy, and are the nuclei of campaign organizations. The family and closest associates of the candidate encourage him and activate others in support of his campaign. However large or small, or simple or complex the organizational base of the campaign organization, the candidate's intimates are at the center, ultimately influencing his decisions and supporting him. Without such a political primary group there would be no candidacy, nor campaign, nor support from other groups.

Interest groups and associations serve candidates in various ways. They support and promote candidates for consideration by the party nominating machinery and play a role in political socialization. Interest groups provide organizational resources, furnish active workers in campaigns, contribute to party finances, and provide propaganda in behalf of party and individual candidates. They also define policies which candidates espouse.

Interest groups and their linkage with political parties influence significantly the part they play in recruitment. Interest groups may become independent sponsors or auxiliaries to the activities of political parties. Well organized parties incorporate interest groups. Loosely organized political parties are fragmented further because interest groups see no need to weld strong centralized party organization.

HOW: SELECTION MECHANISMS

The strategies of sponsors dictate the mechanisms which join them to candidates. These mechanisms may be identified as: *cooptation, agency, conscription, self-starting* and *bureaucratic ascent.*

When sponsors (political parties, interest groups) feel threatened,

[28] William E. Wright, "Comparative Party Models: Rational-Efficient and Party Democracy," in William E. Wright, ed., *A Comparative Study of Party Organization* (Columbus, Ohio: Charles E. Merrill, 1971), pp. 17–54.

they will attempt to enlist support from outside their ranks by coopting individuals as candidates who enjoy high prestige and political influence. In coopting candidates, sponsors trade the control they might exercise over one of their own for better prospects of electing a candidate. Agency is another mechanism whereby interest groups select candidates, usually from within their own ranks. These candidates will act as representatives of their interest groups when they gain office; sponsors are, in effect, "hiring" individuals to promote their interests. Minority political parties or groups may conscript candidates who have little chance to be selected, but who accept service as candidates because they are duty bound to serve the organization.

Thus, selection mechanisms determine whether sponsors will control candidates when they assume office, as Figures 1, 2 and 3 indicate.

FIGURE II–1

Mechanisms of Sponsorship and Control Over Recruitment

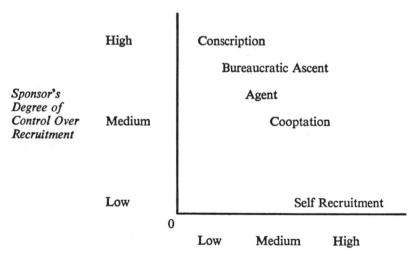

Candidate's Degree of
Control Over Recruitment

Lastly, self-selection is a mechanism found everywhere, but the self-starting candidate enjoys success only under special conditions. The direct primary is favorable for self-starters because party organizations cannot block self-promotion. Indeed, the self-propelled candidate thrives when political parties are so fragmented that he can draw support among followers who are disengaged from strong political attachments.

FIGURE II–2

Mechanisms of Candidacy and Candidate Roles

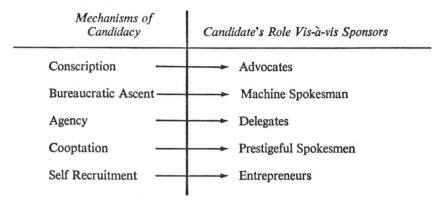

Mechanisms of Candidacy	*Candidate's Role Vis-à-vis Sponsors*
Conscription ⟶	Advocates
Bureaucratic Ascent ⟶	Machine Spokesman
Agency ⟶	Delegates
Cooptation ⟶	Prestigeful Spokesmen
Self Recruitment ⟶	Entrepreneurs

FIGURE II–3

Recruitment Mechanisms and Decision Making

Candidacy Mechanism		*Sponsor's Influence in Decision Making*		
(Sponsor's Role in Instigating Candidacy)		High	Medium	Low
High	Bureaucratic Promotion, Cooptation	+	+	
Medium	Conscription and Agency	+		
Low	Self-Starters			+

Thus, each mechanism reflects the motivation, incentives of candidates, and the sponsors' situation. Where the selection process follows an established pattern, particular mechanisms are regularly used. Where the selection process changes often, the mechanism used will depend upon the tactical and strategic requirements of sponsors and candidates.

Four factors often determine the complexity of the recruitment process: (1) the degree of competitiveness of the parties; (2) the cohesion of party organization; (3) the social homogeneity-heterogeneity of the electorate in a given constituency, and (4) the number of stages in the selection process.

A disparity often exists between the formal stages for the nomination of elective candidates (prescribed by the electoral system) and the informal stages required in practice for the selection of candidates. In practice, the selection of candidates does not go through the same stages in every party. The number of stages depends, in the first instance, upon the electoral system, whether the open or closed primary is employed, or a convention system, or both. Also, the competitive position of the party and its internal cleavages and organization will determine which stages will be decisive in selection. In the most extreme single party constituency, candidates are hand-picked by a small group of leaders. In a district where each party competes evenly with every other party, a number of groups and individuals participate in the nominations and more stages are required to complete the selection process.

In sum, the character of the constituency, the competitive position of a political party, the extent of internal cohesion, and the electoral system influence the relative importance of selection phases. The spectrum includes at one extreme exclusive, centralized, single parties whose nominees are, in fact, appointed by the top leadership of the party. At the other extreme intensive intra-party competition over nomination occurs and the general election is competitive.

The degree of secrecy and publicity also differentiates selection processes. Competitive selection processes are more open to public scrutiny because the competing sponsors require publicity in order to marshall public support and weaken their opponents. Then the electorate may choose from among candidates because the processes of selection have been visible and open. In contrast, secrecy is indispensable to more closed selection processes because the participants are few in number and the stakes are high. Just as public scrutiny and free communication threatens oligarchical control, so does secrecy permit the elites to maneuver deceitfully without exposure and public involvement. Secrecy is conducive to control and is, therefore, cherished by oligarchies.

What effect do the variables we have discussed have on decision-making? When effective political opportunity expands or contracts, or recruitment risk increases or diminishes, and selection processes become more or less competitive, the composition of the activists and the elites is changed. How do such changes affect the third phase of selection process, role assignment?

TO WHAT ROLES: THE STATE LEGISLATOR

The assignment of individuals to specialized roles in decision-making institutions is the end product of the recruitment process. Recruitment influences the distribution of power, the representativeness of elites, elite competence, policy outputs, and the collective norms of elites. The adequacy of decision-making and policy outputs thus tests recruitment and the legitimations of elites.

THE DISTRIBUTION OF POWER. The selection process influences the extent to which decision-making will be responsible and accountable. If aspirants to political roles are drawn from a narrow base of the population, then an exclusive and self-perpetuating oligarchy will fill political roles. If selection processes are competitive and open to entry and public scrutiny, then the decision-makers cannot become a closed oligarchy. The broader the base from which decision-makers are drawn and the more competitive the recruitment, the more likely that elites will be responsible and responsive to the opinions of non-elites.

The recruitment process not only selects individuals for political roles, it also generates political influence. Political parties and groups acquire political influence when they recruit successfully. The recruitment process itself, with its complex coalition formations generates and reduces relative influence, and enhances or reduces the status of individuals, parties, interest groups, and sub-cultures.

ELITE COMPOSITION AND REPRESENTATIVES. The recruitment process determines the social profile of decision-makers and therefore whether their characteristics will seem representative or not. Representation is both symbolic and instrumental. Symbolically, the selection of individuals for elite roles signifies recognition and status for the groups that sponsored and supported them. An elite recruited exclusively from one narrow segment of society simulates such symbolic representation. In the course of recruitment activities, political parties emerged as vehicles for the representation of interest and classes because as sponsors of candidates they built coalitions of interest that were thus given symbolic representation.

The recruitment process also selects the elites for their instrumental skills and policies in decision-making. The occupational and political skills of elites result in certain policy predispositions. Brokers and technicians are not proficient in coping well with issues that involve ideological differences. They prefer questions where the means rather than the ends are the important considerations. The biased perceptions and interests of occupational training and identifications influence policy outlooks. Political skills produce points of view as well as techniques that influence policy decisions.

POLICY OUTPUTS. In assessing the effects of recruitment and decision-making, it is useful to distinguish the instrumental from the expressive dimensions of social action. The instrumental dimension refers to decisions as means to the achievement of ends, or as means of problem-solving. The expressive dimension refers to the effects of decisions upon social and political solidarity and consensus. The instrumental aspect of decision-making refers to the policy outputs: programs of action such as are contained in statutes, administrative orders, and judicial opinions. The expressive aspect refers to the consequences of elite behavior for social consensus. To a larger extent, the expressive aspect depends upon whether decision-makers are (or are believed to bc) representative of the population and enjoy public confidence. The instrumental and expressive dimensions of decision-making are interdependent. Effectiveness in decision-making contributes to social consensus, just as social consensus facilitates effectiveness in decision-making.

Policy outputs are products of a chain of influences forged by the continuity of the principal participants in opportunity, risk, selection, and decision-making. At all points of the recruitment process and decision-making, the same actors participate (e.g., the activists, primary groups, political parties, interest groups, mass media, and the electorate). The same actors determine the sponsorship of decision-makers and to whom they will be accountable. Where opportunity is not exclusive, risk is moderated, selection is open and competitive, then decision-makers will be responsible to their sponsors and the public. Oligarchical selection from an exclusive and narrow base of the population determines that those chosen will answer only to their elite sponsors.

Sponsorship and accountability are thus linked by the similarity of the principal actors in both the recruitment process and in decision-making. If the parties and/or interest groups played significant roles in recruitment, it follows that they will play significant roles in decision-making. The converse is also true: that those active in decision-making did in fact play a significant role in the recruitment process. This symbiotic relationship is not accidental. Parties and interest groups actively sponsor candidates *because* they wish to influence the direction of public policy, and the latter determines who will be selected. The roles of sponsors in the public among the political activists and in decision-making are complementary.

Sponsorship exercises both an antecedent and an anticipated influence on the officeholder. The antecedent influence of sponsors arises from the obligations and dependencies (we call them mechanisms of selection) that candidates and sponsors have incurred in the course of selection and election. Indeed, in many instances such obligations are explicit; interest groups furnish advice, information and assistance in the carrying out of duties and the maintenance of support with the electorate in return for favorable responses by incumbents. Thus, groups and individuals active in recruitment continue to serve as reference groups for officeholders, and thereby influence their decision-making.

The sponsor's influence depends also upon the role he is expected to play in the career of a candidate or an official. A "one-shot" sponsor who withdraws support after one campaign will have less influence than a sponsor who will play an important part in the future career of an officeholder. Thus, the influence of sponsorship on recruitment determines a sponsor's influence on decision-making.

Reciprocally, decision-making influences recruitment by modifying recruitment criteria, role socialization, and role requirements. Because the decision-makers play their roles in particular ways, they reshape the recruitment criteria, role expectations, and political opportunity of others. The public will alter their expectations of performance criteria necessary to the fulfillment of elite roles. Political opportunities will then change because new types of people will become eligible, and sponsors (political parties and/or interest groups) will also seek candidates with new talents and qualifications.

THE COLLECTIVE NORMS OF DECISION-MAKERS. Recruitment processes many hinder or facilitate the ability of decision-makers to work together. The backgrounds and career experiences of would-be decision-makers include their socialization to norms of political conduct and norms of particular roles. If political recruits have been acculturated to political moderation and respect for institutionalized processes, then such norms and styles will be brought to bear in their decision-making roles. Where the criteria and practices of recruitment are congruent with demands made in decision-making roles, then norms will be sustained. If the manner of achieving office contradicts the norms of behavior in office, then behavior that breaks the rules can be expected.

The manner of initial recruitment into political roles may, itself, reaffirm the legitimations of recruitment norms, or it may undermine such norms. Under conditions of high risk in recruitment, individuals and groups are more likely to violate the norms of selection, thus impairing the rules of the game among elites that underlie effective decision-making. The consensus among decision-makers flows from agreements about substantive values and procedures. The latter make possible interim agreements on many issues, despite differences on long-run goals. Procedural agreements include more than just parliamentary procedures, they include as well the informal understandings and courtesies that facilitate communication and create an atmosphere for give-and-take.

RECRUITMENT AND THE FEEDBACK OF DECISION-MAKING. Recruitment is not only an input in decision-making, but it is influenced by the outputs of decision-making. Both policies and decision-making processes generate a train of influences that affect recruitment variables singly and cumulatively. Public policies affect the political strength of competing sponsors and the amount of support they will receive from associations, groups and the electorate. The divisions and coalitions generated in the course of decision-making influence the strategies of candidate recruitment by political parties and factions within parties. Various policies activate (and deactivate) some political activists and the public, e.g., taxation policies can spur new candidates and new groups to enter political competition. Substantive policy changes can increase or decrease political risk, creating new roles and down-grading others. Eligibility for office can be broadened or narrowed by policies that change the allocation of economic resources. Education policy affects the barriers to social mobility that, in turn, affect political opportunity. The feedback of decision-making and policies on recruitment also permit us to view policies as the *starting point of recruitment analysis*. Such a perspective has been neglected in the analysis of recruitment, despite the obvious importance of public policies for each of the recruitment variables we have discussed.

CONCLUSION

The interrelated variables of the recruitment process—opportunity, recruitment risk, selection and its outcomes—enable us to compare recruitment of legislators in the various legislative districts. These variables lead to functional outcomes: certification, selection and role assignment. In the chapters that follow we shall show how these variables identified patterns of selection of the winners and losers in the Oregon election of 1966.

CHAPTER III

Oregon Politics: The Eve of the Campaign

THE MODEL in the last chapter identified the variables we used throughout this study. In this chapter we will apply these variables to the Oregon
recruitment process. We shall discuss certain structural features of the
Oregon economy and polity that affected political opportunity and
the selection process during 1966. In the preceding decade and a half,
the emergence of the Democratic party as a successful challenger to the
long dominant Republican party opened a new chapter in Oregon politics. Population trends, economic developments, FDR's New Deal and
Truman's Fair Deal administrations in Washington and the rise of a new
political generation changed the party balance in Oregon. Such trends
affected party competition in the legislative districts as well as in the
Congressional constituencies and the state as a whole. As a result of
these new trends, by 1966 the Democrats had become the major party
in a number of legislative districts, previously Republican strongholds.
By 1966, social and economic factors and the new balance of parties
enabled us to identify four types of legislative districts: (1) urban one-
party; (2) urban two-party; (3) rural one-party; and (4) rural two-
party. In 1950, we would have found fewer competitive districts.

SOCIAL, ECONOMIC AND POLITICAL CONDITIONS

Oregon has not grown as rapidly as its neighboring states to the
south and north, California and Washington. In 1960, Oregon had one
and a half million inhabitants; in 1970 there were slightly over two million. Immediately after World War II, new immigrants, responding to

the growth of the lumber industry, arrived in large numbers; the influx diminished by 1950. Since then, population in Oregon has grown steadily and more rapidly than the national average. In the wake of population growth, Oregon changed in some respects. Its cities grew larger, hydroelectric power became more abundant because new dams were built, some new industries were established, new government agencies were created. However, the actual character of the state has not changed; even though growth has been greatest in urban areas, Portland, Oregon's largest metropolis, has not acquired a character distinct from the rest of the state, the way Chicago stands apart from the rest of Illinois, and Los Angeles is its own California.[1] Portland still evokes the slower pace and more restrained, conservative behavior of Oregon's smaller cities and rural areas. To understand how Oregon changes with continuity requires an examination of its recent history and social-economic character.

Social and Economic Structure

Extractive industries and tourism constitute the core of Oregon's economy. Forest industries, which include logging and the manufacture of paper, wood pulp, plywood and lumber, make up the largest segment of the state's economy.[2] With such a narrow base, Oregon's economic stability fluctuates with the rise and fall of the lumber and plywood markets. When lumber prices are high, jobs are plentiful; when prices fall, large numbers of loggers and millworkers become unemployed.

When compared with other states, the population of Oregon is relatively homogeneous. For example, the average Oregonians are more educated than the national average. The population above twenty-five years of age in 1960, completed 11.8 school years (median) which was higher than the national average of 10.6 years. Furthermore, Ore-

---

[1] Oregon has a large rural population. Nearly 40 percent of the population lives on farms or in rural, non-farm settings. Approximately two-thirds of the state's residents live in cities of less than 25,000 or in rural areas. The Standard Metropolitan Statistical Areas are Portland, Salem and the Eugene-Springfield areas. Although Salem fell 850 inhabitants short of being classified a SMSA in the 1960 census, during the years since, the Salem area has grown to over 100,000 population. (U.S., Bureau of the Census, *U.S. Census of Population: 1960.* Vol. I, *Characteristics of the Population,* pt. 39, Oregon.)

[2] Approximately 20 percent of Oregon's work force is engaged in extractive industry, while just over 10 percent are employed in manufacturing. The rest are engaged in service occupations or the wholesale-retail trade. The latter categories include the tourist industry which recently has moved close to the forest industry in total revenues. (See U.S., Bureau of the Census, *U.S. Census of Population: 1960;* U.S., Bureau of the Census, *Statistical Abstract of the United States: 1966.*)

gon ranks eighth among the fifty states according to the degree of education of the most and least educated citizens.[3]

Oregon's population is also ethnically and racially homogeneous. In 1960, 2.1 percent of the population was non-white. Across the state, the range in percent non-white was 14.2 percent (from a low of 0.1 percent to a high of 14.3 percent), which compares with an average of 11.4 percent and a range of 67.8 percent (from 0.2 percent to 68.0 percent) for the fifty states. In Illinois, a state close to the national average (10.6 percent), the range among its counties was 36.1 percent (from less than 0.1 percent to 36.2 percent).[4] Ethnic minorities in 1960 and 1966 were small in number and politically unimportant. A few pockets of ethnic culture exist: the Basques in the rangeland counties along the Snake River in Eastern Oregon and several small Scandinavian communities along the Pacific Coast. In 1960 only 4.0 percent of the population was foreign-born, compared with 5.4 percent for the entire nation, and 7.9 percent for the Pacific States.[5] Among the counties of Oregon, the least number of foreign-born are found in Wheeler County (0.6 percent) and the high percentages are found in Clatsop County (8.6 percent). For the state the range is 8.0 percent.

In 1960, Oregon enjoyed an even income distribution when compared to other states. It ranks ninth in equality of income distribution in the nation.[6] The median family income of the counties range from $4,554 to $6,523, a difference of $1,969.[7]

Despite Oregon's apparent homogeneity, geographic and economic factors create regional differences. Farming is concentrated in Eastern, Central and Coastal regions of the state. Although farming is practiced throughout the state, the Willamette Valley is urban and industrialized. Such differences stem, in part, from climatic differences. Eastern and Central Oregon are arid, and devoted to livestock and wheat farming. The Coastal region is mountainous and ample rainfall makes it best suited for logging or dairy farming. Along the Coast, and Eastern Oregon, the land does not support large populations. In contrast, the fertile

---

[3] In terms of educational achievement state-wide, Oregon is tied with Idaho for eighth place. (See U.S., Bureau of the Census, *County and City Data Book: 1962;* U.S., Bureau of the Census, *Statistical Abstract of the United States: 1968,* p. 113.)

[4] U.S., Bureau of the Census, *County and City Data Book: 1962,* appropriate sections.

[5] Ibid., appropriate section.

[6] Thomas R. Dye, "Income Inequality and American State Politics," *American Political Science Review,* LXIII (March, 1969), 157–162.

[7] U.S., Bureau of the Census, *County and City Data Book: 1962,* appropriate sections.

Willamette Valley, located between the forests of the Coast ranges and the Cascade Mountains, has a temperate climate and adequate rainfall. The Valley is therefore ideal for agriculture and lumber, plywood and paper mills. Abundant electric power and easy access to the sea make the Willamette Valley more suited for industrial development than the other regions of the state. The influx of new immigrants from other states into the Willamette Valley brought Easteners, Southerners, and Middle Westerners into this region.

Between 1930 and 1966 the population of Oregon more than doubled. In 1930, the state had a population of 954,000. By 1966 the figure had reached 1,973,000, a gain of 106 percent. In 1970, the census reported the population as 2,091,000. The major increase was recorded in the principal metropolitan center centered around the City of Portland. Between 1930 and 1966 the population of the Portland Standard Metropolitan Statistical Area grew from 393,000 to 908,000, a gain of 131 percent.[8] The wartime migration of people seeking employment in shipyards, electro-process plants, and chemical plants made up a good portion of this growth. Union membership nearly tripled from 1935 to 1966, representing 32.7 percent of non-agricultural employment in the state.[9] In the postwar period, most of the recently-migrated people found jobs in the Portland area and remained.

The population wave that struck Portland splashed over the neighboring counties at the end of the postwar decade. Responding to the rising demand for construction, lumber output and manufacturing, the demand for labor increased in the postwar years. As a result Lane and Douglas, principal lumber industry counties in the Willamette Valley experienced a considerable increase in labor force. Immigration and industrialization were two factors instrumental in the rise of the Democratic party as a competitor with the Republican party.

The Rise of the Democratic Party

Since 1954, a group of new Democratic candidates have won elective political offices traditionally held by Republicans. Richard Neuberger was elected to the U.S. Senate; Edith Green and Charles Porter were elected to the House of Representatives. With the reelection of Senator Wayne Morse as a Democrat in 1956, the Democrats controlled both U.S. Senate seats. In the same year, Democratic candidates won three of the four Congressional seats. For the first time in a score of years, a Democrat was elected governor and Democrats gained a ma-

[8] U.S., Bureau of the Census, *Statistical Abstract of the United States: 1968*.
[9] Ibid.

jority in the lower house of the legislature (see Figure III–1). In 1958, while retaining control of the lower house, Democrats won control of the state senate, although the Republican party recaptured the governorship. These political changes were the cumulative results of particular social, economic and political developments.[10]

The tempo of economic and social changes and their correlative political expressions do not always occur in phase; during crisis periods

FIGURE III — 1

Party Representation in the Oregon Legislature, 1937-57

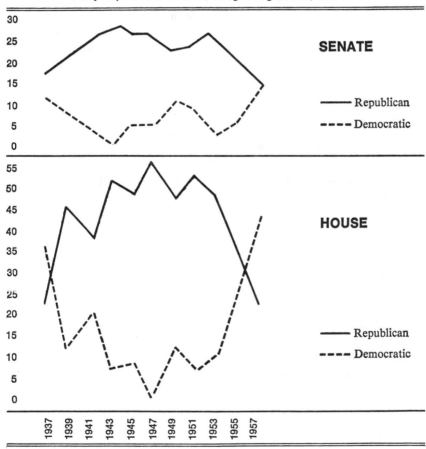

Source: *Oregon Blue Books.*

[10] Lester G. Seligman, "A Prefatory Analysis of Leadership Recruitment in Oregon," op. cit., 153–167.

political processes respond quickly to social demands. More commonly, political effects lag behind social and economic change. So in Oregon, a decade or more intervened between economic changes and the rise of new Democratic party leadership in the fifties.

The Democrats became a majority among the registered voters in the state over a period of twenty years. The confluence of a number of currents created this stream: the factional battle within the Democratic party in the thirties between Democratic Old Guard and New Dealers; the arrival of new Democratic voters responding to the employment opportunities during the war and postwar years; the Truman administration's provision of patronage and financial support to dominant New Deal factions in the state; the continuity with New Deal ideology that the Truman administration sustained; the new political vitality of the CIO-AFL unions; the emergence of young political leadership aspirants among the Democrats; and public disaffection with old Republican leadership. All these factors interacted and cumulatively increased Democratic strength.[11]

Among the economic changes of 1946–49, the Neuberger victory in 1954, and the Democratic victories in 1960, much had happened; while economic prosperity and growth provided opportunities for the young lawyers who were new elite aspirants, the economic recession in Oregon in the early 1950s gave rise to political issues which contributed to victories for Democratic party candidates. In 1954 an economic recession in Oregon made the "tight money" policies of the Eisenhower administration and its opposition to continued governmental development of hydroelectric power leading issues in the state. These issues enhanced support for the Democrats and coupled with the emergence of new leadership in the Democratic party, quickened the party renaissance.

New Elite Aspirants and Political Change

A rising, new group of Democratic state legislators became a middle-level corps of party leaders. Most of these legislators were union officials and young lawyers from the Portland area. The latter, drawn to the state by economic growth, had been politically socialized by the New Deal and soon had become die-hard political activists. As the number of laborers increased, many joined CIO unions, which were more politically active than A.F. of L. unions. The CIO and its political arm, COPE, committed labor's financial and organizational resources to political activity. The leaders of COPE joined hands with a new political generation of leadership aspirants in the Democratic party.

The Democratic party was open to aspiring newcomers and natives

[11] Ibid., pp. 153–166.

alike. Although the need for better "organization" was emphasized by Democratic party leaders, the Party was neither well organized nor cohesive. Had it been, political entry for new political activists might have been more difficult. The direct primary made it easy for new aspirants to file for office. The way was open and inviting to political entrepreneurs,[12] many of whom were lawyers who expected that political activity would benefit their legal practice.

The pattern we have described above may be called "growth politics," in which new political aspirants, an incipient elite, played a key role. When one party dominates the politics of a state, new political aspirants are blocked by veteran leaders who hold safe seats. Yet, in the resurgent minority party, recruitment opportunity is more inviting. The influx of new and younger adherents into the minority party creates a generational cleavage. The young leader aspirants thrive on the cleavage because it defines the struggle between conservative old-guard and liberal "young turks." The factional battle *within* the minority party becomes the crucible of party changes *between* the two parties. The internal struggle within the minority party later redefines the ideological differences *between* the Democrats as liberals and the Republicans as conservatives. As the Democratic party became increasingly competitive with the Republican party, the ideological differences between the parties became sharper.

The direct primary system facilitated the candidacy of both entrepreneurial and sponsored political aspirants. The diffuse roles and fragmented party organization of the Democrats enabled younger elements to appeal directly to the party voters as they battled for party leadership. In such a context, long-standing party "loyalty" or "service" meant little, but political skill and ambition were at a premium. The direct primary has been criticized because it makes organizational and programmatic cohesion difficult.[13] However, when the primary is evaluated in the context of economic growth and elite recruitment, then the easy entry that the primaries allow keeps recruitment channels open and makes parties responsive to new economic and social groups.

The Structure of Political Parties in Oregon

1956 marked the beginning of an era of two-party competition. Since then, registered Democratic voters have exceeded the number of registered Republicans. In 1966 (the year in which this study was con-

[12] Lester G. Seligman, "Political Change: Legislative Elites and Parties in Oregon," *Western Political Quarterly,* XVII (1964), pp. 177–187; and Seligman, "A Prefatory Analysis of Leadership Recruitment in Oregon."
[13] Frank J. Sorauf, *Party and Representation* (New York: Atherton, 1963), pp. 95–96.

ducted) Republicans controlled two of the four seats in Oregon's congressional delegation, the lower house of the state legislature, the governorship and two of three state-wide offices.

The strength of each party in the legislature had been evenly balanced during the last twelve years; actual party competition within the legislative districts had been exceptional.[14] Today one party *(Republican or Democrat) dominates over 70 percent of the legislative districts in the state;* hence, the elections in the competitive district shift the balance of power in the legislature. For state-wide offices and in presidential elections Oregon is "competitive," but not in its contests for the U.S. House of Representatives or the State legislature.

The party registration of Oregon voters does not always correspond to their voting preferences. In recent elections, Republicans have enjoyed substantial Democratic support (they consistently receive more votes than there are registered Republicans). To be sure, some Republican voters support Democrats. However, if only half as many Republicans voted for Democrats as vice versa, nearly 4 out of 10 voters in Oregon would cross party lines in an average election.[15]

The generally accepted explanation for this puzzling leaning toward party irregularity is that voters in the West are ruggedly independent. If this were true, then party registration would fluctuate, and it does not. A more realistic explanation is that voters split the ticket because differences among candidates are often marginal. The shifting voter may also respond to candidates, who because of weak party organization are free of commitments to a party platform, and therefore offer blurred images to the public.

Although one party dominates in most legislative districts, neither majority or minority party is well-organized. Oregon statutes prescribe the organization and governance of political parties. The participation of party-registered voters is required in the selection of precinct

[14] Competition is measured by election outcomes. Districts in which one party has been successful over 80 percent of the time since 1956 in state representative races are considered noncompetitive. Ranney, for example, classifies Oregon as a two-party competitive state. He uses a modified version of the Dawson and Robinson measure of competitiveness (see Richard E. Dawson and James A. Robinson, "Inter-Party Competition, Economic Variables, and Welfare Policies in the American States," *Journal of Politics*, XXV [May, 1963], pp. 265–289). Ranney bases his classification on the popular vote for governor, party balance in the state house and senate, and the number of terms in which the Democrats controlled the house, senate and governorship. See Austin Ranney, "Parties in State Politics," in Herbert Jacob and Kenneth N. Vines, eds., *Politics in the American States* (Boston: Little, Brown, 1965), pp. 63–67.

[15] Oregon, Secretary of State, *Official Abstract of Votes* (Salem, Oregon: Office of Secretary of State, 1958, 1962 and 1966 eds.). Data were for gubernatorial elections.

committeemen; they, in turn choose county officials who then elect state central officials. But these are legal requirements that more often exist only on paper.

Party work confers low prestige and offers few rewards, which makes it difficult to staff party positions in Oregon. Many positions of precinct committeemen are filled by individuals who have received a few unsolicited write-in votes. In the state as a whole, year after year 60 percent of the positions of precinct committeemen remain vacant. In no legislative district are more than 75 percent of the precinct posts filled and only in four districts are half of the precincts filled. This is as true in urban as it is in rural districts.[16]

A comparison between party organization in Oregon and states like Pennsylvania shows striking contrast. In Pennsylvania the greater the density of the population the more organized is the political party.[17] Pennsylvania party organizations are made up largely of patronage employees. As Sorauf describes it:

Old-style political machines, with their armies of committeemen and party workers, prevail in many small towns and cities, as well as in the metropolitan centers of the state.[18]

The loose party organization in Oregon is the product of two movements, Populism and Progressivism, that abolished many patronage positions and instituted the direct primary, the initiative, the referendum and recall. These measures were directed against "machine" party organization.[19] Since then, party organization has been regarded with suspicion, an attitude which interest groups quickly exploited. Oregon has active labor and farm organizations, and well-organized business

[16] The correlation between the number of precinct positions filled in a district and the density of the population is .07. Number of precinct committeeman posts filled, our measure of party organization, was obtained through a poll of county clerks in Oregon. Others have suggested that party organization in Oregon is weak. See Darryl Wilson, "A Study of Political Aspiration in the Oregon Legislature" (unpublished Master's Thesis, University of Oregon, 1960), pp. 1–4; and Lester G. Seligman, "Political Recruitment and Party Structure: A Case Study," *American Political Science Review*, LV (March, 1961), 86.

[17] Sorauf, *Party and Representation*, p. 48.

[18] *Ibid.*, p. 14.

[19] Several studies have documented Oregon's history of Populism and Progressivism. See, for example, M. Harrington, "The Populist Movement in Oregon" (unpublished Master's Thesis, University of Oregon, 1935); A. H. Pike, Jr., "Jonathan Bourne, Jr., Progressive" (unpublished Ph.D. dissertation, University of Oregon, 1957); H. Poulton, "The Progressive Movement in Oregon" (unpublished Master's Thesis, University of Oregon, 1949); and Lester G. Seligman, "A Prefatory Analysis of Leadership Recruitment in Oregon," pp. 153–167.

and utility lobbies. Fragmented party organizations have made parties less capable of active recruitment of candidates. In Pennsylvania, party organizations recruit over 80 percent of the candidates, while in Oregon, parties recruited only 35 percent of the candidates.[20]

Sorauf claims that "where the parties have not mastered the primary, non-party groups have controlled it."[21] In Oregon, this does not seem to be true. Occasionally, a party faction may influence recruitment in more than one district. Oregon's leading interest groups play a key role in recruitment, but they, too, do not control nominations.[22] Groups made up of the candidate's friends, citizens' committees, service organizations, the League of Women Voters, and even occasional Country Club Set or Fraternal Lodge Cliques promote and sponsor candidates. In states like Pennsylvania, the party machine designates and handpicks candidates; in Oregon, candidates "emerge" from various groups and party circles.

The primary elections in both states reflect contrasting party organizations. Historically, the direct primaries were introduced first in one-party states to wrest the control over nominations from party caucuses and conventions and give them instead to the party electorates. In Pennsylvania:

> . . . the parties have not had to resort to elaborate preliminary caucuses or even, in many instances, to formal pre-primary endorsements. Nor has the state seen the rise of extra-party organizations to re-establish discipline in the primary. Plainly, Pennsylvania parties, strong and vital by any standard, have not been greatly discomfited by the primary. In fact, one can reasonably argue that they have turned it to their purposes by making it another hurdle for the unanointed candidate. . . . The very party organizations which the primary was created to break, the strong and vigorous organizations, are those most capable of turning the primary to their uses.[23]

The electoral system in Oregon has dissolved party organization. Over 60 percent of Oregon's state representatives have been elected in multiple-member constituencies, most of which are the urban counties of the Willamette Valley. In the multi-member districts, elections are a free-for-all. If a district has three legislative seats, the three candidates who receive the largest number of votes are elected, regardless of their

[20] Sorauf, *Party and Representation,* pp. 101–102.
[21] *Ibid.,* p. 119.
[22] Harmon Ziegler and Michael Baer, *Lobbying* (Belmont, Cal.: Wadsworth, 1969), *passim* for an analysis of the strength and functions of interest groups in four states, including Oregon.
[23] Sorauf, *Party and Representation,* p. 119.

party affiliation. Consequently, each candidate competes not only with candidates from the opposing party, but also with those of his own party.[24]

The electoral requirements in multi-member districts fragment party organizations in two ways. First, candidates must appeal for votes to the largest audience, since they compete with candidates of both parties. Hence, candidates usually do not identify closely with party labels and partisan issues. They act as if they were in business for themselves. Each candidate forms his own campaign organization, which dissolves after the election. Second, no incentive exists for candidates to cooperate with each other. The idea that candidates should run on a "ticket" smacks of political discipline and is, therefore, rejected. Moreover, some candidates claim that a "ticket" would be only as strong as the vote-getting ability of its least popular member. Few candidates are willing to ally with other candidates, even of the same party, because they may lose and drag them down.[25]

Election Laws and Legislative Districts

The election laws prescribe complex formulae for electing Oregon state legislators. Legislative districts fall into five categories (Table III–1). As a rule, the boundaries of legislative districts coincide with county lines, except for nine of the twenty-eight districts which are multi-county constituencies. All nine districts elect one representative and most of them are found in the sparsely settled Eastern, Central or Coastal regions of the state.

In 1966 eleven districts were coterminous with county lines and were single-member constituencies. The remaining eight were multi-member districts concentrated in the populous Willamette Valley. Seven of the eight were single-county, multi-member constituencies. They elected between two and five representatives each. The eighth, Multnomah County, included the Portland metropolitan area and was divided into five subdistricts. The subdistricts were multi-member and elected three or four representatives each. Multnomah County also elected one representative at large.

In multi-member districts, candidates run according to a "position

---

[24] This feature of Oregon's election laws was changed just before the 1966 election and was replaced by a "position numbering system" which will be described at length below. This change introduces a compounding factor into the study of the 1966 election, since there is no way of estimating its impact. However, there seemed to be little, if any, change in the level of party organization from 1964 to 1966.

[25] The at-large position was eliminated by the 1967 legislature and was assigned to one of the subdistricts.

TABLE III–1

Legislative Districts in Oregon

Single-Member, Multi-County	*Single-Member, Single-County*	*Multi-Member, Single-County*	*Multi-Member, Subdistricts*	*At Large*
14.* Benton, Lane	1. Clatsop	4. Washington (3)**	6. Multnomah, West (3)	6. Multnomah at large
17. Coos, Curry	2. Columbia	7. Clackamas (4)	6. Multnomah, South (3)	
21. Crook, Deschutes, Jefferson	3. Tillamook	11. Marion (4)	6. Multnomah, East Central (4)	
22. Hood River, Wasco	5. Yamhill	12. Linn (2)	6. Multnomah, North (3)	
24. Union, Wallowa	8. Lincoln	13. Lane (5)	6. Multnomah, East (3)	
25. Baker, Grant	9. Polk	15. Douglas (2)		
26. Harney, Malheur	10. Benton	19. Jackson (3)		
27. Klamath, Lake	16. Coos			
28. Gilliam, Morrow, Sherman, Umatilla, Wheeler	18. Josephine			
	20. Klamath			
	23. Umatilla			
Number of Districts = 9	Number of Districts = 11	Number of Districts = 7	Number of Subdistricts = 5	Number of Districts = 1
Number of Legislators = 9	Number of Legislators = 11	Number of Legislators = 23	Number of Legislators = 16	Number of Legislators = 1

* Indicates representative district number.
** The figures in parentheses are the number of representatives from multi-member districts.

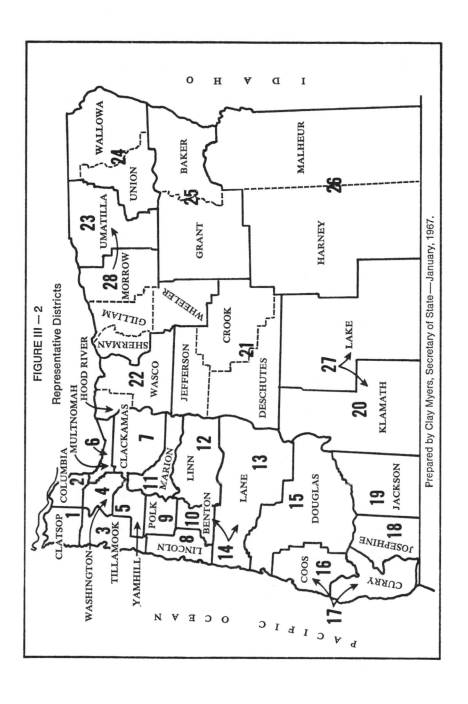

FIGURE III — 2

Representative Districts

Prepared by Clay Myers, Secretary of State—January, 1967.

numbering" system which was first introduced in the 1966 campaign. Each legislative seat was numbered and candidates in each primary file for a numbered position. The primary election reduced the field to one candidate per position from each party. In the general election, the candidates of each party who won the primary for *position one* opposed each other; the same was true for *position two,* and so on. The position-numbering system was designed to focus the competition directly on the candidates representing each party; it was also intended to give the voter a clearer choice, and a greater influence on recruitment, to party organization. To date, position-numbering has had little effect on party organization in Oregon, although such judgments are premature.

Prior to the year 1966, the last reapportionment of the Oregon Legislature had been in 1957, and representation remained remarkably equitable despite marked population increase during the previous decade. In 1966, the four most populous districts, in which 53 percent of the population over 21 years of age reside, elected 31 of Oregon's 60 state representatives.[26] There are several instances of gerrymandering. The subdistricts in Portland were created to give the Republican party (which trails the Democrats in registration by a substantial margin) greater representation from Multnomah county. Subdistrict lines were drawn so that two of the five subdistricts (with seven of the seventeen seats from the county) were considered safe Republican districts. It is clear that position-numbering districts has had little effect on party contests. Both parties seemed satisfied with the current apportionment, and redistricting did not become an issue in 1966.[27]

THE SOCIAL AND ECONOMIC PARAMETERS
OF RECRUITMENT

The manner in which social and economic factors translate into electoral competition defines the parameters of the recruitment process. Social structure and the economy create social cleavages that interest groups and political parties crystallize and organize. How political parties will express such cleavages determines whether one or two parties will function and to what extent they will compete. The resources available to the principal participants in recruitment and the tactics they will employ will determine the intensity of party competition. We will show how

[26] U.S., Bureau of the Census, *U.S. Census of Population: 1960;* and Oregon, Secretary of State, *Official Abstract of Votes, op. cit.* (1966).
[27] The attempts at redistricting that have occurred since 1957 have been aimed at dividing the state's multiple-member districts into a number of single-member constituencies.

the economic and social diversity of a legislative district shapes political competition in Oregon's thirty-three legislative districts and subdistricts.

Measures of Economic and Social Diversity and Party Competition

The concepts of economic diversity, social diversity and inter-party competition were operationalized by using factor analysis. "Economic diversity" proved so complex that even adding indicators of urbanization, industrialization and income would not measure it. Adding indicators necessitated judgments about diversity that begged the question. We faced two problems in operationalizing diversity and competition: (1) Were these concepts empirically relevant in Oregon? (2) If so, which indicators best measured these variables and how much weight should be assigned to them?

The first problem was solved by using factor analysis as a technique for theory testing rather than data reduction.[28] It was hypothesized that through analysis, factors called "social diversity," "economic diversity," and "inter-party competition" would be identified. Then factor loadings and estimates of communality would allow us to select the indicators that together make up each factor and assign the appropriate weights to each indicator. If meaningful factors did not emerge, then the empirical relevance of the concepts would be in doubt. This method proved an objective way of measuring diversity and competition in Oregon.

Table III–2 is the rotated factor matrix of an oblimin rotation.[29] Although several types of rotation were employed, the oblimin method using the biquartimin simplicity criterion most closely approached "simple structure."[30] The factor correlation matrix in Table III–3 indicates that the factors are roughly orthogonal, although an oblique rotation was selected. Thus each factor loading indicates roughly the degree to which a given measure is correlated with a factor.[31]

[28] R. J. Rummel, "Understanding Factor Analysis," The Dimensionality of Nations Project, No. 7 (Honolulu: University of Hawaii, undated, mimeographed), p. 16.

[29] Harry H. Harman, *Modern Factor Analysis,* 2nd ed. (Chicago: University of Chicago Press, 1967), Ch. 15 for a technical discussion of the rationale underlying an oblimin rotation.

[30] *Ibid.,* Ch. 2 for a discussion of Thurston's notion of "simple structure." Simple structure refers to a factor matrix in which each indicator loads on one and only one factor.

[31] Since the factors are virtually independent, we can choose a cutting point based on significance level. For our purposes, we considered an indicator related to a factor if it is associated at the .01 level. With 32 of Oregon's 33 districts included in the sample, factor loadings greater than or equal to ±.47 are significant at the .01 level.

TABLE III–2

Rotated Factor Matrix of Structural Data[32]
(Oblimin Rotation)

Variables	Factor I Economic Diversity	Factor II Social Diversity	Factor III Partisan Competition
Median Family Income	*.85*	−.13	.02
% Work Force in Industry	*.80*	−.11	−.12
Median Years in School	*.95*	.38	.09
Population in Cities, 2,500+	*.79*	.25	−.12
Population in Urban Areas	*.70*	.44	.01
Population Density	*.50*	*.62*	−.19
% Protestant	.42	*−.65*	.15
Length of Residence	.01	*.75*	−.11
% of Mobile Population	−.15	*−.59*	.25
Intra-Party Competition	.16	*.82*	−.07
% Native-White Population	−.40	*−.58*	.23
Median Age	−.40	*.70*	−.13
% Majority Party Victories: 1958–1966	.12	−.08	*−.78*
% Majority Party Advantage in Voting: 1962 & 1966 average	−.17	.10	*−.89*
% Majority Party Victories: 1962 & 1966	.03	−.07	*−.87*

Note: Italics are significant factor loadings.

TABLE III–3

Factor Correlation Matrix[33]

Factors	Factor I	Factor II	Factor III
Factor I	1.00		
Factor II	0.26	1.00	
Factor III	−0.08	−0.04	1.00

Median family income, percent of the work force in industry, and three measures of urbanization loaded positively on Factor I. We have labeled this factor "economic diversity," although it might be called "economic urbanism," recognizing the close relationship between economic development and the level of urbanization in Oregon. In addi-

[32] All communalities were greater than .67; the first three unrotated factors explained 72 percent of the variance and the third factor explained 12 percent of the variance.
[33] A significance test of the largest correlation (0.26) yields $F_{1.31} = .074$.

tion, median years in school loaded strongly on Factor I. This is not surprising in light of the close association between education and the supply of manpower suited for industrial occupations. All indicators of social differences among Oregon's population loaded on Factor II, with the exception of median years in school. These include length of residence, percent native white population, percent Protestant, percent migrant, and median age of the population.[34] Two other indicators loaded on this factor: intra-party competitiveness and density of the population. The first, intra-party competitiveness, is not related significantly to the inter-party competition factor. Instead, it seems to be a function of the particular constellation of social differences in a district, or perhaps the extent to which these cleavages are translated into intra-party political conflict. The second, density of the population, is a measure of urbanization. This second factor we call "social diversity," although like Factor I, it could be called "social urbanism," recognizing the relationship between social differences and the density of population.

Each of these factors is a complex dimension and is related to different aspects of urbanization as well as different constellations of social or economic cleavage. Social diversity, for example, indicates the social differentiations of the population, and is also strongly related to the density of the population. In Oregon, the densely populated areas have more racial and ethnic groups than less densely populated areas. The social diversity factor separates even the most urbanized districts from all others. The network of social cleavages indicated by high social diversity is found in the populated Portland metropolitan area and to a lesser extent in the legislative districts which include Salem and Eugene, respectively. Only these areas may be called "urban," resembling those found nation-wide in larger metropolitan areas. The rest of the legislative districts are ethnically homogeneous, consisting of White Protestants of Northern European extraction. These constituencies have stable populations except for some transient farm workers and loggers.[35]

[34] The term "migrant" may be misleading. The definition of *migrants* in the 1960 Census was: "Persons who lived in different counties in the U.S. in 1955 and 1960."

[35] Although the factor analysis suggests that urban residents have a longer average length of residence in Oregon, when farm or non-farm place of residence is controlled, distribution of average length of residence changes. Farmers are the most stable element of the population, urban or rural, while rural, non-farm residents move frequently. This finding, together with the distribution of percent migrant (which also loads on Factor II) suggests that rural, non-farm residents account for the low average length of residence in rural areas. These people, mostly loggers

Economic diversity measures the number of economic cleavages in a district, and also indicates the level of industrialization and the proportion of the population living in cities and towns. Thus, economic diversity is linked more to the size of the population of urban areas than its density. In Oregon, the threshold of economic diversity divides rural and agrarian areas and small towns from the other districts. Industrialization, income, and education are strongly related to the proportion of the population residing in cities and towns of over 2,500 residents. Consequently, districts with no large cities, but where most citizens live in towns over 2,500 have economic characteristics that resemble larger metropolitan districts more than rural districts.

Generally, social diversity differentiates the most urbanized districts from all the others, while economic diversity distinguishes the most rural, economically diverse districts from all others. Thus, urbanization is not unidimensional in Oregon. Variations in the density of the population parallel changes in the distribution of social differences, while changes in the size of the urban population accompany changes in the level of economic development.

All indicators of inter-party competition loaded significantly on Factor III. Two of these indicators measure inter-party balance during off-years, since this study was conducted during an off-year election. The other indicator measures election outcomes in all elections since 1958. Although it did not load as highly as the others, the differences between it and the off-year measures are not statistically significant. Later on, we shall use inter-party competition as one component of a typology of patterns of effective electoral competition. The degree and kind of competition between the parties and within each party, are, of course, closely related and determine what recruitment stages will, in the end, prove decisive.

---

and farm workers, live in one place only a short time and move frequently from county to county more often than any other segment of the population, urban or rural.

Data about legislators complement this finding. In almost all instances, candidates resided in their districts at least five years. The majority of urban candidates had lived in their districts between five and fifteen years. In rural areas, however, nearly all candidates, winners and losers alike, had lived in the district at least fifteen years, with many reporting that their families had resided in the county for several generations. The politically active segment in these districts seems to be made up of long-resident local merchants, professionals and farmers. The geographically mobile people who pass through these counties exert little or no impact on politics. Many do not stay long enough to establish themselves in local politics. The "newcomers" that remain in the community are probably "long-time residents" before they become informed, interested, active and accepted in local affairs.

As a last step in the factor analysis, scores were computed for each factor. These scores gave an interval ranking of districts so that factor scores for Factor I, for example, provide an interval measure of the level of economic diversity in each legislative constituency.[36]

Distributions of Economic and Social Diversity

We expected the economic diversity of our area and its social diversity to be closely associated, but they proved independent of each other. The correlation between social and economic diversity for 32 of the 33 legislative districts is .26.[37] If the economic and social diversity factor scores are dichotomized and cross-tabulated, the probability of a random relationship between the two factors is significant (Table III–4).

A closer examination of the districts in each cell in Table III–4 reveals that the districts which are socially *and* economically diverse include subdistricts in the Portland metropolitan area and the surrounding suburban districts. The exception is Marion county, which contains the state capital, Salem. Similarly, districts that are low in *both* social and economic diversity are located in the more rural Eastern Coastal regions, where logging or farming are the major occupations. Most of the districts of Southern Oregon and many in the Willamette Valley outside

TABLE III–4

Relationship Between Economic Diversity and Social Diversity
(Percentages)

| *Economic* | *Social Diversity* | |
Diversity	*High*	*Low*
High	50%	50%
Low	50%	50%
Total	100%	100%

[36] Rummel, "Understanding Factor Analysis," pp. 31–33 for a description of the derivation and use of factor scores.

[37] The correlation of .26 is not significant at the .05 level. It is impossible to determine precisely the thresholds of urbanization because the data are constrained to the categories used by the Census Bureau. However, the factor analysis indicates that the greatest difference in industrialization occurs between districts which have few residents living in cities and towns and districts which have most of their citizenry clustered in towns even as small as 2,500. Increases in the size of towns in a constituency have relatively small marginal effect on economic diversity. Similarly, the socially diverse districts tend to have extremely dense populations (on the order of 1,000 people per square mile). Density of this magnitude is found in Oregon only in the Northern Willamette Valley. Virtually all other districts fall well below 500 residents per square mile.

of Portland and Salem are *mixed* cases. Some have diversified economies, but are socially homogeneous. In other districts, the distribution of social cleavages resembles that found in large metropolitan areas, but they are not industrialized.

The districts that represent mixed cases show the complexity of urbanization. Apparently, urbanization affects social and economic diversification at different rates even in one district. Before an area acquires the social and economic characteristics of large metropolitan areas like Portland, two thresholds must be crossed. The first occurs when a significant proportion of the population reside in towns or cities. The concentration of population into incorporated areas accompanies industrial growth. The second occurs when the population density increases, regardless of whether people live in municipal areas, unincorporated suburbs or residential neighborhoods.[38]

Thus, as population becomes concentrated in cities and towns, we cannot assume that the density of the population increases. Some legislative districts, especially those in the Willamette Valley outside of Portland and Salem, are densely populated, but few people live in towns of 2,500 inhabitants or more. The coastal districts, those in Southern Oregon, and several in Eastern Oregon have populations that are concentrated in cities and towns, but population density is low. In general, the *most urbanized* districts are socially and economically diversified, and the *least urbanized* districts are not. Half of the constituencies are both diversified and homogeneous. In half the legislative districts, social and economic diversity are correlated directly, but the remaining districts are *mixed* cases.[39]

Partisan Competition in Oregon

The decisive stages of selection competition in a district fall into one of four patterns: (1) instigation alone is the contested selection

[38] It must be emphasized that "more" or "less" densely populated and "higher" and "lower" proportions of the population living in cities and towns are relative to the range of these dimensions found in Oregon.

[39] These conclusions are supported when the level of economic or social diversity is controlled. When the most extreme cases on either dimension are considered (those districts ranking highest and lowest in economic or social diversity), there is a strong positive correlation between social and economic diversity. In the remaining districts, the two factors are negatively related.

The correlation between economic and social diversity controlling for levels of *social diversity* is .89. This result was obtained by selecting the six most and the six least socially diverse districts and correlating their social and economic diversity scores. The results of a similar control on *economic diversity* is .86. The twelve districts in each case represent slightly more than one-third of the total in Oregon. In the remaining constituencies in each instance, the correlations were —.25 and —.21 respectively.

stage; (2) instigation and the primary election are contested; (3) instigation and the general election are contested and (4) all stages of recruitment are contested.

What determines these patterns of political competition? Studies by V. O. Key and others have shown that as a single party comes to dominate a district, competition increases in that party's primary. However, when two parties are likely to compete closely in a general election, then the primary election within each party attracts fewer candidates.[40] The evidence in Oregon does not support Key's findings. The correlation between primary and general election competitiveness in Oregon's legislative districts is —.10 (see Table III–5).[41]

Table III–6 shows that approximately one-fourth of Oregon's legislative districts fall into each category of contested selection stages. Cell I contains districts where competition occurs at all stages in the recruitment process. Cell II shows the percent of districts where instigation

TABLE III–5

Patterns of Competition: General Election Competitiveness
and Primary Election Competitiveness

General Election Competitiveness	Primary Election Competitiveness	
	High	*Low*
High		
	53% (8)	47% (7)
Low		
	41% (7)	59% (10)

$X^2 = 1.00$ with 1 d.f. $N = 32$
$P > .05$ (insignificant)

---

[40] V. O. Key, Jr., *American State Politics* (New York: Knopf, 1956), pp. 171–181; Leon D. Epstein, *Politics in Wisconsin* (Madison: University of Wisconsin Press, 1958), p. 201; Malcolm E. Jewell and Samuel C. Patterson, *The Legislative Process in the United States* (New York: Random House, 1966), p. 84; and Austin Ranney, "Parties in State Politics," pp. 74–77 contain comprehensive summaries of these studies.

[41] A correlation of —.10 yields $F_{1.31} = .313$ which is not significant at the .05 level. Primary competitiveness was measured by taking the ratio of the number of candidates who compete in a district's primary to the number of primary election positions in a district. If, for example, a district elects one legislator, there are two primary election positions, one for each party. If four candidates file, the district's primary competitiveness score is 2.00. Data on primary competition were drawn from Oregon, Secretary of State, *Official Abstract of Votes* (Salem: Secretary of State, 1958–1966 editions). The measure of inter-party competition is based on the partisan competition factor. Factor scores were computed which give an interval ranking of inter-party competition among the districts of the state.

TABLE III–6

Patterns of Decisive Selection Stages:
Competitiveness in Primary and General Elections
(Percentages)

Competitiveness in General Election	*Competitiveness in Primary*		
	High	*Low*	*Total (N = 32)*
High	Cell I 53%	Cell II 47%	100%(15)
Low	Cell III 41%	Cell IV 59%	100%(17)
	$X^2 = 1.0$, n.s.		

and the general election are contested selection stages. Candidates from constituencies classified in Cell III compete during instigation and the primary election. The instigation stage is the only contested one in districts shown in Cell IV.

The data indicate that party competition alone does not explain the patterns of primary competition found throughout the state. In fact, a slight tendency prevails for contested primaries to occur in competitive rather than safe districts. Eighteen of the thirty-two districts do not fit the pattern that Key describes.

Other factors must account for the distribution of primary and general election competition in Oregon. We shall consider a number of such factors, especially the relationships between economic and social diversity and patterns of competition.

Economic and Social Diversity Determine Patterns of Competition

Key suggested that where incumbents sought reelection, few candidates would challenge them in the primary. Similarly, because incumbents are familiar to voters, they are less likely to be opposed in the general election, are usually well financed and organized, and enjoy the support of party officials who value their legislative seniority.[42] Again, these indicators are not always the case in Oregon. In 1966, fifty of the sixty incumbents ran for reelection to the Oregon House of Representatives. Of these, forty-five were reelected and five were defeated, one in the primary and four in the general election. In the general election, 88 percent of the incumbents were opposed, compared with 90 percent of the non-incumbents. Over 40 percent of the incumbents were opposed in the primary while approximately 60 percent of the non-

[42] Key, *American State Politics,* pp. 97–118, 171–181.

incumbents ran in contested primaries. In both cases, the differences were not significant although they followed the expected direction. Thus, on the basis of these findings, incumbency does not explain recruitment competition in Oregon.

Some studies have proved that urbanization, the diversity of the population, per capita income, and the economic resources of an area are related to political competition.[43] All such variables reflect economic and social diversity and determine the social and economic cleavages in a district. As a constituency becomes economically and socially diverse, the political cleavages increase. When such cleavages crosscut, the intensity of political conflict is diminished. Conversely, when cleavages reinforce each other, then the intensity of political conflict increases (Table III–7). *Taken together, the number and configuration of cleavages and their interrelationships determine political competition and the particular contested stages of the recruitment process that will be decisive.*[44]

Unfortunately, little solid information is available on whether cleavages crosscut or reinforce Oregon's legislative districts. Only the measures which precisely indicate the total number of cleavages were readily available. Consequently, it was projected that the degree of diver-

TABLE III–7

Diversity, Configurations of Cleavages, and Decisive Selection Stages

District Type	Economic & Social Diversity	Configuration of Cleavages	Decisive Selection Stages
Urban One-Party District	High	Reinforcing	Instigation & Primary Election
Urban Two-Party District	High	Crosscutting	Instigation, Primary, & General Election
Rural One-Party District	Low	Crosscutting	Instigation only
Rural Two-Party District	Low	Reinforcing	Instigation & General Election

[43] Fred I. Greenstein, *The American Party System and the American People* (Englewood Cliffs, N.J.: Prentice-Hall, 1963), pp. 55–57; Angus Campbell, *et al., The American Voter* (New York: Wiley, 1960), Chs. 15–17; Key, *op. cit.,* Ch. 2; and Ranney, "Parties in State Politics," pp. 67–70, 74–77.
[44] See Table III–7, this page for a more complete representation of the relationships among patterns of decisive selection stages and number and configuration of cleavages.

sity *partially* predicts only contested selection stages. In highly diverse districts, competition for office is likely during candidacy instigation and the primary *or* during all stages of recruitment. Alternatively, competition is limited to the instigation stage alone *or* to the instigation stage and the general election in less economic or socially diverse districts.

Table III–8 indicates the significant relationship between social diversity and patterns of the contested selection stages. Therefore we have identified districts where all stages of recruitment or instigation and the primary election are contested selection stages. The measure of strength of relationship (E) suggests that approximately 65 percent of the variance in the interval social diversity scale is involved in the relationship with patterns of political competition.[45]

With a single exception, the most diverse districts, those with a good deal of competition during initiation and the primary, are in the Portland metropolitan area. Legislative districts where *all* stages of recruitment are contested are less diverse. With a single exception, these districts are located in the Willamette Valley and include Eugene and Salem, Oregon's second and third largest cities. Districts where instigation and the general election are contested, rank third in social diver-

TABLE III–8

Social Diversity and Patterns of Contested Selection Stages

| | Contested Selection Stage | | | |
	Instigation	Instigation & General Election	Instigation & Primary Election	Instigation, General & Primary Elections
Mean Factor Scores for Social Diversity	$\overline{X} = 154.8$ (N = 10)	$\overline{X} = 209.7$ (N = 7)	$\overline{X} = 373.2$ (N = 7)	$\overline{X} = 274.3$ (N = 8)

$$F_{3 \cdot 28} = 17.22, \quad p < .001$$
Correlation Ratio $E = .805$, $E^2 = .65$

[45] Although analysis of variance indicates whether a statistically significant relationship exists between two dimensions, it does not measure the strength of the relationship. Consequently the correlation ratio *E* was selected as a measure of strength of relation. *E* was preferred to ETA and the intra-class correlation coefficient because its interpretation is extremely straight-forward. E^2 is the ratio of the explained or between-category sum of squares to the total sum of squares. Thus, the interpretation of E^2 is directly analogous to that of a coefficient of determination. In general, *E* measures the degree to which the interval scale is homogeneous within the nominal categories as compared with the total variability in the interval scale. See Hubert M. Blalock, Jr., *Social Statistics* (New York: McGraw-Hill, 1960), pp. 266–267.

sity, and are scattered throughout the rural districts of the state, but include Klamath Falls, Medford, The Dalles, and Pendleton, all cities of over 10,000 population.[46] The socially homogeneous districts, in which a contest occurs only during instigation are the farming areas of Eastern and Central Oregon and the sparsely populated Coastal counties.

As Table III–9 shows, no significant relationship prevails between economic diversity and contested selection stages. There is no apparent pattern to the ranking of mean economic diversity scores. Several explanations are possible. The level of economic development in Oregon is not as great as in some other states. The ecology of Oregon's industry is atypical: the two leading industries, tourism and the forest industry, are dispersed widely around the state. Oregon's mountains and beaches are appealing to tourists and are located in sparsely settled areas. Similarly, lumber and paper mills are situated close to sources of raw materials, again in rural areas. Industry is concentrated in the Portland Metropolitan region but other districts have their share as well.[47] The distinctive political milieus of Portland, the "mill towns," and resorts, account for the weak relationship between measures of economic diversity and contested selection stages.[48]

TABLE III–9

Economic Diversity and Patterns of Contested Selection Stages

	Contested Selection Stage			
	Instigation	*Instigation & General Election*	*Instigation & Primary Election*	*Instigation, Primary & General Elections*
Mean Factor Scores for Economic Diversity	$\overline{X} = 157.0$ (N = 10)	$\overline{X} = 142.3$ (N = 7)	$\overline{X} = 232.3$ (N = 7)	$\overline{X} = 162.4$ (N = 8)
	$F_{32 \cdot 8} = 1.20$, $p > .05$ Correlation Ratio $E = .332$, $E^2 = .110$			

[46] The nominal classification of effective selection stages is derived from the cross-tabulation of primary and general election competition (Table III–5 above).
[47] U.S., Bureau of the Census, *U.S. Census of Population: 1960*.
[48] One out of four people in Oregon is employed in the lumber industry. Of these, 67 percent live in small towns or rural areas. Unfortunately, the census does not distinguish between tourist trade and other types of service and proprietary occupations. Consequently, there is little systematic data on the number of people employed in the tourist industry or the ecology of the industry.
    The operational problems of separating districts with complex multiple-industry economies from those with a simpler, single-industry base are nearly all types

Issues of the 1966 Campaign

Election outcomes in the state, ebb and flow with the tides of national politics. Public interest increases when political issues strike close to home, or some dramatic political candidates come along, or a close contest develops.

Even the informed American involves himself in the affairs of state with a high degree of selectivity. The great quadrennial contest for the presidency may catch his fancy, but in the election of a state legislature or the deliberations of the local school board he is often monumentally uninterested. If state and local government, especially, does not titillate, shock or frighten, it might as well be taxing Zulus or subdividing Mars as far as he is concerned.[49]

During presidential elections, some political issues link national problems with local issues and penetrate the thick layer of private preoccupations which insulate the citizen. A presidential candidate's coattails may extend even to the local school board elections. During off-years, state and local candidates and issues lower the public's political horizons to parochial matters. For these reasons, we chose an off-year election (1966) to conduct this study. At such times, local influences on recruitment are more easily identified. But even in off-years, national issues or unusual local events may alter customary recruitment patterns. The issues in the Oregon election in 1966 were as follows: taxation, national resources, conservation and the War in Vietnam.

In Oregon, like in so many states, taxation is the perennial issue, often the only issue. Oregon levies no sales tax and relies for revenue on property taxes and a state income tax. Over the 1950s the public had demanded that the property tax be reduced. This is especially true in the urban areas where property taxes were highest. On several occasions, the legislature had referred a tax package to the voters that combined

---

of forest products under manufacturing, for example. Under the forest industries classification fall primary activities like logging and secondary manufacturing such as the production of paper, lumber and plywood. The manufacture of furniture and similar products is also included in this category. Census classifications of other types of industry raise similar problems.

Moreover, it is impossible to determine from census data if all manufacturing in a constituency, even if it is of only one kind, involves one or several factories and businesses. In general, although it might be desirable to develop means of classifying qualitative differences in the industrial base of a constituency, appropriate data are not available for legislative constituencies in Oregon. The end result is that the economic diversity factor separates districts that have some industry from those that do not.

[49] Sorauf, *Party and Representation op. cit.*, pp. 4–5.

property tax reduction with a sales tax, but such measures were calmly defeated. The 1965 legislature passed a measure that provided limited property tax relief, but this proved to be insufficient, because demands for property tax reduction became even more insistent since then. Several token attempts were made by an initiative to limit the rate of property taxation to 1.57 percent of true cash value. Opponents of these measures argued that such a policy would severely reduce the tax base of most municipalities and school districts. The drive to place the 1.57 percent limitation on the ballot in 1966 failed, for lack of a few hundred signatures.

Property taxation was the salient issue of the 1966 election. Many citizens felt that if the next legislature did not find an alternative source of revenue and significantly reduce property taxes, the 1.5 percent tax limitation initiative would be passed in the 1968 election. Almost all legislative candidates declared their support or opposition to the tax limitation measure. Some candidates proposed property tax relief through a sales tax or an increase in the personal income tax. The issue aroused such interest that several candidates reported that their concern with this issue alone impelled them to become candidates.

Another major issue of the 1966 campaign was the ownership of natural resources, a problem which includes many smaller issues: taxation of forest and grazing lands, water rights, conservation of resources, tourist facilities, wilderness areas, and water and air pollution. These issues were all quite basic to the economy of the state which at that time, derived its principal income from logging, farming and tourism. Controversy developed in 1966 because the federal government owned over half of the land in the state, including a large part of the prime timber and grazing lands. State officials, the timber industry and federal officials differed over the logging policies of the Forest Service and The Bureau of Land Management. The conflict had been aggravated because federal lands were exempted from property or timber taxes, although the federal government paid a subsidy in lieu of property taxes. Much of the state was not on the tax rolls in 1966, which shifted the tax burden to private timber lands, much to the dismay of the timber industry. Local school districts that contained federal acreage were deeply concerned, because their budgets depended upon federal-state-private agreements on logging policies or timber taxes.

During the 1966 campaign, tourism and the ownership of portions of Oregon's beaches became an important issue. The beaches in Oregon were and still are, public property. However, in some cases high tide lines changed sand drifts or rivers filled estuaries, thus making property boundaries ambiguous. In 1966, several private developers wanted to build a number of motel complexes along the Oregon coast. As construction progressed, beaches were covered with gravel, roads were built on the sand, and beach sand was used as fill around the motel sites. These practices raised the question of legitimate the ownership of beach-front property. A group called "save our beaches" was formed. A group of private developers and their supporters promptly formed an opposing group. The conflict centered around two major issues: should the public or private interests own the beaches, how important was tourism and what were the costs of tourism to the environment? The 1965 legislature resolved the issue by authorizing a survey to permanently fix beach-front property lines.

The War in Vietnam was the third major issue of the 1966 election. In the race for the U.S. Senate of that year, Mark Hatfield opposed the war and Robert Duncan supported it. Hatfield was Governor of Oregon and Duncan was then Congressman from Oregon's Fourth Congressional District. It was expected that the contest would become a referendum on Vietnam policy, but Hatfield played down the Vietnam issue and emphasized his record as Governor. Despite Duncan's persistent attacks on Hatfield's antiwar position, Vietnam did not become as prominent an issue as had been predicted. Consequently, the Vietnam issue had little impact on state legislative campaigns. Seldom, if ever, did a candidate for the Oregon House ally himself publicly with either Senatorial candidate. The Vietnam war was not an issue of debate in any of the contests for state legislator. Like other off-year elections in Oregon, the state legislative races focussed on local issues.[50]

CONCLUSIONS

The rise of the Democratic party in the mid-1950s inaugurated a new pattern of competitive politics in Oregon. The Democrats benefited from new immigration, industrialization and urbanization in the state. Just as overall growth and social-economic change in the state were responsible for political development, so was it true in each legislative district.

We examined the relationship between the social and economic

---

[50] This conclusion was supported, although unsystematically, in interviews with state representative candidates. No candidate mentioned that Vietnam had a marked impact on his campaign. However, this was in response to a question asking candidates to list factors they felt most important to the outcomes of their elections. Candidates were not asked specifically whether the War in Vietnam had an effect on their chances of winning.

diversity of Oregon's legislative districts and their patterns of electoral competition. The pattern of political competition changes as districts become more socially diverse and densely populated. The social diversity of a district's population determines whether the primary election, the general election, or both will be contested. The social structure of a district determines how many barriers a candidate must cross on the way to the state legislature and thereby constrains the aspirations and strategies of political aspirants.

CHAPTER IV

The Initiation of Candidacy

WHEN A PERSON considers candidacy for the state legislature, sponsors almost invariably influence his decision. The majority of candidates are sponsored. That is, individuals and groups encourage a prospective candidate in ways that range from subtle courtship to irresistible pressure. A few "self-starters" become candidates without such encouragement, but even these need and actively solicit sponsorship eventually.

The role of sponsors helps explain why the pool of potential candidates in each legislative district is small. Opportunity to run for public office is distributed unequally and achieved only after crossing three thresholds. The first is *formal certification,* which defines the legal qualifications for officeholding, i.e. those who *may* run for office. In the United States, every citizen who satisfies minimum age and residence qualifications may seek offices ranging from school board member to the Presidency. But only a few such individuals are also *effectively certified,* i.e. have the social status, sponsorship and skills to consider candidacy.[1] These are the citizens who *can* run. Finally, there are those who *will* run, who are not only ready and able, but also willing. These factors restrict office-seeking to a select few. The odds against an aver-

---

[1] See Lester G. Seligman, "Political Parties and the Recruitment of Political Leadership," in Lewis J. Edinger, ed., *Political Leadership in Industrialized Societies* (New York: Wiley, 1967), pp. 298–299; and James D. Barber, *The Lawmakers* (New Haven: Yale University Press, 1965), pp. 10–15, for similar conceptions of political certification. See also Chapter VI below for a more detailed discussion of factors influencing certification and the preselection that precedes filing for office.

age Oregonian filing for a seat in the Oregon House of Representatives are approximately ten thousand to one!

In this chapter, as we examine how individuals actually become candidates, we will consider the following questions: (1) What are the instigative mechanisms which lead candidates to file and what styles of candidacy do they produce? (2) Who sponsors candidates and what influence do such sponsors have in the decision to run? (3) In making this decision, how do candidates perceive the rewards and risks of candidacy? and (4) How does the social and political structure of constituencies determine the interactions and incentives at the inception of candidacy? In answering these questions, we will highlight the interactions between candidates and their sponsors as the candidates decide to run.

PATTERNS OF COMPETITION AND INCENTIVES

In chapter III, we discovered that the number and configuration of social cleavages in a constituency interact to produce four distinct patterns of political competition.[2] Each pattern represents a political milieu with characteristic types of candidates who enter candidacy in particular ways.

In *Urban One-Party Districts,* two phases of selection are competitive: candidate instigation and the primary election. Numerous social and political cleavages divide the population into two parties. But one political party enjoys a substantial advantage in voter registration. Only within the majority party does effective competition occur and show up during *instigation* or the *primary election.*

In *Urban Two-Party Districts,* all phases of selection are competitive. In such districts, social and political cleavages overlap. Some run parallel to party lines and balance the parties more or less evenly. Other cleavages cross party lines and create active intra-party competition. Shifting coalitions of individuals, factions and interest groups raise many issues during instigation and the primary election. These issues and those which divide the parties become the focus of competition during the general election. In these districts, competition prevails during *all selection phases.*

In *Rural One-Party Districts,* only the instigation phase is contested. The populations of these districts are quite homogeneous. The few social or political cleavages overlap and have little if any bearing on the issues which divide the national parties. In this setting, conflict is low

[2] See Chapter III, pp. 58–61 above.

key, moderate, and rarely expressed in open political competition. Consequently, the *instigation phase* is decisive because candidates often run unopposed or with token opposition in the primary and general elections.

In *Rural Two-Party Districts,* instigation and the general election are the two crucial phases. As in the rural one-party districts, the citizens of these districts do not display marked social or political differences. Consequently, little public competition should prevail. However, the existing cleavages are reinforcing or cumulative and become the focus of legislative competition. If the issues coincide with national party lines, public competition reaches a peak during the general election. More often, the issues are local, but the general election remains a decisive recruitment phase because it is more visible than the primary, and party labels conveniently identify the opposing factions.[3] Consequently, only *instigation* and the *general election* are decisive phases.

Each configuration of social diversity and political competition creates distinct recruitment patterns. In urban two-party districts, a candidate must divide his efforts among several stages of recruitment, while in rural one-party districts, all his efforts are bent on one phase. For some candidates in some districts, the recruitment process is long, uncertain and costly; for others it is short, certain and relatively inexpensive.

The social structure of a particular district shapes the "style" or character of its political life and can determine how attractive public office will be to potential candidates. If we treat the number of candidates who file as a crude measure of district incentives, then the incentives to run for office are greatest in Oregon's urban constituencies (Table IV–1 and IV–2). The urban one-party district offers the

TABLE IV–1

Social Heterogeneity and Number of Candidates Per Seat
(N = 33)

Social Diversity	Number of Candidates Per Seat				
	One	*Two*	*Three*	*Four —*	*Average*
High	0%	18	41	41	3.68
Low	38%	50	12	0	1.88
	$X^2 = 18.24, p < .001$				

[3] See Barber, *The Lawmakers,* pp. 127–129; and Arthur J. Vidich and Joseph Bensman, *Small Town in Mass Society,* Anchor Books (New York: Doubleday, 1958), p. 122.

greatest incentives (followed by the urban two-party areas), because the urban candidate can easily make his political aspirations coincide with his private career.[4] Like a politician, the businessman, realtor or insurance agent seeks prominence and publicity, which a political campaign surely provides. Moreover, urban legislative seats are stepping stones to higher office and attract the politically ambitious.

Small rural communities offer few incentives to potential candidates. People know one another, and the community is tied together by interlocking networks of primary social groups. Any outbreak of political conflict becomes intense and disruptive. Consequently, "the value attached to being a good neighbor and the rewards of amicable intra-community relations are greater than the rationally perceived gain from various conflicts."[5] Since political rivalry breaks these primary relationships, community norms disapprove of open political conflict and inhibit most potential candidates.[6] The result is *rural one-party constituencies* where the candidates run either unopposed or with mild token opposition.

In some rural areas, social cleavages are cumulative, and the conflict finds expression in a sharp contest between the two parties. The public competition which ensues is both intense and personal. One candidate who had challenged a veteran incumbent in one of these *rural two-party districts* described the disruptive effects as follows:

> I'm having lots of second thoughts now. I ran . . . because a lot of people around here are mad about the way [Incumbent] has thrown his weight around on a number of issues.
> But I know [Incumbent] pretty well, and a lot of his friends are my friends. We meet nearly every day when the legislature isn't in session, and both of us belong to the same organizations. This campaign is opening a lot of sores and they'll be slow to heal. No matter who wins, both of us will be worse off.

Such open competition tears apart old friendships and divides the constituency into rivalrous factions. Candidates from these rural two-party districts risk their community standing and reputation when they run.

---

[4] When social diversity was related to the number of candidates per seat, controlling for competition, we found that diversity and competition each independently influence the number of candidates.

[5] Richard I. Hofferbert, "Elite Influence in Policy Formation: A Model for Comparative Inquiry" (a paper presented at the annual meeting of the American Political Science Association, Washington, D.C., 1968), p. 22.

[6] See Vidich and Bensman, *Small Town in Mass Society,* Chapter V and pp. 121–123; Frank J. Sorauf, *Party and Representation,* p. 109; and Barber, *The Lawmakers,* pp. 122–127.

Many potential candidates are discouraged from filing because they shy away from conflict that becomes so personal.

Other aspects of the rural constituencies deter individuals from becoming candidates. The man who seeks state legislative office can expect few social or financial payoffs. In a small community, the farmer, attorney or realtor does not need publicity. Also, the constituency is too small to be a staging area for the politically ambitious. Local leaders can aspire to the Oregon State House, or possibly the Oregon State Senate, but no higher.

Each political milieu draws particular elements into politics, the products of patterns of incentive and sponsorship endemic to each district. The conventional notion that a candidate throws his hat into the ring only after he has chosen the most opportune moment, weighed his chances of winning, and planned his strategy, is true only in some constituencies. There is greater diversity in the way individuals become candidates.

Each candidate's initial recruitment as well as his subsequent campaign strategy depends upon three factors: one that applies to all candidates–(1) the incentives and opportunities for the advancement that a district offers its candidates; and two that apply to each individual candidate–(2) the goals and motivations of the candidate himself; and (3) the candidate's relations with his sponsors.

If one must generalize, each candidate (both serious contenders and advertisers) would like to make a respectable showing. This is a relative matter, however. A respectable showing is that vote that protects a candidate's standing and self-esteem. It falls between the optimal results and the most embarassing ones.

Incentives are a key factor in each candidacy. Some individuals regard campaigning and officeholding as onerous and unattractive. Others consider public office so rewarding that they are blind to its disadvantages. The balance of rewards and risks that candidates perceive is at once both an objective and subjective matter. In each legislative district, candidacy bestows particular objective rewards and risks which each candidate perceives in his own way. In part, the candidate's position in the district's social structure determines how he will respond to such incentives. For example, the publicity of the campaign attracts young attorneys in urban districts. By contrast, in the same districts, a respected businessman, physician or the scion of an old family will rarely become a candidate, because they don't need the recognition that public officeholding affords. Ultimately, each potential candidate is receptive or resistant to sponsors depending upon whether and what he stands to gain or lose. Some individuals seize opportunities to run, others need coaxing, and still others reject categorically the suggestion that they become candidates.

INCENTIVES, SPONSORSHIP AND STYLES OF CANDIDACY

Candidates in Oregon displayed two basic styles. Some were *reluctants,* while others were *enthusiasts.*[7] The reluctants had been pressed into service by others. The enthusiasts found office-seeking so rewarding that they needed little or no encouragement to run. *Enthusiasts* included completely unsponsored candidates and others who had made up their minds to run before they were urged to do so by their sponsors. The remaining candidates were labeled *reluctants* because they ran only because other people convinced them that they should (Table IV–3).

TABLE IV–2

Patterns of Competition and Number of Candidates Per Seat
(N = 33)

Patterns of Competition	Number of Candidates Per Seat				
	One	Two	Three	Four+	Average
Rural One-Party District	60%	30	10	0	1.50
Rural Two-Party District	0%	71	29	0	2.29
Urban One-Party District	0%	14	28	58	3.97
Urban Two-Party District	0%	22	45	33	3.59
	$X^2 = 28.67$, p $< .001$				

Generally speaking, most rural candidates were reluctants, which reflects the low incentives of the rural districts (Table IV–4). Conversely, the majority of the urban candidates were enthusiasts, although important exceptions existed which we will discuss below. Many enthusiasts were self-starting candidates, while others served as spokesmen for interest groups. Still others earned a chance to run by working their way

[7] As used here, the term "reluctant" shares some similarity with Barber's use of the term. Barber's reluctants were unwilling to run for reelection, found legislative service less than fully satisfying, and had their roots in small towns and rural areas. We use the term "reluctant" to refer to individuals who were unwilling to run in the first place, generally found legislative service unrewarding, and who came from rural communities. Thus, although different dimensions were used to classify reluctants in the two studies, the reluctant category appears to refer to much the same style of candidate. See Barber, *The Lawmakers,* Chapter 4.

TABLE IV–3

Styles of Candidacy in Oregon
(N = 109)

Styles	%
Enthusiasts	49
Reluctants	51
	100%

up through the ranks of parties or groups.[8] A mixture of political and private goals impelled the enthusiasts. Those who were genuine contenders for office marshalled support and publicized the issues during the campaign. At the same time, they exploited candidacy to advance their political careers, enhance their social status, and further their private occupations. To achieve these objectives, they actively sought to enlist sponsors for their personal campaign organizations.

Other enthusiasts were simply self-promoting entrepreneurs. They exploited the campaign to publicize themselves in order to gain clients in their private occupations. One such advertiser explained, "I'm not a real candidate. I run simply because it's good for business." Such advertisers were usually self-starters who waged a minimal campaign and bowed out after the primary election.

Virtually all enthusiasts, whether advertisers or genuine contenders, responded sensitively to district incentives. They filed because they expected tangible profit from running. Consequently, this style of candidacy was found almost exclusively in the urban legislative districts of Oregon.[9]

Reluctant candidates ran for less tangible reasons. Many reluctants agreed to file only after their sponsors had appealed to their sense of civic responsibility, party loyalty or obligations to some interest group. Without such pressure most of these individuals would not have run because the rewards of candidacy offered them so little. Nearly all minority party candidates in urban one-party districts were reluctants. They ran to provide symbolic opposition to the dominant party or faction in the district. They were the political martyrs of the campaign. The minority party leaders drafted them and promised money and workers to help them make a respectable showing. Occasionally, a reluctant candidate

[8] For a more detailed discussion of mechanisms of recruitment and styles of candidacy, see Lester G. Seligman, "Political Recruitment and Party Structure: A Case Study," *American Political Science Review*, pp. 77–86.

[9] Altogether, 17 of the 22 advertisers ran in the urban districts. All five of the advertisers in the rural districts refused to be re-interviewed after they lost the primary, whereas all of the urban advertisers agreed to the post-primary interview.

filed in an urban two-party district. Almost invariably, these men were prominent civic leaders who already enjoyed considerable prestige and influence. We call them the *notables*. They agreed to run under protest, yielding to strong pressure. Party leaders and other sponsors sought to *coopt* them because their prominence and public esteem is a decided advantage in a close urban election. Such notables were not strongly identified with their sponsors. They needed their sponsors less than their sponsors needed them. The notables weren't interested in a political career. Few found legislative service rewarding and many retired after one or two terms.[10]

The coopted notables and the minority martyrs were not the only reluctant candidates. Virtually all rural legislative candidates were pressured into running. They ran for office simply because no one else would. Low district incentives detered the politically ambitious and reduced the number of potential candidates. Because potential hopefuls were scarce, sponsors and "kingmakers" carefully cultivated individuals who might run. All segments of the community or faction joined forces to convince a chosen individual to file. Once in office, incumbents were encouraged to seek reelection one term after another because suitable replacements were hard to find.

The reluctant candidates point up the importance of sponsorship in recruitment. Strictly speaking, only the reluctant candidates are actually instigated by sponsors. But sponsorship is important to the enthusiasts in the other stages of selection—the primary and general elections. We found that in all constituencies, sponsors began preparing for the campaign several months before the filing deadline.

At first, we had difficulty in classifying the various sponsors because we had expected to find only two types of sponsors: political parties and pressure groups. We had anticipated that the party organizations and interest groups would instigate most candidates, and that particular sponsors and candidates would join together because of their ideological affinities. However, party and group-sponsorship activities were not so consistent. In one district, a labor union urged a liberal Democrat to run, while in another district, the same union supported a conservative candidate. In a third district, labor and employer groups, civil rights and conservative veterans' organizations supported the same candidate. In some bizarre instances, an interest group would encourage *both* opponents.

Moreover, "party" sponsorship proved to be a misleading concept. The county party organizations were often so undermanned that the

---

[10] Only one of the coopted candidates who won in 1966 continued in politics, and he ran for higher office.

regular party organization or party recruiting committees did not exist. Seldom were the parties solely responsible for initiating a candidate. More often, the parties shared instigation with interest groups, or as was frequently the case, a candidate would have an elaborate campaign organization, but no party or associational sponsors!

These instigative patterns illustrate the "free-for-all" quality of recruitment in states like Oregon where party organization is fragmented. Oregon's parties and free-wheeling interest groups do not control recruitment. Each candidate must form his own campaign organization. In doing so, he may accept associational or party help, but he is apt to build the campaign organization around a nucleus of people he knows and trusts, e.g. relatives, friends, colleagues, and the like. Consequently, the candidates' primary groups become crucial instigative agents. They encourage him, advise him, solicit support, and bolster the candidate's resolve during the delicate days of candidacy initiation.[11]

In some instances, a candidate's primary group was linked indirectly to his party or to an interest group. As one candidate explained:

I've been friends with the guy who talked me into running for a number of years. He's also been the business agent for [labor union] for nearly 20 years. When he asked me if I would be interested in running, I wasn't sure whether *he* wanted me to run or the *union* wanted me. (emphasis added)

Although the parties and interest groups occasionally used a friend or colleague as an intermediary, especially if the candidate was reluctant to run, they usually approached candidates directly.

The importance of primary group initiation in Oregon led us to classify each instigating sponsor into one of two categories: primary or secondary group. Secondary group sponsors were divided again into party instigators and other secondary organizations (a residual category).[12] The classification describes sponsorship more accurately in states like Oregon where parties share recruitment functions with other organizations, primary groups, and many candidates are self-recruited.

---

[11] This finding reinforces other research on primary group influences on individual orientations and behavior. See, for example, Sidney Verba, *Small Groups and Political Behavior* (Princeton: Princeton University Press, 1961), pp. 22–29; Leon Festinger, et al., *Social Pressures in Informal Groups* (New York: Harper, 1950), Chapters 5 and 6; and Edward A. Shils, "Primary Groups in the American Army," in Robert Merton and Paul Lazarsfeld, eds., *Studies in the Scope and Method of "The American Soldier"* (Glencoe, Ill.: Free Press, 1950).

[12] We divided the secondary sponsors into party and other secondary organizations simply so that party activity in Oregon might be compared with other states. In most districts, the parties were no more significant than interest groups in initiating and sponsoring candidates, and in many instances, were less so.

DISTRICT COMPETITION AND INSTIGATION PATTERNS

Sponsors must consider the strength of incentives for candidacy that operate in each legislative district. Where candidacy is unenticing, potential candidates are more reluctant to run and sponsors must actively encourage them. Where public office is more rewarding, sponsors can easily find suitable candidates because numerous enthusiasts seek their support. Consequently, most candidates were actively encouraged in the rural constituencies, but not in the urban ones (Table IV–5). Moreover,

TABLE IV–4

Patterns of Competition and Styles of Candidacy
(N = 109)

Patterns of Competition	Reluctants	Enthusiasts
Rural One-Party District	65%	35
Rural Two-Party District	83%	17
Urban One-Party District	33%	67
Urban Two-Party District	46%	54
$X^2 = 10.92$, p < .02		

primary group sponsors were more active in the rural districtcs (Table IV–6). Primary groups encouraged over 80 percent of the rural candi-

TABLE IV–5

Patterns of Competition and Instigation
(N = 109)

Patterns of Competition	Instigated	Not Instigated
Rural One-Party District	94%	6
Rural Two-Party District	89%	11
Urban One-Party District	64%	36
Urban Two-Party District	60%	40
$X^2 = 10.26$, p < .02		

dates, and party recruiters urged over 70 percent of the rural candidates to run. By contrast, less than half of the urban respondents reported that primary groups, party recruiters, or interest group representatives had asked them to run.

Moreover, the urban sponsors gave their encouragement selectively. They concentrated their efforts on the reluctant candidates and generally ignored the enthusiasts. For example, in the urban one-party districts, a total of fourteen minority party candidates ran. Of the fourteen, party recruiters approached eleven, and all fourteen had sponsors of one kind or another. Thus, the minority party candidates were *party-instigated*. By contrast, only five of the twenty-five majority party candidates were sponsored at all.

In the urban two-party constituencies, intensive efforts were made to instigate the "notables." We found that thirteen candidates in these districts were coopted, that is, sponsors convinced prominent individuals to become candidates.[13] Party recruiters talked to all thirteen, and primary groups encouraged all but one. Moreover, interest groups instigated eleven. *Only eight other candidates in the urban two-party districts were encouraged to run by anyone.*

The sponsors' activities become clearer when we consider the *number* of sponsors of each type who encouraged the candidates (Table IV–7). Some candidates had many primary group or party sponsors, while others had few or none at all. A candidate faced more intense instigative pressure when many people, both friends and representatives of his party or interest groups urged him to run.

As a rule, the instigating sponsors in rural areas consisted of the candidate's friends and neighbors, including close associates who belonged to such local organizations as the Farm Bureau, the Grange, Cattlemen's Associations, Chambers of Commerce, and local fraternal and civic clubs. The pressure of so many of the candidate's friends and col-

TABLE IV–6

Patterns of Competition and Sources of Instigation
(N = 109)

Patterns of Competition	Primary Group		Political Party		Interest Group	
	Yes	*No*	*Yes*	*No*	*Yes*	*No*
Rural One-Party District	82%	18	71%	29	65%	35
Rural Two-Party District	83%	17	72%	28	67%	33
Urban One-Party District	38%	62	46%	54	36%	64
Urban Two-Party District	46%	54	40%	60	29%	71
$X^2 = 16.50$, p < .001			$X^2 = 7.86$, p < .05		$X^2 = 10.01$, p < .02	

[13] "Coopted candidates" were defined operationally as individuals who (a) were reluctant to run; (b) were unusually well-known, successful, and respected according to the accounts of other candidates and the sponsoring groups in the constituency; and (c) were not closely associated with any party, group or faction in the district, again according to the reports of other candidates and the sponsors.

leagues made it nearly impossible for him to refuse. In the same districts, party initiation was perfunctory. Most candidates told us that the county chairman talked to them, but could offer only moral support in the upcoming campaign. Party recruitment committees were seldom active, and the Young Democrat and Republican organizations were more interested in state-wide and national races.

Only a few urban candidates had very many sponsors. Those that did, i.e. the "martyrs" of the minority party and the coopted "notables" in the competitive urban districts, had more diverse recruitment groups than their rural counterparts. Numerous friends, relatives, work associates, party recruiters, and, in the case of the coopted candidates, interest group sponsors combined to instigate their candidacies. The organized sponsorship that parties and interest groups could give was especially important to both types of urban reluctants because they feared that the campaign and risk of making a poor showing in the election, might jeopardize their reputations and community standing. Only with adequate backing from various organized sponsors could they make a respectable showing in the election. The coopted candidates sought firm commitments of financial assistance, campaign workers and endorsements *before* they filed. They negotiated the campaign strategy and financing with their party and group sponsors, and consented to run only after they were assured of enough resources to launch effectively and maintain the campaign. The minority party candidates dealt exclusively with their party leaders and their objectives were quite different from the coopted notables. The minority party candidates hoped only to lose with dignity, whereas the coopted notables sought assurances that they would *win*.

The urban enthusiasts entered the race. In uninvited urban two-party districts, the enthusiasts, incumbents and challengers alike, initiated their own candidacies, solicited sponsors and formed their own personal campaign organizations. Incumbents in the urban one-party districts simply filed and did little else. They were secure in office and waged only *pro forma* campaigns. These majority party incumbents were elected quietly in primary elections that elicited little public interest and low turnout. The name-familiarity of such veteran incumbents gave them a decisive advantage. A challenger must wage an intensive campaign to catch the attention of enough voters to win. Only when a seat was vacant were incentives sufficient to draw enthusiasts who were serious candidates. Even then, campaign efforts often had little bearing on the outcome. When the field consisted of unknown candidates, the primary election was like a lottery. An unusual name, or a name identified with a familiar one, a catchy slogan in the Voter's Pamphlet (distributed to each voter) or a chance factor such as position on the ballot often proved decisive.

The incumbents' commanding advantage in the urban one-party districts created opportunities for advertisers and political entrepreneurs. They entered the race unasked and were content to remain unsponsored because all they sought was publicity. As one self-promoter explained:

I don't expect to win, and what's more I don't want to. This is the third time I've run against Mr. [Incumbent]. He's ... been in the House since the early Fifties. I don't have a snowball's chance of beating him out.

Every election, I pay the filing fee and buy a page in the [Voter's] Pamphlet. They put in my picture, and I write up who I work for and where I work, and they publish it all. When you're in the insurance business like I am, every little bit helps. I figure every election is worth ten or twenty policies.

Another such candidate stated:

I run because when you're an attorney, it's the only way you can advertise. When someone needs an attorney, they look in the phone book and they choose a name they recognize. Around here I want them to know my name.

PREDISPOSITIONS TO CANDIDACY

Enthusiasts and reluctants have different expectations and outlooks. The enthusiasts are buoyed by high expectations about the campaign or their political careers, a perspective the reluctants do not share. Each candidacy style creates opportunities and dilemmas for sponsors. In dealing with the reluctants, sponsors must search for candidates and pressure them to run. In dealing with enthusiasts, sponsors can safely wait for the candidates to come to them. But sponsors may find a superfluity of enthusiasts when the reluctant notables are what they need.

Whether or not a potential candidate responds to a sponsor's inducements depends upon the candidate's perceptions of risks and benefits. The privileges of office alone do not assure an adequate number of candidates. Each would-be candidate makes his own assessment as to whether the incentives to run are sufficient or not. What constitutes an incentive for a particular candidate depends in part on his motivation for politics, and is rooted in his early socialization. Our research did not probe such motivation directly. But motivation underlies various orientations to politics: a commitment to an issue or ideology, a deep sense of civic responsibility, or an instrumental orientation toward politics as an avenue to power or income.

Such orientations color each individual's expectations about political activity and predispose him to view political roles as gratifying or unrewarding. During each of three waves of interviews, we asked the candidates how they assessed the personal costs and benefits of candidacy and service in the State Legislature. The questions explored how political activity affected the candidate's occupation, his relationships with family and friends, and his or her social affiliations in various clubs and organizations.[14] During the pre-primary election interviews, the candidates were asked to *anticipate* how the campaign and election would affect them personally; in the later interviews candidates reported their *actual* gains and losses.[15] From their responses, we constructed separate personal costs and benefits indices.[16] We expected the indices to be inversely related, so that candidates who perceived high costs would report low benefits and *vice versa*. However, the indices were independent of each other rather than reciprocal. Such a finding is consistent with experimental research which reported that perceived risks are more salient than benefits when decisions are made under conditions of uncertainty.[17]

Since the social structure and competitive pattern determine the incentives to run in each district, we expected that they would be related to what its candidates expected to gain or lose. But it had been found that the degree of political competition and the candidates' perceptions of risks and benefits were not related at all! Incentives *per se* did not determine the candidates' perceptions (Table IV–8).[18] Instead, anticipated gains and losses were shaped by the *interaction* between the candidates' desire to run and incentives. Each candidate's expectations of gains and losses depended on *how strongly the candidate wanted to run* (e.g. whether enthusiast or reluctant) and the *particular incentives*

[14] See Appendix B for appropriate questionnaire items.

[15] We found a great deal of consistency among candidates' anticipated costs and benefits and their reports of actual costs and benefits after the primary and general elections. Their responses were so consistent that we could develop a single index of costs and another for benefits incorporating both anticipated and actual costs and benefits.

[16] See Appendix A for a description of the procedures used to construct these indices.

[17] See Kogan and Wallach, "Risk-Taking as a Function of the Situation, the Person, and the Group," in *New Directions in Psychology*, III (New York: Holt, Rinehart and Winston, 1967), p. 143.

[18] Social and economic diversity also proved to be unrelated to anticipated costs and benefits.

TABLE IV-7

Patterns of Competition and Number of Instigators by Sources
(N = 109)

Patterns of Competition	Total Number of Instigators of All Sources		Number of Primary Group Instigators		Number of Party Instigators		Number of Interest Group Instigators	
	Large	Small	Large	Small	Large	Small	Large	Small
Rural One-Party District	69%	31	79%	21	17%	83	55%	45
Rural Two-Party District	81%	19	87%	13	46%	54	58%	42
Urban One-Party District	32%	68	20%	80	83%	17	43%	57
Urban Two-Party District	62%	38	62%	38	100%	0	55%	45
	$X^2 = 11.35, p < .01$		$X^2 = 16.84, p < .001$		$X^2 = 23.43, p < .001$		$X^2 = .63, p < .80$	

that were found to be attractive. The incentives the candidate selected depended, in part, on his or her social and economic position in the community and his competitive advantage or disadvantage as compared to other candidates. Thus, if a candidate wanted to run, he or she expected beneficial results even if the incentives were small. Certain incentives made the candidate more expectant and optimistic. Weakly motivated candidates, perhaps because of a distaste for politics or the pressure of other commitments, expected to gain little even when the incentives were great. Fewer incentives made them more pessimistic and resistant to persuasion.

In sum, a candidate's perceptions of costs and benefits seemed to result from the following set of influences. *When a candidate was predisposed not to run and at the same time had few incentives, he anticipated high costs and low benefits.* Thus, the urban coopted candidates and the majority of rural contenders were both reluctant and had weak incentives to run. They perceived high costs and low benefits (Table IV–9).

A candidate strongly predisposed to run, and with rewarding incentives expected high costs and high benefits. Most urban enthusiasts who were serious contenders for office anticipated that they would experience substantial costs in return for the high benefits of candidacy. They reported that the campaign and legislative service would enhance their prestige and popularity among their friends and associates, and bring added success to their occupations. Yet they expected the campaign to be a gruelling affair that would demand much in time and energy. Most predicted that legislative service would seriously disrupt their family life and social activities and would necessitate some special arrangements in their work. Consequently, most entered the race fully expecting to gain *and* lose.

TABLE IV–8

Patterns of Competition and Anticipated Benefits and Costs
(N = 109)

Patterns of Competition	Anticipated Benefits		Anticipated Costs	
	High	Low	High	Low
Rural One-Party District	59%	41	59%	41
Rural Two-Party District	41%	59	41%	59
Urban One-Party District	49%	51	44%	56
Urban Two-Party District	59%	41	62%	38
$X^2 = 1.38$, n.s.			$X^2 = 3.13$, n.s.	

Some candidates gave ambivalent responses: *highly motivated candidates faced with incentives that were moderate or low, or reluctant candidates faced with substantial incentives.* The advertisers, typically enthusiasts who entered a race with limited incentives that matched their limited objectives, tended slightly to expect high benefits, and almost all of them anticipated low costs. The urban minority candidates were reluctant, but had small incentives. As the minority party spokesmen, they could reap benefits from the publicity of the campaign so long as they avoided the stigma of an overwhelming loss. In general, they reported low benefits and low costs, which suggests that they expected to gain or lose little by serving as martyrs.

Although the sponsors sought to add inducements to the candidates, *sponsorship did not change the candidates' preconceptions about how they would fare in the campaign and thereafter* (Table IV–10). The candidates perceptions about benefits and costs were unrelated to whether or not they were sponsored or how many sponsors they had. In fact, the most strongly instigated candidates, the reluctants, were the ones who were the most pessimistic. In the short run, instigative pressure did not change attitudes and predispositions that had taken root in early socialization and had been reinforced by long experience in the district. Neither could it change the candidate's basic understanding of district politics, nor the information about what candidacy and legislative service does and does not have to offer.

However, sponsorship did perform a critical function. *Without sponsors, many candidates would not have run, generally because their experience and predispositions convinced them that it was undesirable*

TABLE IV–9

Styles of Candidacy and Anticipated Benefits and Costs
(N = 109)

Styles of Candidacy	*Anticipated Benefits*		*Anticipated Costs*	
	High	*Low*	*High*	*Low*
Reluctants:				
Rural Reluctants	34%	66	38%	62
Urban Coopted Candidates	31%	69	92%	8
Urban Minority Candidates	36%	64	29%	71
Enthusiasts:				
Advertisers (Urban & Rural)	55%	45	9%	91
Other Urban Enthusiasts	71%	29	65%	35
$X^2 = 11.33$, p $<$ .05			$X^2 = 30.81$, p $<$ .001	

to do so. Many candidates filed simply because other people talked them into running. This encouragement was most influential if it came from their primary groups. At the instigation stage, primary group approval was a necessary precondition of candidacy for reluctant candidates. For them, their family, friends and neighbors exerted one kind of influence and secondary groups exerted another. The candidate valued his or her relations with his primary groups *intrinsically,* but valued secondary groups for their *instrumental* value to his or her campaign. Only after the idea of running was cleared with family and friends did the reluctant candidate assess what he might lose or gain by becoming a candidate. When members of a potential candidate's primary groups approved and encouraged his candidacy, he often ran, even though he had little chance of winning. When family and friends opposed candidacy, even a virtual shoo-in would not file, though he had firm promises of finances, organizational backing and every reason to believe that running would improve his income, prestige and influence.

The role of primary groups became clear when we asked the sponsored candidates to assess the differential influence of the various sponsors who initiated their candidates. Primary group sponsors proved important to candidates among all types of districts. As we typically expected, all rural candidates who were influenced by their primary groups were reluctants. Moreover, all but two of the urban candidates who were similarly influenced were either minority party candidates in the one-party districts, or coopted candidates in the two-party districts. The same urban reluctants were also likely to report party instigation as

TABLE IV–10

Sources of Instigation and Anticipated Benefits and Costs
(N = 109)

Sources of Instigation	Anticipated Benefits		Anticipated Costs	
	High	Low	High	Low
Primary Groups:				
Yes	50%	50	48%	52
No	55%	45	55%	45
Political Party:				
Yes	56%	44	46%	54
No	48%	52	57%	43
Interest Groups:				
Yes	58%	42	50%	50
No	48%	52	52%	48

influential. Thus, the rural reluctants ran if they could count on their primary groups to back them, while the urban reluctants needed both the moral support of those close to them, and the resources of secondary groups like their party to wage the campaign. In both instances, primary group encouragement was crucial.

SUMMARY AND CONCLUSIONS

When we focus on the instigative patterns in Oregon's four types of legislative districts, the following pattern emerges. In rural areas, the incentives to candidacy are weaker, and therefore a variety of sponsors approach candidates and urge them to run. The unsponsored candidate is a rarity. Whereas, in urban areas, where the incentives are greater, enthusiasts are found more frequently, and only the urban reluctants required strong instigation.

In rural areas, party is not a significant factor, because party organization is so diffuse and fragmented. Primary groups play an important role, but they blend into secondary associations because the distinction between friendship groups and secondary organizations is blurred. In urban areas, the number of sponsored candidates is fewer, and sponsorship focused only on the reluctant notables and minority party candidates. Primary groups instigate these candidates, and so do their parties. Minority candidates are reluctant because they face certain defeat. The coopted candidates need inducement to run because they are already "established" and bring prestige and proven appeal to the voters.

When candidates file they have particular expectations about what they will gain and risk losing. The expectations are created both by the candidate's desire to run and by the incentives his district offers him. The candidate's anticipated costs and benefits are unaffected by sponsors' efforts. Instead, the candidates' knowledge of politics and office-seeking in the district, tempered by political attitudes and orientations rooted in his political socialization shape his expectations.

CHAPTER V

Support and Reinforcement

THE DEADLINE FOR filing for office marks the official start of the campaign. The behind-the-scenes negotiation and maneuvering of instigation cease, and the public sees the newly-announced candidates and sometimes their sponsors for the first time. As this new phase of the recruitment process begins, the candidates mobilize their sponsors in order to broaden their support among the voters. The original circle of family, friends, and others who initiated the candidacy evolves into a full-fledged campaign organization. As the campaign unfolds, the candidate recruits additional backers or new sponsors come forward and offer their support. Together, the initial and later sponsors make up each candidate's coalition of campaign support.

Mutual interdependence unites the candidate with his sponsors. Candidates need the support of influential individuals and groups, and these supporters, in turn, enhance their political influence by sponsoring promising candidates. Even when their candidate is defeated in the primary or general election, the campaign itself gives sponsors an opportunity to articulate their positions before a wide audience and win new adherents. Moreover, should their candidate win, they expect him to represent them in the legislature.

Sometimes a distinction is drawn between recruitment politics and pressure politics. Recruitment politics refers to attempts to place or replace the men in power, while pressure politics describes attempts to influence those already in power. But the distinction becomes empty when recruitment politics and pressure politics are one and the same. The obligations a candidate incurs to a group during his campaign remain with the newly elected lawmaker in the legislature. The coalition of support that initially recruited a candidate will make demands on the fledgling legislator, and the new state representative or senator, in turn, needs the support of the sponsor in the next campaign. Consequently, today's sponsors become tomorrow's legislative lobbyists. It is no surprise that legislative decisions often can be traced back to influences that form during the earliest phases of recruitment.

In the pages that follow, we will see if the same people who initiate candidates go on to support them during the campaign. Then, we will consider how social and political factors determine the patterns of campaign support in the various constituencies, and show that the kind and amount of support that candidates receive shape their perceptions of the risks: the net gains and losses they encounter.

PATTERNS OF SUPPORT IN THE PRIMARY AND GENERAL ELECTIONS

Candidates expect the individuals and groups that first persuaded them to run to support their campaigns. Our data show the largest proportion of instigators did in fact actively sponsor their candidates in the primary and general election campaigns (Table V–1).[1] The few cases where such support was not forthcoming were either veteran incumbents or first-time candidates. Veteran incumbents often lose their dependency on those originally responsible for their candidacy, and with successive terms in office reconstruct their coalition of support and discard the original group. Similarly, after several terms, sponsors may find that they no longer need the services of an incumbent and direct their support elsewhere. Since novice candidates, especially, require the continuous support of those who instigated them, it was these rookie candidates who complained most bitterly if their original sponsors let them fend for themselves. Such candidates encountered the greatest difficulty mobilizing support in the primary campaign, when sponsors of all kinds were less active.

---

[1] "Active supporters" or "sponsors" refers to the individuals and groups, if any, who contributed most to a candidate's campaign, according to the evaluation of the candidate himself. After the primary election, our respondents were asked whether they received support from others during the campaign. Those who said "yes" were asked to name the sponsors who contributed the most, describe their relationship with the sponsor, report who he represented, if anyone, and indicate his position in the community, the type of support given, and the overall contribution to the outcome of the election. This procedure was repeated with the post-general election panel. Thus, our discussion of sponsorship centers on the close circle of active and dedicated individuals who comprised the core of each candidate's campaign organization.

TABLE V–1

Instigation and Support in the Primary and General Election
(Percentages)

Sources of Instigation	Subsequent Support			
	Primary Election		*General Election*	
	Yes	*No*	*Yes*	*No*
Primary Groups:				
Yes	70%	30	100%	0
No	44%	56	96%	4
Party:				
Yes	70%	30	98%	2
No	25%	75	90%	10
Other Organizations:				
Yes	89%	11	100%	0
No	60%	40	92%	8
	(N = 109)		(N = 72)	

Studies in other states have shown that the primary and general elections do not engage political activists to the same degree. When the primary or general election outcome is a foregone conclusion, the interest of the activists and the electorate diminishes. Only in the constituencies with competitive primaries and contested general elections do campaign organizations form early and remain active.[2]

By contrast, competition has only modest influence on support activities in Oregon (Tables V–2a, b).[3] During the primary campaign, *sponsors were most active in districts which had little or no primary competition.* These findings suggest that the need for support varies inversely with the incentives of candidacy rather than with competition *per se.* In areas with noncompetitive primaries, i.e., the rural constituencies, candidacy is less attractive. Nearly all candidates filed for office originally only because of pressure from sponsors, and required continued reinforcement during the campaign. In the rural one-party districts, supporters sought to bolster their reluctant candidate's determination

[2] V. O. Key, Jr., *American State Politics,* pp. 171–181; Leon D. Epstein, *Politics in Wisconsin* (Madison: University of Wisconsin Press, 1958), p. 201; Malcolm E. Jewell and Samuel C. Patterson, *The Legislative Process in the United States* (New York: Random House, 1966), p. 84; and Austin Ranney, "Parties in State Politics," in Herbert Jacob and Kenneth Vines, eds., *Politics in the American States,* pp. 74–77; contain comprehensive summaries of these studies.
[3] See Chapter IV, pp. 73–74 above for operational definitions of primary group, party, and interest group sponsors.

TABLE V–2a

Patterns of Competition and Sources of Support in Primary Election
(N = 109)

Patterns of Competition	*Primary Groups*		*Political Party*		*Interest Groups*	
	Yes	*No*	*Yes*	*No*	*Yes*	*No*
Rural One-Party District	82%	18	77%	23	82%	18
Rural Two-Party District	72%	28	56%	44	67%	33
Urban One-Party District	49%	51	36%	65	74%	26
Urban Two-Party District	46%	54	49%	51	71%	29

and reduce his costs of candidacy. In the rural two-party districts, where the opponents usually were spokesmen for local factions, the candidates needed solid factional support if they were to make a show of strength. Consequently, most rural candidates received considerable support from their sponsors during both the primary and general election campaigns, even though the primaries were uncontested and the general election was competitive in less than half of the rural constituencies.

Alternatively, fewer sponsored candidates ran in the urban primary elections. This was due in part to the presence of numerous advertisers who waged modest unsponsored campaigns, gained some public notice, and hoped to lose. Such men cannot be regarded as *bona fide* candidates, for they gained more by losing than winning. However, many serious candidates also had few sponsors. Although these men often faced their stiffest challenges in the primary, many had great difficulty mobilizing support for their primary campaigns. This reflects the political vacuum which frequently surrounds primary campaigns for legislative or local office. In Oregon, as in many states, the public is generally apathetic about primary races, and the primary campaign gets only token coverage by the press. Consequently, the would-be voter had little opportunity and even less incentive to learn about the various candidates. More often than not, the voter marked his ballot (if he voted at all) on the basis of name familiarity. Under these circumstances, many sponsors remained aloof from the primary campaign, since they could do little to change their candidate's chances of winning. Incumbents and other prominent figures regularly won with or without sponsorship, and even a massive effort could not guarantee the victory of an unknown. Moreover, since the urban campaigns were lengthy, expensive affairs, many sponsors preferred to wait until after the primary, when the front runners had emerged, before committing their resources.

Since their activities would not change the primary results, the urban sponsors who did participate in the primary campaign gave their support selectively to the candidates who had the best chance of winning and/or needed some moral support. Such candidates were, of course, incumbents and the urban reluctants, i.e., minority contenders and coopted notables.[4] Like their rural counterparts, the urban reluctant candidates were given support in the primary to demonstrate the confidence and solidarity of their backers. Interest groups occasionally backed incumbents during the primary campaign, but such support was given and received as down payment for expected services rendered in the legislature.

As the general election approached, new sponsors, drawn by their desire to be on the winning side, and different from the ones who instigated the candidate, came forward with pledges of support. The primary election did not change the number of serious candidates in the rural districts since they all ran virtually unopposed. However, in the urban constituencies, most advertisers and a few serious challengers were defeated. Those who won the primary received strong support in the general election campaign. Sponsors were most active in rural two-party districts and least active in urban one-party areas, where the legislators were elected, in effect, in the primary. In the rural one-party and urban two-party districts, campaigning was fairly intense, but for different reasons. Sponsors continued their strong reinforcement through the general election campaign in one-party rural districts. Contestants in the urban two-party constituencies attracted support because they were locked in close, publicized inter-party races.

To illustrate more clearly the contrasting activities and strategies of the candidates and their sponsors, we will examine in greater detail the amount and the source of support, if any, each candidate received. We determined the amount of support contributed by each sponsor in the following way. If a candidate told us he was sponsored during the primary or general election campaigns, we asked him *who* his sponsors were, *how many* sponsors of each type he had, e.g., how many interest group backers, and *what* they did. We found that some sponsors did little more than offer encouragement, while others contributed money or advice, canvassed neighborhoods, addressed circulars, or conducted polls. From such responses, we constructed two indices of *level of sup-*

---

[4] Specifically, the incumbents were supported because of their strong chance of reelection. Sponsors gave support to the notables for two reasons: to reinforce their determination to run and because of their excellent chances of election. The support that the minority candidates received from their parties was intended as reinforcement only.

port. The first index (A) is a tally of the number of friends, party workers, and associations that helped each candidate.[5] The second ranks the type of support they gave: (1) financial contributions; (2) manpower, e.g., canvassing and work in the campaign headquarters; and (3) encouragement and advice (which are more superficial). If a sponsor contributed money *and also* worked on the campaign, we rated his support as "strong." Anything less was rated "weak" support.

Tables V–3a, b, c, d show the association between patterns of competition and the support that the candidates received from various sponsoring agents in the general election. Only the sponsored candidates were considered in this table. We found that rural party sponsorship was perfunctory or disorganized in the primary, although the parties backed over half of the candidates (Table V–2a above). The county chairman occasionally helped a candidate. Other party officials went through the motions of working in the primary campaign, but were unwilling or unable to devote much time to it. The general election campaign apparently mobilized the rural party "machinery," such as it was. However, it was clear in the interviews that rural party organizations remained dormant during the general election, while various groups and organizations campaigned in the *name* of the party. The upsurge in party activity was the result of the identification of local factions with party labels, rather than a rejuvenation of the party organization itself.

In rural one-party districts, candidates received consistent and active support from various groups and associations throughout the primary and general election campaigns. By contrast, in the rural two-party districts, primary group support was forthcoming only during the

TABLE V–2b

Patterns of Competition and Sources of Support in General Election
(N = 78)

Patterns of Competition	Primary Groups		Political Party		Interest Groups	
	Yes	No	Yes	No	Yes	No
Rural One-Party District	93%	7	86%	14	93%	7
Rural Two-Party District	100%	0	92%	8	92%	8
Urban One-Party District	100%	0	95%	5	95%	5
Urban Two-Party District	93%	7	86%	14	93%	7

[5] We computed the mean number of primary group sponsors the candidates had, and then divided the candidates into two categories: those with a large number of primary group sponsors and those with few. The mean was used as a cut-point. The same procedure was used to classify the number of party and interest group sponsors.

primary campaign. During the general election campaign, local associations and interest groups took over campaign work. Up to this point, the candidates' friends and neighbors had been instrumental in instigating their candidacies and had worked for them during the primary campaign. However, as the general election approached, the sponsoring circle of friends and neighbors dwindled and withdrew as secondary organizations of various kinds took over the support of candidates.

The apparent change in the complexion of support in rural two-party districts is only an accident of classification. Throughout the three waves of interviews, we tried to learn how well each candidate knew his sponsors and supporters. In some instances, the candidate had never met some of his supporters before the campaign, others he knew only casually, and still others were close friends, relatives, or work associates. Accordingly, we classified sponsors into primary and secondary groups: family, close friends and associates into primary groups, and the rest were classified as secondary group sponsors. However, candidates in the rural constituencies knew virtually all of their sponsors and supporters well, because the political activists in such districts constitute a small group. By the time a person from a rural constituency becomes a candidate, he or she should be well known in political circles. Consequently, those we labelled "primary group supporters" were the candidates' closest friends and relatives, and all others were classified as "secondary group supporters" even though they were friends or acquaintances of the candidate.

As the general election drew near, candidates in the rural two-party districts showed a marked change in the way they viewed the contest and in the way they perceived their relationships with their supporters. During the initial phases of recruitment, these candidates regarded the encouragement and sponsorship of primary groups as an expression of friendship and loyalty. But with the advent of the general election campaign, when the voters were actually to choose their representative, lines of opposition hardened. Candidates in these usually close-knit rural communities increasingly defined the contest as one that divided the community into "we-they" blocs. "They" referred to the opposing candidate and the local faction or factions that supported him. Each member of the community was forced to align himself with one of the opposing groups and was designated either a friend or an enemy. The opposing forces acquired labels, such as Baptists v.s. Methodists, Elks v.s. Moose, the names of denominations and the various secondary associations prominently aligned with each side. For example, one candidate stated

... [T]he whole election boils down to which side is going to win. I'm not running for myself. Well, I guess you could say that I'm running so that I can represent this district in the legislature, but that's only a small part of it. We want a legislator, but we also want our people on the county commission and on some of the city councils around here. For a long time the county Chamber [of Commerce] has had things their way ... the people who own the stores and businesses that the ranchers use. We're tired of getting the short end of things ... of high prices and [land] zoning [policies] and property taxes that seem to help everybody but the ranchers.

Things have come to the boiling point. We're organizing. All the farm organizations are in on this and we're going to try to get a change all the way from state senator to dogcatcher. My campaign is only a part of what I like to call a community effort, and it's really been uphill because they've been doing their damndest to stop us.

Another respondent from a rural two-party district said:

This election means a lot more than if I win or lose. If I lose, that means they win, and if I win, it means that our side wins.

The cleavages these respondents describe make the distinction between primary and secondary relationships artificial. The election competition described above resembled two extended families engaged in a feud and supported by associations on each side. The election was perceived as a struggle between the leaders of the county Chamber of Commerce and leaders of farm organizations. "Chamber" and "farm" organizations are labels which symbolically identify the parties in conflict. The election referred to above had become the focus of a profound cleavage in an Oregon community that usually smothered conflict with a smooth facade of harmony. Not all the issues at stake pertained to the "Chamber v.s. farm" conflict, but these secondary groups symbolized the cleavages, bolstered the respective parties in dispute, and forced individuals in the community to choose between the two sides.

For these reasons, the terms primary and secondary group inaccurately classify the activists who worked in the general election campaign in the rural two-party districts. In the urban districts and the rural one-party districts, the classification of sponsors into primary and secondary groups proved useful. In these districts, candidates continued to perceive future sponsors according to how close or distant they were from them, and drew clear distinctions between their closest friends and associates and other sponsors. In the rural one-party districts, the candidates were very sensitive about who gave them their support in the general election, and less concerned with how many sponsors they had. The primary-secondary group distinction was relevant, but of lesser importance to the candidates in the urban districts. The urban candidates, especially the reluctant ones, wanted their family and friends to give at least tacit assent to their candidacy. Once such primary group approval was assured, they sought enough support from other sources to win or at least to make a respectable showing. Consequently, in the urban districts, candidates were as concerned with how much sponsorship and support they received as they were with who their sponsors were.

In the urban districts, sponsors carefully matched their strategies with the terms of competition and candidate incentives. Each sponsor backed the candidate(s) who seemed to offer the best chance of providing a return on their investment, although such support often was intended to reinforce a much-needed, hesitant candidate who might withdraw, rather than to mobilize the electorate. As a result, campaigns became public rituals in urban one-party districts. Only the minority party nominees received steadfast support from their sponsors throughout the primary and general election campaigns. Incumbent candidates, because of the independence created by their commanding advantage, seemed poor investments to most sponsors in the urban one-party districts. The advertisers, of course, were ignored by most sponsors. The hotly contested, well-publicized races in urban two-party districts attracted considerable public attention. Even here, however, sponsors were highly selective. Incumbent legislators seeking re-election and coopted notables shared the bulk of support. The local party organizations usually endorsed the incumbents seeking re-election in the general election. The incumbents' families and friends worked in both the primary and general election campaigns, although they were less active in the primary. In general, in the urban two-party districts, the greatest efforts were expended in behalf of the notables, even if they were regarded as certain winners. For the ear-marked, coopted notables, sponsors and volunteers offered their services; the campaign coffers were full; and billboards, newspaper ads, and leaflets flooded the constituency.

During the instigation stage, these coopted candidates were reluctant to run, and their experiences during the campaign did little to increase their enthusiasm. One such candidate summed up the campaign as follows:

I don't think it's worth it. Right now, I'm chairman of the United Fund, I work on the Planning Commission, I run the Elk's Little League, I'm on the city council, and I try to take time out from all this to keep my practice going. Then they asked me to run for the House, as if I wasn't doing enough around [name of city]. I don't know what the [expletive deleted] they want from me. I'm interested in our local problems, but all my friends want me to go to Salem and spend most of my time deciding if timber taxes are high enough or . . . if motel owners on the Coast are using too much sand.

I don't need to be a legislator. I don't need the money—they don't pay much anyhow. As far as I'm concerned, I'm doing important enough things around town now. And on top of all this, I have to go through this campaign business and give a talk to my friends at the Chamber [of Commerce] and at Rotary and at the League of Women Voters rally. The same people are at all these, and the voters don't seem to care. But if I'm elected, they'll expect miracles.

A coopted candidate from another district complained:

This whole campaign is a waste of time and a fraud. My campaign manager tells me I have to be a good candidate and he keeps mentioning my image. What's all this got to do with whether . . . I'll be a good representative? Four months ago, the County Chairman [of his party] told me I ought to run because people know me and respect me and trust me. All my friends fed me the same line. Now they want me to be something I'm not. It's dishonest.

Still another stated angrily:

If I had known what I had to put up with, I would never have let them talk me into running. I've spent the better part of my life serving on committees for charities and generally doing my part to make this county a better place to live. What do I get? My wife gets threatening phone calls. [His opponent] calls me everything in the book. Worst of all, I have to stand in front of crowds and be criticized by people who don't know me for things I've never said and for stands on issues I've never heard of. I've had it. They'll never get me to run again.

Another notable said:

I can hardly wait for this campaign to be over. I feel like I'm marking time. I like to get things done . . . to accomplish something, and nothing constructive is happening in the campaign. I hope things are different in the legislature.

The distaste for campaigning was understandable. Coopted candidates were commonly successful businessmen or lawyers, accustomed to a direct and decisive discourse in business relationships. Evasive campaign rhetoric, the cloying conduct and showmanship of candidates made them uncomfortable. "Image-making" irritated them, and pandering to a crowd repelled them. Nevertheless, to the delight of their supporters, most of the notables won handily. However, most found legislative service hardly more rewarding than the campaign. All but one of the successful coopted candidates in 1966 withdrew in 1968, and the other was elected to a higher state office.

Interest groups played a key role in the instigation and sponsorship of candidates in all districts. Indeed, the pervasiveness and intensity of interest group activities were among the most salient features of the 1966 election. Throughout the primary and general election campaigns, Oregon's interest groups followed the strategy of "covering-all-bets." Nearly all candidates (except the advertisers) reported that they had received token assistance from interest groups in the primary campaign. Even seemingly hopeless campaigns were backed by some interest group sponsors. Often the same group quietly helped both opponents in a race, awaiting the outcome of the primary election before they decided whom to support in earnest.

As the general election approached, interest groups assessed the chances of the various candidates, then supported the front runners and abandoned the others. However, most interest groups did not withdraw completely from what they regarded as "losing" causes. They still gave token support to almost all candidates hedging against the slight chance that a dark horse might win. Such token support earned them chances of fence-mending and assured a favorable relationship with the unexpected winner.[6]

THE IMPACT OF SPONSORS' ACTIVITIES

Candidates were asked to evaluate the contribution of each sponsor in regards to the effectiveness of their campaigns and the election results. The candidates differentiated among their supporters in the following way. They usually singled out one or two sponsors who had been especially helpful in launching their campaigns. Other sponsors were described as dedicated and hard-working, but less effective. Still others they characterized as hangers-on, who exploited campaign publicity more for their own benefit, rather than the candidate's.

When the candidates discussed each sponsor's contribution to the election outcome, their statements were sometimes surprising. Tables V–4a, b show that a candidate's evaluations of sponsors' effectiveness were *unrelated* to whether or not the candidate was opposed. After the

---

[6] It is interesting to note that where such "dual support" occurred, the candidates in question were usually unaware that some of their interest group sponsors were also quietly supporting their opponent.

TABLE V–3a

Patterns of Competition and Number of Sponsors in the Primary Election
(N = 79)

Patterns of Competition	Primary Groups		Political Party		Interest Groups	
	Large	Small	Large	Small	Large	Small
Rural One-Party District	72%	28	31%	69	64%	36
Rural Two-Party District	69%	31	30%	70	67%	33
Urban One-Party District	21%	79	64%	36	65%	35
Urban Two-Party District	69%	31	82%	18	67%	33

Note: Data include only those candidates who received support.

primary, the candidates were almost unanimous in declaring that their sponsors had little influence on the primary election outcome. This is understandable where the primary is uncontested, but why should the candidates in urban areas, where the primaries are competitive, tell us their supporters had little effect on the election outcome?

The candidates' remarks provide some clues. One grizzled veteran of six terms in the House described the primary campaign in his urban one-party district as follows:

> After you've been in the House as long as I have, you really don't have to do much campaigning. I'd bet you long odds that I'd win the primary even if I didn't lift a finger. It's not that I've been a special kind of representative. I like to think I've done a good job, . . . but that's not the point. Unless you really pull some boners, the voters don't know what you do in Salem. They just get accustomed to you being their representative.
>
> When the primary election comes around, most of them don't pay much attention to the campaign, and in this subdistrict, only about half of the Democrats vote in the primary. Those that do know my name, and when they see it on the ballot, I'm who they vote for.

When asked why he bothered to campaign at all, this candidate replied:

> I guess I do it because I feel I have an obligation to get out and meet the voters, those that are interested. It's strange, but I guess you might also say that I owe it to the fellows who are running against me.

On the other side of the fence, an opponent of this incumbent (an advertiser) complained that:

> If I really wanted to win the primary, it would cost me nearly as much as running for Congress from Portland. Even if I could pull together ten times the money and had enough people working for me to really go door-to-door as I should, I would still probably lose. People just aren't interested,

for one thing, and [incumbent] is well known and respected. In this part of Portland, voting for him is as natural as breathing.

He went on to say:

I could have filed for Position Two [a vacant seat], but even then my chances wouldn't be much better. The problem is the same. People aren't interested. It isn't the guy who works the hardest that's going to win. The winner is the man with the most luck.

Such remarks emphasize the importance of name-familiarity in urban primaries. The primary evokes little public interest and challengers have a poor chance to reach the voters. Individuals who are well known and incumbents enjoy a tremendous advantage. When the field consists entirely of unknowns, support has little bearing on the outcome of the election.

After the general election, all candidates, winners and losers alike, reported that their sponsors had an appreciable impact on the election outcome. It is understandable that candidates in the urban and rural two-party districts should consider their support important. But in rural one-party districts, for example, each legislator virtually is elected when he files, and the general election is only a formality. Why should he consider his sponsor's efforts crucial? The answer lies in the way candidates perceive the election outcome. In rural one-party districts, the support a candidate received served to reduce the costs of running rather than to influence the election results. Candidates regarded their election victory as a flattering expression of public approbation. As they saw it, a successful campaign which resulted in a large voter turnout was an expression of widespread support. After his second unopposed campaign, a successful candidate in one of the rural one-party districts said

I did very well in this election. I got 5,000 more votes than last time.

The winning majority-party candidates in urban one-party districts held a similar view. For them, a substantial margin of victory in the general election represented success, but winning by a slim margin over the minority party opponent was equivalent to losing the election. The minority party candidates in these districts also considered their sponsors' efforts quite essential. They valued the support received as reinforcement and compensation for the costs of the campaign as much as its effect on the election outcome. A defeated minority party candidate felt his campaign was successful if he did not lose public esteem and his work did not suffer too much. If his sponsors had helped him avoid such campaign costs, this was more important than the election out-come itself.[7]

CAMPAIGNING: WHO GAINS AND WHO LOSES?

The Oregon candidates were amateur politicians. Until they decided to run for office, most candidates regarded politics as an avocation which they enjoyed, yet could set aside when their work or personal affairs became pressing. But when they became candidates, many learned how demanding the campaign could be. Office-seeking offers personal and political advantages, but it also exacts personal costs. The campaign affects, for better or worse, each candidate's job, family, friendships, reputation and community standing. As one veteran legislator put it:

No matter how you look at it, if you're fool enough to want to go to Salem, you've got to take the bad with the good. I guess everybody only half-believes us when we say our only interest is serving our districts. I'm in this business for what I can get out of it, within reason. And that doesn't mean that the district has to suffer. It's just that for every advantage I get for being in the House, I pay a price. Every two years I have to campaign, which means dipping into savings again, making arrangements with my boss, and sometimes I don't see my wife and children for a month at a time. During sessions, I'm away from home again three or four days a week.

It's only natural and right that we should gain something personally. If we couldn't, nobody would run.

Candidates seek an acceptable balance between the personal costs and benefits of political activity. Serious contenders hope that winning will recoup their costs or that a respectable showing will enhance their prestige, influence and social status. But many new legislators find that legislative service is not worth the investment. As the high rate of voluntary resignation among state legislators attests, only a few go on to pursue a lifetime career in public office.

We asked a series of questions about the consequences of running for office and serving in the legislature. The responses were used to construct separate indices of personal costs and personal benefits.[8] These indices may point out to us whether and how candidates enhance their benefits and reduce their costs. From their responses, we might

---

[7] The minority party conscripts had no illusions about their chances of victory. When we asked them shortly after they filed about their chances of winning the general election, all admitted that they expected to be defeated easily by their majority party opponent.

[8] See Chapter IV, p. 79 above for a description of these indices.

also learn whether the rookie candidate perceives his outcomes differently from the experienced legislator.

If a candidate can mobilize various group and organizational sponsors for his campaign, they will help defray the campaign costs. Primary groups, because their members are close to a candidate, influence personal gains and losses for the candidate even when their resources are meager. Interest groups and party organizers can provide the management, staff, and finances that established organizations can offer. Each type of sponsor contributes in its own way to the reduction of costs.

Table V–5 shows that both primary group and secondary group sponsors influenced the candidates' assessments of benefits, but not costs. The candidates who were sponsored were more apt to report high benefits than those who were not sponsored. This relationship is most apparent in the primary election because virtually all candidates received support for their efforts in the general election. In both elections, the candidates apparently did not relate the costs they incurred to the particular individuals or groups that gave or withheld support.

This finding has important implications. If the intensity of the support is positively related to the candidates' perceptions of benefits, but not to their perceptions of costs, a candidate should try to attract the largest coalition of sponsors who will give active support. Kingdon's study of candidates in Wisconsin found that

> relatively few politicians feel that their coalition members expect much of them in return for their support. They do not, therefore, think of the process of coalition building as one in which they offer favors to members in return for support. . . . But the candidate will not tend to feel that he has paid any large cost in order to gain their support because the things he feels they expect in return are regarded largely as simple continuation of his normal behavior. In the mind of the candidate, then, coalition building

TABLE V–3b

Patterns of Competition and Number of Sponsors in the General Election
(N = 83)

Patterns of Competition	*Primary Groups*		*Political Party*		*Interest Groups*	
	Large	*Small*	*Large*	*Small*	*Large*	*Small*
Rural One-Party District	77%	23	83%	17	69%	31
Rural Two-Party District	31%	69	67%	33	67%	33
Urban One-Party District	45%	55	29%	71	19%	81
Urban Two-Party District	70%	30	64%	36	67%	33

is a process in which he adopts a stance or pattern of behavior and groups fall in with him or not as they see fit.[9]

Sponsorship may not influence each candidate's personal costs, but the possibility remains that it is the *amount* of support, rather than the source that offsets such costs. As a candidate's campaign coalition increases in size, and more money and workers are activated in his behalf, the candidate will have fewer personal expenses. Moreover, such broad based and highly active sponsorship will enhance his prestige and reputation. Consequently, what a candidate gains or loses may depend on how strongly he is sponsored, rather than "who" his sponsors are. Our analysis shows, however, that the strength of sponsorship had no appreciable effect on the candidates' costs in the primary campaign, although the sponsors' efforts enhanced the amount of personal benefits the candidates experienced (Table V–6). In the general election campaign, the efforts of primary group supporters affected costs, but the backing of secondary associations had little effect on personal costs. Apparently, candidates' costs correspond generally to subtle variations in candidate-sponsor relations in the various districts that arose from the different sponsoring role of primary and secondary groups. When patterns of competition were controlled, we discovered that the rural candidates and those from urban one-party districts matched the Wisconsin pattern, at least with respect to all the secondary group sponsors. Rural candidates felt little obligation to repay their party and interest group backers, and consequently secondary group sponsors influenced the level of benefits they received, but not their costs. Candidates in urban two-party districts actively sought organized support and assiduously cultivated their party and interest group sponsors. Such sponsorship affected both their benefits and their costs since the larger

TABLE V–3c

Patterns of Competition and Intensity of Support in Primary Election
(N = 79)

Patterns of Competition	Primary Groups		Political Party		Interest Groups	
	Weak	Strong	Weak	Strong	Weak	Strong
Rural One-Party District	43%	57	100%	0	57%	43
Rural Two-Party District	46%	54	90%	10	42%	58
Urban One-Party District	95%	5	50%	50	92%	8
Urban Two-Party District	88%	12	59%	41	87%	13

[9] John W. Kingdon, *Candidates for Office: Beliefs and Strategies* (New York: Random House, 1966), pp. 65–66.

their support coalitions became and the stronger the support they received, the higher their benefits and costs.

Almost all candidates in the urban two-party districts were serious contenders running in close races, which made organized backing crucial. Most sought to mobilize the broadest constellation of interests and groups in their behalf. The various campaign organizations that we analyzed proved to be a curse to some candidates and a blessing to others. Many candidates spent much time simply dealing with internal dissention within their coalition. Likewise, incumbents from these districts told us that servicing their constituents' and sponsors' requests took much of their time in Salem.

If a political career in such districts was more strenuous, it also held out brighter prospects. In Oregon, urban two-party districts are the best springboards to higher office because such populous districts are large enough and provide sufficient visibility for later attempts at statewide or congressional seats. Such constituencies are also good training grounds for sharpening political skills, building campaign organizations, and achieving political notoriety. But career risk is high because the chances of winning are smaller and only the most skilled and devoted politicians can endure. Those that hope for political career advancement must work hard to build the broad coalitions of support that are essential to their political success.[10]

By contrast, in rural districts candidates said that they did not feel obligated to accede to the demands of party and interest group sponsors because such sponsors were not separate and distinct from the political activists in the entire district. A lifetime spent in the local community led candidates to conform with their sponsors' positions concerning district and statewide issues. Their sponsors only reinforced the candidates' views and actions. It was implicitly assumed that the candidate would protect the district's interests in the legislature.

In the urban one-party districts, primary groups were not active sponsors. Support was limited almost exclusively to party organizers and interest group sponsors. Incumbents in such districts felt little obligation to their coalition of support because they didn't need it to win. Incumbents who were assured of their election in the primary could afford to let their sponsors come to them. Because the other candidates in the urban one-party districts had little chance of winning, they too felt little obligation to their backers. Their sponsors knew when they supported them, that no immediate payoffs could be expected.

---

[10] Over the past 15 years, all of Oregon's Governors, U.S. Senators, and several Congressmen, launched their careers in such urban two-party districts.

For such reasons, secondary group support is unrelated to personal costs in both elections, with the exception of candidates in the urban two-party districts. But the support of primary groups affects such deprivations during the general election campaign in all areas. If a candidate's family and friends were not among his active sponsors, he experienced high costs. If some, but not all of his close friends and relatives took part, his personal costs were reduced. However, if many of those close to him joined his campaign and his organization became a family and neighborhood effort, he found the campaign less threatening.

It is clear that primary groups play a special role in electoral politics. Each candidate needs the reassurance of his family and friends. The campaign tests his relationship with those close to him. If they don't respect his ability and support his ambitions, his self-esteem is threatened and the campaign becomes a painful experience, *no matter who else supports him or if he wins or loses.* But his family and friends must not get too involved either. If they do, and his campaign becomes a way of showing their respect and affection, the candidate bears a heavy burden. He must then strive to live up to their high opinion of him and repay their support. This creates a dilemma. If he loses, he fails those closest to him. If he wins, can he fulfill his friends' expectations of him as a legislator? Can he possibly achieve everything in Salem they are telling the voters and themselves he will do? If he wins, he may disappoint some of his friends; if he loses, he must bear responsibility for their defeat as well. As one candidate put it:

I didn't know all my friends would get involved. It's kind of frightening. They're telling everybody what a great guy I am. The trouble is, I think they believe it too. They make me out as some sort of god. They think I'm going to go to Salem and take over the state. I'm only one man and I can't do everything. . . . But if I lose, I don't know how I'm going to live with myself.

Another candidate, a veteran incumbent, said:

I learned long ago to keep my family out of the campaign. They haven't much experience with this sort of thing, but they still insist on giving advice, and I have to listen to it and try to explain to them why I'm not going to do what they want. I never talk politics at home for the same reason. If I ever let them work for me, and I lost, I'm afraid they'd blame themselves, and that would make me feel miserable. It just doesn't pay to get your family involved.

Candidates do not view their primary groups as mere instruments of electoral success. To win the election, but lose the respect of family and friends is too great a price to pay. Our respondents perceived their primary and secondary groups differently. The more secondary group support they received, the better the chances of extrinsic benefits—winning the election, enhancing their social status, promoting their occupations. If the party or interest groups offered support, it was received gladly because it increased the chances for personal and political gains and usually entailed little cost. But primary group support involved both intrinsic benefits and intrinsic costs. It was not the amount of support that was important but the expression of support by a friend. As the incumbent above suggested, some candidates avoided jeopardizing their personal relationships by not permitting their primary groups to take part.

Thus, the size and composition of each candidate's coalition influences the way the campaign will threaten or enhance his family life, job, friendships, prestige, and self-esteem. We counted the number of sponsors in each category of support (i.e., primary groups, party organizations, and interest groups) that worked on each candidate's campaign. From these figures we computed the number of categories of support which had a large number of sponsors for each candidate. This measure summarized the size of each campaign coalition and the breadth of the social and political spectrum from which they were drawn. Table V–7 shows the relationship between this measure and the personal costs and benefits candidates faced in the campaign.

In both campaigns, if candidates had many and diverse sponsors, they perceived high benefits. Support influenced candidates' costs in a more complex way. In the primary, candidates tended to perceive low costs if they had very few sponsors or, paradoxically, if their campaign coalition was broad and diversified. Candidates with medium-sized, fairly diverse coalitions experienced higher costs. The candidates with the fewest backers were, for the most part, advertisers, a few urban minority candidates, and several majority party winners in the urban

TABLE V–3d

Patterns of Competition and Intensity of Support in General Election
(N = 73)

Patterns of Competition	*Primary Groups*		*Political Party*		*Interest Groups*	
	Weak	*Strong*	*Weak*	*Strong*	*Weak*	*Strong*
Rural One-Party District	15%	85	8%	92	8%	92
Rural Two-Party District	23%	77	8%	92	8%	92
Urban One-Party District	82%	18	48%	52	62%	38
Urban Two-Party District	22%	78	16%	84	36%	64

one-party districts. For such candidates, the primary was a formality. The advertisers desired little support, minority candidates were unopposed, and the majority party winners, all of whom were incumbents, were virtually assured of victory and did not need sponsorship in the primary. Consequently, the primary created few personal costs for these candidates, despite the fact that their campaigns drew few sponsors of any kind, simply because there was no need or desire to conduct more than a *pro forma* campaign.

For most of the remaining candidates, the primary was an opportunity to test the resources and devotion of their sponsors. The rural candidates were especially anxious about the size and composition of their support coalition. For them anything less than a solid community effort was distressing or threatening because they had little to gain from running but the respect and gratitude of their friends and associates.[11] If the campaign was not a display of public admiration, it was a serious blow.

The urban candidates, especially those in the two-party districts, also tested the actual size and dedication of their primary campaign coalition, but for a different reason. The showing such urban candidates made in the primary, especially their capacity to attract organized support indicated their chances in the general campaign. If, on the one hand, their coalitions were neither large nor diverse, then their chances of victory diminished and their personal and political costs rose. On the other hand, if they made a strong showing in the primary, they gained confidence and their costs were reduced.

With the advent of the general election, the relationship between intensity of support and personal costs changed subtly. As the intensity of support increased and candidates' coalitions became larger and more diverse, both their benefits and costs increased. The direct relationship between the size and diversity of each candidate's campaign organization and his personal costs can be attributed in part to the rising costs of coordinating his sponsors. As one candidate put it:

[11] During the course of our interviews with them, most of the rural candidates discussed in great detail the gratification they derived from the support of their friends and colleagues. Often, each sponsor was described in depth, his relationship with the candidate was spelled out, including the length and closeness of the friendship. It was clear that these candidates regarded such support as an indication of their esteem in the community. When such support was not forthcoming from a friend, faction, or group in the local area, the rural candidates were likely to volunteer this information and to discuss it with a great deal of anxiety. By contrast, seldom did the urban candidates of any type dwell at such length on their sponsoring coalitions, nor did they express anger or bitterness when support was denied them by an individual or group in the community which they had hoped would sponsor their campaign.

My headquarters are a madhouse! People are walking all over one another. I have about 14 self-appointed assistant campaign managers, and each has his own idea about running things. To top it all off, I've got people from both business and labor working for me. Sometimes they seem more interested in arguing with one another than working for me. I spend more time acting like a referee than a candidate.

The management of the campaign coalition is not the only source of personal costs. The campaign for the general election calls for more sophisticated political skills than the primary. The primary election has eliminated most advertisers and political novices, leaving the field to incumbents, conscripts, and a few experienced challengers or "perennial" candidates. A candidate's prior experience with campaigning and office-holding influences the way he perceives the campaign. When we controlled for political experience, we found that novices perceived high benefits and low costs, while the more experienced candidates, especially incumbents, perceived low benefits and high costs (Table V–8). Incumbents, one might say, and this is probably true for other veteran candidates, have experienced deprivations and inconveniences to a degree unsuspected by the novice. Office-holders encounter costs that they did not anticipate before they took office.[12] In addition, the more experience one has as a candidate, especially in the general election, the more likely that candidate is to feel neglected, because the attention of the media and the attentive public is focused on the candidates running for statewide and national office.

Legislative candidates often have difficulty obtaining adequate funds from sponsors and must be willing to finance part of their campaign from their own funds. Kingdon found that in Wisconsin ". . . candidates for the State legislature, unlike candidates for higher-level office, operate in something of a felt vacuum, a situation in which they are comparatively neglected by the press and the voters."[13] Thus, we can understand why incumbents and experienced candidates would report high costs associated with the campaign and legislative service; they know them from firsthand experience. So it is that political experience influences candidates' perceptions of personal benefits and deprivations. The novice candidate, naive and idealistic, expected to gain much and lose little. Experience had tempered the expectations of political veterans who expected smaller gains and higher costs.

The general election outcome itself, by the same token, affected candidates' personal advantages and losses. As a group, those who were de-

[12] James D. Barber, *The Lawmakers* (New Haven: Yale University Press, 1965), pp. 246–249.
[13] Kingdon, *Candidates for Office*, p. 52.

feated in the primary were most apt to report high benefits and low costs. These losers were almost exclusively advertisers whose defeat was an expected part of their political adventures. General election candidates, both winners and losers, contrast sharply with the losers in the primary. A majority of general election candidates experienced low benefits during the campaign. However, the defeated general election candidates were more likely than their successful counterparts to report low costs.

At this point, it is difficult to disentangle the effects of political experience on the costs and benefits that can be attributed directly to the success or failure of the candidate. When we control for incumbency, it appears that both the candidates' prior political experience *and* their showing at the polls influenced their perceptions of personal gains and losses (Table V–9). Incumbents generally reported low benefits and high costs, but the defeated incumbents unanimously reporting high costs and low benefits. The less experienced, nonincumbents were more sensitive to whether or not they won or lost. Predictably, losers in the primary (the advertisers) reported high benefits and low costs. However, those who competed in the general election gave contradictory reports depending upon whether or not they had won or lost. New candidates who won in the general election perceived low benefits and reported high costs, while the new candidates who were defeated in the general election experienced greater benefits and fewer deprivations. Thus, victorious candidates, especially incumbents, found the campaign gruelling and expected that legislative service would have a detrimental effect on their jobs, family life and social obligations. Many felt that they had gained little from the privilege of serving in the legislature.

Some of the defeated in the general election savored the publicity and the experience that campaigning afforded them. Not all of these candidates were serious contenders. Many were minority candidates who expected defeat. Generally speaking, their sponsors took care of their costs. Of the fourteen minority candidates we interviewed, all reported low costs, while eleven experienced high benefits. The twenty-three remaining candidates who were defeated in the general election of 1966 were all reluctants. They were either contestants in rural two-party districts or coopted losers in the urban two-party districts. Like their successful opponents, they did not find the campaign personally beneficial and experienced high costs.[14] Thus, reluctant candidates who faced close contests experienced low benefits and high costs regardless of whether

---

[14] Sixty-one percent of the reluctant general election losers reported *both* low benefits and high costs.

TABLE V-4a

Patterns of Competition and Importance of Various Sources of Support in Primary Election
(N = 109)

Patterns of Competition	*Primary Groups*		*Political Party*		*Interest Groups*	
	Important	*Not Important*	*Important*	*Not Important*	*Important*	*Not Important*
Rural One-Party District	8%	92	8%	92	14%	86
Rural Two-Party District	15%	85	40%	60	33%	67
Urban One-Party District	5%	95	36%	64	14%	86
Urban Two-Party District	23%	77	35%	65	21%	79

TABLE V-4b

Patterns of Competition and Importance of Various Sources of Support in General Election
(N = 109)

Patterns of Competition	*Primary Groups*		*Political Party*		*Interest Groups*	
	Important	*Not Important*	*Important*	*Not Important*	*Important*	*Not Important*
Rural One-Party District	92%	8	100%	0	92%	8
Rural Two-Party District	85%	15	92%	8	92%	8
Urban One-Party District	82%	18	95%	5	86%	14
Urban Two-Party District	89%	11	100%	0	82%	18

they won or lost. Advertisers and conscripts found the campaign rewarding and paid little for the chance of running.[15]

Such findings suggest that a subtle blend of factors influences the personal gains and deprivations that candidates attribute to political activity. They are as follows: (1) *the character of the candidates' support,* i.e., the intensity of support and the size and composition of their support coalitions; (2) *prior political experience of the candidate,* which leads the more experienced politician to be less optimistic about what he is in a position to gain or lose from running for office and serving in the legislature; and (3) *the candidates' chances of victory,* which make those out of contention exploit at small cost the visibility and publicity of the campaign for personal gain. Serious contenders are less fortunate however, because they must cope with the reforms of competition itself, the organizational problems of their coalition, the possible odium of defeat.

SUMMARY AND CONCLUSIONS

Each district's competitive pattern determines which sponsors will support the various candidates. The level of support they receive depends on the attractiveness of political office, and these incentives, in turn, are a product of the social structure and competitive structure of the district. Candidacy is not a rewarding experience for most rural candidates, nor does it have much to offer urban minority candidates or civic notables who have been coopted into running. Such reluctant candidates require much support to enter and remain in the race. Under these conditions, their sponsors work as hard at keeping their standard-bearers in the contest as they do in trying to defeat their opponents. In fact, the most intense primary election support was given to reluctant candidates, *most of whom were running in uncontested primaries.*

Generally speaking, candidacy is more enticing in the urban districts. Political and monetary inducements are greater, so that many candidates will run with little initial support. In such political milieus where advertisers and other pseudo candidates flourish. Running for office brings more rewards than winning. In rank order, candidates in rural two-party districts received the most extensive and intensive support, followed by their colleagues in rural one-party districts. Organized

---

[15] The advertisers and minority party conscripts displayed remarkably similar patterns of costs and benefits. Sixty-five percent of the minority party candidates and 64 percent of the advertisers reported both high benefits and low costs. The evidence is convincing that running for office is a rewarding experience for the majority of candidates who were out of serious contention.

support is least in urban one-party districts, while the urban two-party constituencies run a close second. Overall, primary campaigns are more low-key, and candidates have fewer sponsors than in the general election campaign.

A continuous chain links the instigation and support phases of recruitment. Between seventy and ninety percent of the candidates were supported in the primary campaign by the individuals and sponsors who originally instigated their candidacies. Instigators were active in over ninety-five percent of the campaign organizations during the general election campaign.

The analysis of support during the primary election reveals the antiparty bias so characteristic of Oregon politics. Only a small proportion of candidates received party support, compared to the large number who were sponsored by their friends and neighbors or by interest groups.

Most candidates find that running for office affects not only their political influence and stature, but also their family life, job, social relationships with their friends, and their reputation in the local community. Some candidates have much to gain and little to lose from running. Others experience lower benefits and higher costs. Generally speaking, a candidate's personal gains and losses depend in part on who sponsors him and how intense his support is. As long as the candidate's campaign organization is not too large and unwieldy, or his primary groups do not make his candidacy a *cause celebre,* he is likely to find office-seeking a rewarding experience and his investment light. However, prior experience has led veteran candidates to expect inconveniences and deprivations that rookie candidates have not yet experienced. Consequently, candidates with much campaign experience, and incumbents, tend to report greater costs and fewer benefits than new challengers. Finally, the candidates who fully expect to win and make a concerted effort in the campaign find that in some ways, their efforts are unrewarded, regardless of whether they win or lose. By contrast, the candidates who are never in contention, i.e., the advertisers and minority candidates, use the campaign for private purposes. As a result, they experience greater rewards and fewer deprivations.

TABLE V-5

Sources of Campaign Support and Candidates' Personal Benefits and Costs

Sources of Primary Campaign Support

Benefits and Costs in the Primary Campaign	Primary Groups Yes (N=62)	Primary Groups No (N=45)	Party Yes (N=53)	Party No (N=54)	Interest Groups Yes (N=78)	Interest Groups No (N=29)	Any Source Yes (N=89)	Any Source No (N=18)
Benefits								
High	66%	33%	66%	39%	62%	28%	60%	17%
Low	34	67	34	61	38	72	40	83
	$X^2 = 13.23$, P < .001		$X^2 = 7.90$, P < .01		$X^2 = 9.77$, P < .01		$X^2 = 11.03$, P < .001	
Costs								
High	58%	42%	47%	56%	47%	62%	53%	44%
Low	42	58	53	44	53	38	47	56
	X^2 = n.s.		X^2 = n.s.		X^2 = n.s.		X^2 = n.s.	

Sources of General Campaign Support*

Benefits and Costs in the Primary Campaign	Primary Groups Yes (N=74)	Primary Groups No (N=3)	Party Yes (N=69)	Party No (N=8)	Interest Groups Yes (N=72)	Interest Groups No (N=5)	Any Source Yes (N=75)	Any Source No (N=2)
Benefits								
High	51%	0%	51%	38%	53%	0%	51%	0%
Low	49	100	49	62	47	100	49	100
Costs								
High	47%	100%	48%	62%	50%	40%	48%	100%
Low	53	0	52	38	50	60	52	0

* All Chi-squared (X^2) for this table are insignificant.

TABLE V-6

Level of Support by Source and the Candidates' Personal Benefits and Costs

Number of Primary Campaign Supporters

Benefits and Costs in the Primary Campaign	Primary Groups			Party			Interest Groups			All Sources		
	None N = 43	Few N = 25	Many N = 39	None N = 54	Few N = 24	Many N = 29	None N = 29	Few N = 26	Many N = 52	None N = 18	Few N = 41	Many N = 48
Benefits												
High	26%	68%	72%	39%	71%	62%	28%	58%	64%	17%	44%	73%
Low	74	32	28	61	29	38	72	42	36	83	56	27
	$X^2 = 20.71$, P < .001			$X^2 = 7.77$, P < .02			$X^2 = 10.65$, P < .01			$X^2 = 18.50$, P < .001		
Costs*												
High	49%	48%	56%	56%	54%	41%	62%	35%	54%	44%	46%	58%
Low	51	52	44	44	46	59	38	65	46	56	54	42

Types of Primary Campaign Support

Benefits and Costs in the Primary Campaign	Primary Groups			Party			Interest Groups			All Sources		
	None N = 45	Weak N = 47	Strong N = 15	None N = 54	Weak N = 38	Strong N = 15	None N = 29	Weak N = 61	Strong N = 17	None N = 18	Weak N = 64	Strong N = 25
Benefits												
High	27%	72%	67%	39%	71%	53%	28%	61%	65%	17%	58%	64%
Low	73	28	33	61	29	47	72	39	35	83	42	36
	$X^2 = 20.81$, P < .001			$X^2 = 9.28$, P < .01			$X^2 = 14.49$, P < .01			$X^2 = 11.24$, P < .01		
Costs*												
High	47%	53%	53%	56%	47%	47%	62%	43%	65%	44%	50%	60%
Low	53	47	47	44	53	53	38	57	35	56	50	40

* All Chi-squared for costs are insignificant.

TABLE V-6 (Continued)

Level of Support by Source and the Candidates' Personal Benefits and Costs

Number of General Campaign Supporters

Benefits and Costs in the General Campaign		Primary Groups			Party			Interest Groups			All Sources		
		None N=3	Few N=31	Many N=43	None N=8	Few N=29	Many N=40	None N=5	Few N=36	Many N=36	None N=2	Few N=33	Many N=42
Benefits	High	0%	29%	67%	38%	38%	60%	0%	36%	69%	0%	27%	69%
	Low	100	71	33	62	62	40	100	64	31	100	73	31
		$X^2 = 13.77$, P < .01			$X^2 =$ n.s.			$X^2 = 12.94$, P < .01			$X^2 = 15.02$, P < .001		
Costs	High	100%	29%	60%	62%	43%	51%	40%	38%	63%	100%	38%	59%
	Low	0	71	40	38	57	49	60	62	37	0	62	41
		$X^2 = 10.27$, P < .01			$X^2 =$ n.s.			$X^2 =$ n.s.			$X^2 =$ n.s.		

Types of General Campaign Support

Benefits and Costs in the General Campaign		Primary Groups			Party			Interest Groups			All Sources		
		None N=3	Weak N=29	Strong N=45	None N=8	Weak N=16	Strong N=53	None N=5	Weak N=25	Strong N=47	None N=2	Weak N=15	Strong N=60
Benefits	High	0%	34%	62%	38%	31%	57%	0%	47%	55%	0%	33%	55%
	Low	100	66	38	62	69	43	100	53	45	100	67	45
		$X^2 = 8.55$, P < .02			$X^2 =$ n.s.			$X^2 =$ n.s.			$X^2 =$ n.s.		
Costs	High	100%	31%	58%	62%	50%	47%	40%	48%	51%	100%	40%	50%
	Low	0	69	42	38	50	53	60	52	49	0	60	50
		$X^2 = 8.15$, P < .02			$X^2 =$ n.s.			$X^2 =$ n.s.			$X^2 =$ n.s.		

TABLE V–7

Number of Sources of Support with Many Sponsors and Campaign
Benefits and Costs in the Primary and General Elections

Campaign Benefits and Costs in the Primary		*Number of Sources of Support with Many Sponsors*			
		None N = 36	*One* N = 36	*Two* N = 20	*Three* N = 15
Benefits					
	High	33%	56%	65%	73%
	Low	67	44	35	27
			$X^2 = 9.14, P < .05$		
Costs					
	High	36%	69%	65%	27%
	Low	64	31	35	73
			$X^2 = 13.18, P < .01$		
Campaign Benefits and Costs in the General		*Number of Sources of Support with Many Sponsors*			
		None N = 19	*One* N = 14	*Two* N = 27	*Three* N = 17
Benefits					
	High	26%	29%	48%	94%
	Low	74	71	52	6
			$X^2 = 20.10, P < .001$		
Costs					
	High	32%	29%	63%	65%
	Low	68	71	37	35
			$X^2 = 9.00, P < .05$		

TABLE V–8

Incumbency, Election Outcomes, and Campaign Costs and Benefits

Campaign Benefits and Costs		*Incumbency*	
		Incumbents N = 42	*Non-incumbents* N = 71
Benefits			
	High	40%	58%
	Low	60	42
		$X^2 = 3.15, P < .10$	
Costs			
	High	67%	42%
	Low	33	58
		$X^2 = 6.30, P < .02$	

Campaign Benefits and Costs		*Election Outcomes*		
		Primary Losers N = 17	*General Losers* N = 40	*General Winners* N = 56
Benefits				
	High	88%	48%	43%
	Low	12	52	57
			$X^2 = 11.10, P < .01$	
Costs				
	High	41%	43%	61%
	Low	59	57	39
			$X^2 = $ n.s.	

TABLE V-9

Winners and Losers and Their Perception of Benefits and Costs, Controlling for Incumbency

Campaign Benefits and Costs		*Incumbents*				*Non-incumbents*		
		*Primary. Losers** $N = 0$	*General Losers* $N = 3$	*General Winners* $N = 39$	*Primary Losers* $N = 17$	*General Losers* $N = 37$	*General Winners* $N = 17$
Benefits	High	0%	0%	44%	88%	51%	41%
	Low	0	100	56	12	49	59
Costs	High	0%	100%	64%	41%	38%	53%
	Low	0	0	36	59	62	47

* Although one incumbent lost his primary race, he refused to be interviewed.

CHAPTER VI

Recruitment, Opportunity and Selection

IN SOME DISTRICTS in Oregon and throughout the country, the legislative campaign reaches a dramatic climax. A deluge of advertisements in newspapers, radio, and television blanket the constituency as the candidates mobilize their workers for a frantic election-eve effort. In other districts, electoral politics fails to catch the public's fancy, and the various campaign organizations fail to get off the ground. Contrary to widespread belief, only some candidates spend election night anxiously awaiting the voters' decision. Many others are elected, in effect, the day they filed or have already won office by winning in the primary. Still others were certain they would be defeated before they became candidates.

On election night itself, the way each candidate watches the returns indicates with some accuracy the character of his campaign. If all the candidates are not anxious on election night about the outcome of the election, it is because electoral competition in their districts assigns different odds of becoming elected to every contender. Each competitive pattern determines its special mode of candidate instigation and support and requires a particular set of electoral strategies. Each competitive pattern attracts candidates with diverse motivation, incentives and credentials, draw together circles of activists and interest groups as sponsors, and bring particular electorates into the successive phases of the recruitment process. Thus, legislators are selected through a variety of processes. Activists and groups always play an important part, but the competitive structure of the district may exclude part, or even the overwhelming majority, of the citizens from participating effectively in the selection of their legislator.

In this chapter, we will consider the attributes of the individuals who became candidates, and those who were eventually elected as legislators. Each candidate's social and economic background, political experience and socialization, and ties to the constituency tell us something about the candidate's district. We will see how a candidate's credentials mesh with various modes of initiation and support. In particular, we will try to discover whether the social characteristics of Oregon legislative candidates influenced their chances of success, their party affiliations, their candidacy instigation, and the support they actually received. Combining such factors will give us the structure of political opportunity in the Oregon legislative constituencies, not only at the point when individuals decide to run, but also how the recruitment process, throughout all its phases, selects and rejects individuals. We will demonstrate how each district's social, economic, and political structure erects a particular pattern of recruitment restriction.

THE SOCIAL PROFILE OF THE LEGISLATIVE CANDIDATES

Trends in the background characteristics of Oregon candidates reflect infusions of "new blood" into the political elite brought about by social and economic change. The recruitment process translates social and economic changes which affect the electorate into changes in political leadership. Whether such changes in society alter the characteristics of those certified to run for office is a function of what we have called political opportunity.

The social background of candidates clearly shows inclusions and exclusions and thus is an indicator of political opportunity. Numerous studies have shown that state legislators are not a cross-section of the electorate they represent.[1] If proper representation means that each element of the population is included in the State legislature in direct proportion to its relative size in the population, then all State legislatures confer biased representation. Moreover, in no state are those who become candidates a microcosm of the electorate. Recruitment is always biased and selective. The real questions are whether the selection criteria employed and its results are in accord with democratic values. Thus, the social characteristics of the candidates, and the ways they vary

[1] See, for example, Frank J. Sorauf, *Party and Representation* (New York: Atherton, 1963), pp. 61–75; John C. Wahlke et al., *The Legislative System* (New York: Wiley, 1962), pp. 69–133; Samuel C. Patterson and G. R. Boynton, "Legislative Recruitment in a Civic Culture," *Social Science Quarterly*, L (September, 1969), pp. 243–263; and Victor Hjelm and Joseph P. Pisciotte, "Profiles and Careers of Colorado State Legislators," *Western Political Quarterly*, XXI (December, 1968), pp. 471–500.

with each type of legislative district will measure the bias of effective political opportunity in Oregon.[2]

Demographic Characteristics of Oregon Legislative Candidates

In general, legislative candidates in Oregon were similar to legislators in other American states in their demographic characteristics. Table VI–1 presents data on sex, age, place of birth, residence and religion of candidates, by their party affiliation and the results of the election.

There are no legal barriers which prohibit women from seeking a legislative position, yet women were clearly under-represented among all the Oregon candidates. Roughly 9 percent of the candidates were women, which compares quite favorably with legislators in other states.[3] Of the ten women candidates in our sample, seven were defeated.[4] Thus, legislative recruitment is heavily biased in favor of male candidates. Traditional social norms about male and female roles tended to discourage women in Oregon from seeking public office.[5] Some studies have shown that the Democrats are more hospitable to women candidates than the Republicans.[6] However, in Oregon, male candidates predominated in both parties.

Legislative candidates are selected from particular age groups, rather than proportionately from all age groups. Studies conducted in Pennsylvania, Wisconsin, Colorado, and Indiana have shown that state legislators are usually in their forties and fifties.[7] Oregon candidates

---

[2] Parenthetically, social background of candidates should tell us something about the attitudes and behavior of candidates. Edinger and Searing have argued that the social background of political elites tells us their political socialization and may thus predict elite attitudes and behavior. See Lewis J. Edinger and Donald D. Searing, "Social Background in Elite Analysis: A Methodological Inquiry," *American Political Science Review,* LXI (June, 1967), pp. 428–445; and Donald D. Searing, "The Comparative Study of Elite Socialization," *Comparative Political Studies,* I (January, 1969), pp. 471–500. It should be noted, however, that several studies have found that background characteristics of political elites do not seem to be efficient predictors of political attitudes. Chong Lim Kim, "Attitudinal Effects of Legislative Recruitment: The Case of Japanese Assemblymen," forthcoming, October, 1974, issue of *Comparative Politics.*

[3] The percentage of women among the Pennsylvania candidates was 5.2 percent and 8 percent of the Colorado candidates. See Sorauf, *Party and Representation,* p. 66; and Hjelm and Pisciotte, "Profiles and Careers of Colorado State Legislators," p. 699.

[4] Two women were incumbents who lost.

[5] Sorauf, *Party and Representation,* p. 67.

[6] Ibid., p. 67.

[7] Ibid.; Malcolm E. Jewell and Samuel C. Patterson, *The Legislative Process in the United States* (New York: Random House, 1966), p. 114; and Hjelm and Pisciotte, op. cit., pp. 699–702.

TABLE VI–1

Demographic Characteristics of Candidates
(Percentages)

Characteristics	Total	Winners		Losers	
		Republican	Democrat	Republican	Democrat
	N = 107	*N = 31*	*N = 20*	*N = 24*	*N = 32*
Sex:					
Male	91%	93%	95%	88%	88%
Female	9	7	5	12	12
Age:					
26–35	19%	29%	15%	13%	19%
36–45	33	19	40	37	38
46–55	29	33	25	25	31
56–65	16	19	15	21	9
66 or older	3	0	5	4	3
Place of Birth:					
Oregon	44%	58%	35%	29%	47%
Other States	53	42	65	68	50
Other Countries	3	0	0	8	3
Residence:					
City	67%	58%	75%	83%	60%
Town	23	23	20	13	31
Farm	10	19	5	4	9
Religion:					
Episcopalian	9%	13%	10%	4%	6%
Lutheran	6	0	5	8	9
Presbyterian	16	29	15	13	6
Methodist	9	10	10	0	16
Congregational	4	0	10	4	4
Other Protestant	21	13	20	42	16
Catholic	11	10	5	8	19
Jewish	13	10	5	17	19
No Affiliation	11	16	20	4	6

proved no exception. Two factors pointed out the predominance of the middle aged among the Oregon candidates. First, middle-aged persons project an image of maturity and experience which enhances their appeal to the public. Second, middle-aged persons are more likely to be prominent and successful in their occupations, (which makes them able to run is also conducive to political success.[8]) As in other states, Oregon's

[8] Jewell and Patterson, *The Legislative Process in the United States,* p. 114; and David B. Walker, "The Age Factor in the 1958 Congressional Elections," *Midwest Journal of Political Science,* IV (February, 1960), pp. 1–26.

Democrats tended to recruit younger candidates than did the Republicans.[9] We expected the older candidates to hold an edge over their younger opponents, but there was no appreciable difference between the winning and losing candidates in their ages.

All but one of the 1966 candidates were white. According to the 1960 census figures, the nonwhite population constituted only 1.1 percent in Oregon, and most were concentrated in the Portland metropolitan area. The number of registered black voters is too small to elect a black legislator, although there have been black candidates from time to time. Oregon candidates were predominantly native-born Americans. Nearly one-half of them were born in Oregon and the rest were born in other American states. Only three percent of the candidates were born in foreign countries. Thus, the legislative candidates mirror Oregon's white, native-born population.

The Republican and Democratic candidates differed in several respects. The Democratic party has been more hospitable to candidates born outside the state, and clearly our study illustrates that this has not jeopardized their chances at the polls. Over half of the victorious Democrats were born outside of Oregon, while over sixty percent of the triumphant Republicans were native Oregonians. This statistic reflects the growing Democratic strength in urban areas of the state which have experienced a large influx of new residents in recent years. The urban strength of the Democrats is borne out by the fact that winning Democrats were more likely to live in urban areas than were successful Republicans.

In the nation as a whole, Catholic and Jewish voters disproportionately support the Democratic party and Protestants seem to support the Republicans.[10] However, Oregon Republican and Democratic candidates did not differ appreciably in their religious preferences, nor did winners and losers. This reflects the predominantly Protestant makeup of Oregon's population. Over sixty percent of the candidates were Protestants; and the remainder were divided evenly among Catholics, Jews, and those with no religious identification.

In sum, the demographic profile of Oregon candidates seems similar to that of legislators in other American states. The candidates were predominantly middle-aged, male, white Protestants, many of whom were natives of the state.

[9] Sorauf found in his Pennsylvania study that the Democratic party tended to recruit its candidates from relatively younger age groups (Sorauf, *Party and Representation,* p. 66).

[10] Ibid., pp. 68–69.

Career Background and Preparation

No characteristic of American legislators has been more extensively studied than their educational attainment. All studies point conclusively to the fact that state legislators are well educated. It is no surprise then, that more than eighty-five percent of the Oregon legislative candidates received at least a college-level education (Table VI–2). Moreover, one-third had earned an advanced degree. In comparison with other states, Oregon candidates were more highly educated. For

TABLE VI–2

Career Background and Preparation
(Percentages)

Background Profiles	Total N = 107	Winners		Losers	
		Republican N = 31	Democrat N = 20	Republican N = 24	Democrat N = 32
Education:					
Grade School or Less	1%	0%	5%	0%	0%
High School	10	3	10	12	16
College	55	58	50	50	59
Advanced or Professional Degree	34	39	35	38	25
(1)					
Occupation:					
Higher Executive, Proprietors, Major Professionals	37%	55%	35%	42%	19%
Business Managers, Lesser Professionals	32	29	35	29	35
Administrative Personnel, Small Business Owners	20	16	15	25	26
Clerical & Technical Workers	6	0	10	4	7
Skilled Workers	5	0	5	0	9
Others	1	0	0	0	4
Income:					
$5,000 or Less	5%	0%	10%	4%	6%
$5,001–$10,000	24	16	15	22	41
$10,001–$15,000	27	26	25	31	25
$15,001–$25,000	26	26	35	39	12
$25,001 or Over	18	32	15	4	16

Note: (1) Occupational categories were derived from the *Index of Social Position* developed by A. B. Hollingshead.

TABLE VI–2 (Continued)

Background Profiles	Total	Winners		Losers	
		Republican	Democrat	Republican	Democrat
	N = 107	N = 31	N = 20	N = 24	N = 32
(2)					
Class Status:					
Upper Class	2%	3%	0%	0%	3%
Upper Middle Class	37	42	42	36	29
Middle Class	49	48	48	64	42
Lower Middle Class	8	7	5	0	16
Working Class	4	0	5	0	10
(3)					
Social Mobility:					
Upwardly Mobile	45%	34%	56%	57%	42%
Stationary	49	66	39	38	52
Downwardly Mobile	4	0	5	5	6

(2) The respondents were asked to rate their own social status. Therefore, the status categories were based on subjective rankings.

(3) The respondents were asked to compare and rank their own status with that of their father's. Thus social mobility is measured subjectively.

example, the percentage of college educated legislators in Ohio was 77 percent, 74 percent in Tennessee, 68 percent in Wisconsin, 73 percent in Indiana, and 51 percent in Pennsylvania.[11] Nationwide, the Republican candidates were slightly more educated than the Democratic candidates, although these differences were not significant in influencing the results of the election. In Oregon, winners and losers did not differ in educational attainment; both groups were equally well educated.

Most of the Oregon candidates pursued high-status occupations. Thirty-seven percent of them were business executives, proprietors, and major professionals (attorneys, physicians, college professors, and engineers); 32 percent were engaged in prestigious managerial and lesser professional occupations. In this respect, Oregon is no exception to the general rule that high-status occupational groups are favored for legislative candidacy. Moreover, as in other states, Oregon Republicans tend to recruit their candidates from higher-status occupations than do the Democrats.[12] Thus, the two major political parties recruit from somewhat different occupational groups. However, there is little difference in occupational status between the winning and losing candidates of both

[11] See Wahlke et al., *The Legislative System,* p. 489, and Sorauf, *Party and Representation,* p. 69.
[12] Sorauf, Ibid., pp. 75–81.

parties. This is understandable because almost all candidates had high-status occupations.

It is not surprising that the annual incomes of the candidates were substantially higher than the average family income in the state. In 1960 the median family income in Oregon was about $5,900; the comparable figure for the candidates was $13,000. Thus, higher-income groups were over-represented among the candidates. As expected, more Republicans earned a high income than did the Democrats. However, the winning and losing candidates indicated roughly the same income distributions. This is surprising because a high income, associated with a high-status occupation and substantial education, should make it easier for the candidate to raise campaign funds or organize campaign machinery. Consequently, we expected that candidates with high incomes would have better chances to win than others. However, the data have shown consistently that the levels of income, education, and occupation have no significant bearing on the outcome of the election.

Measured by education, occupation, or income, the 1966 Oregon candidates had relatively high social status. It is also noteworthy that the candidates self-rated their social status as high. When asked to identify their social positions on a six-point status scale, 85 percent classified themselves as middle-class or above.[13] No matter whether objective or subjective measures of social class are used, the overwhelming majority of the candidates were middle-class. Despite some differences in education, occupation, and income, both the Republicans and the Democrats regarded themselves as high in social status. Indeed, their social status derived from their private occupations, not from their status as candidates.

Political offices serve as effective avenues for social advancement. A number of studies indicate that state legislators are socially mobile. Patterson reported that nearly half of the Wisconsin legislators were upwardly mobile when compared with their parents' social status.[14] Eulau and Koff found that approximately one-third of the legislators in California, New Jersey, Ohio, and Tennessee were upwardly mobile.[15] In Oregon, forty-five percent of the candidates stated that their present social status was higher than that of their parents. Thus, legislative office

[13] The question and codes for responses were as follows: "If you were to place yourself in a social class, which of the following would suit your current position? (1) Upper Class; (2) Upper Middle Class; (3) Middle Class; (4) Lower Middle Class; (5) Working Class; (6) Lower Class."

[14] Samuel C. Patterson, "Inter-Generational Occupational Mobility and Legislative Voting Behavior," *Social Forces,* XLIII (October, 1964), pp. 90–93.

[15] Heinz Eulau and David Koff, "Occupational Mobility and Political Career," *Western Political Quarterly,* XV (September, 1962), p. 511.

attracts upwardly mobile persons. Among the winning candidates, more Democrats were upwardly mobile than the Republicans. A party that is gaining strength, as we have shown, creates opportunities for advancement and attracts upwardly mobile persons.

In sum, the career backgrounds of the Oregon candidates show them to be members of the successful middle class. They were well educated, held prestigious occupations, and earned incomes substantially higher than the median income of families in Oregon. Most legislators ranked themselves as members of the upper middle or middle classes. Legislative candidates are not ordinary citizens; neither are they a group born to privilege. They are the children of the middle class or have achieved middle-class status.

Political Socialization

The political attitudes, values, and beliefs of legislative candidates derive in large part from their political socialization. Recent studies show that legislators are likely to have grown up in more politicized family and school environments than the average citizen, and acquire an interest in politics and the habit of participation at a relatively early age.[16] To what extent were the family and school environments of the Oregon candidates politicized? How did they become involved in political activity initially? What agencies stimulated their interest in politics over the years?

Wahlke and his associates reported that "an interest in politics is probably related to the opportunity to hear about it or directly experience it."[17] Thus, having parents, relatives, or close friends in politics is likely to facilitate an individual's own awareness of and familiarity with politics. A large number of the Oregon candidates of both parties had such opportunities in their families (Table VI–3). Over forty percent of them recalled that when they were young, one or more members of their immediate family were active in politics. Consequently, many of these candidates acquired an interest in politics at an early age from members of their primary groups. We expected that winning candidates might have had more politicized family backgrounds than losing candidates, but our evidence on socialization does not show this to be true. However, a substantially greater proportion of the winning Democrats had a family history of activism than did the successful Republicans.

The legislative candidates as a rule, became active in politics in their youth. Over three-fourths of them recalled that they held either an

[16] Jewell and Patterson, *The Legislative Process in the United States,* pp. 105–106.
[17] Wahlke et al., *The Legislative System,* p. 82.

TABLE VI–3

The Political Socialization of Candidates
(Percentages)

Socialization Experiences	Total	Winners		Losers	
		Republican	Democrat	Republican	Democrat
	N = 107	N = 31	N = 20	N = 24	N = 32
Immediate Family Members Active in Politics:					
Yes	43%	39%	69%	38%	38%
No	57	61	31	62	62
NA	(7)	(3)	(4)	(0)	(0)
Political Activity While Going to School:					
Yes	77%	81%	70%	70%	84%
No	23	19	30	30	16
NA	(2)	(0)	(0)	(1)	(0)
First Political Activity:					
Party Work	33%	30%	25%	35%	43%
Campaign Work for Candidate	35	43	35	43	20
Filed for Office	25	27	20	22	27
Supported Issues	7	0	20	0	10
NA	(5)	(2)	(0)	(1)	(2)
Sources of Continuing Political Interest: Party or Political					
Figure	20%	16%	20%	25%	20%
Issues	39	35	40	50	32
Personal or Group Advantage	8	0	10	4	19
Sense of Civic Duty	33	49	30	21	29
NA	(5)	(2)	(0)	(1)	(2)

elective or appointive office when they were students. The candidates of our study grew up in politically active families, but as they were maturing, they also participated in politics. Republican and Democratic candidates do not differ in this respect, nor do the winning and losing candidates.

Once a person develops an interest in politics, he must choose some activity in which he can express this interest. We asked our respondents, "Do you remember what kind of activity you engaged in when you first entered politics?" For some candidates, involvement with issues or

125

officeholding were initial activities; for many others, party or campaign activity triggered political participation. A study of four American states reported that 45 percent of the legislators in California, 66 percent in New Jersey, 44 percent in Ohio, and 44 percent in Tennessee first broke into politics through party or campaign activity.[18] In Oregon, 68 percent of the candidates began their political careers by working for their parties or for particular candidates. Thus, the evidence is convincing that political parties and the electoral process are the two most important socializing agents for the activists in American political life.

Republican and Democratic candidates entered politics in similar ways, with the exception that some Democrats were drawn by political issues (20 percent), while none of the Republicans were. No marked difference existed in the types of initial political activity between the winning and losing candidates. Win or lose, most of the Oregon candidates began their political careers through party- or campaign-related activities.

By the time a person becomes a legislative candidate, he has usually been involved in public affairs for some time. Some individuals participate because of a deeply ingrained sense of civic duty. Others are deeply attached to their party or a particular public figure. Still others perceive political activity primarily as a means of achieving some personal or group advantage. Still others are drawn into politics because of a particular issue they advocate. When we asked the Oregon candidates what had prompted their participation in politics over the years, nearly 40 percent replied that particular issues had been primarily responsible for their public activity. One-third of all the candidates reported that a sense of civic duty, a desire for good government, or an obligation to guard their district's interests had been of primary importance. Only 20 percent of the candidates mentioned their parties or prominent public figures as the prime reasons for their involvement. Less than one in ten stated that they used politics for personal or group advantage. Thus, the Oregon candidates as a group participated year after year because of a high-minded sense of civic duty or a deep involvement with issues. This reflects the progressive heritage in Oregon which has fostered a deep mistrust of any political "organization" and an association with "dirty" machine-type politics. The data show no appreciable differences between winners and losers, or Republicans or Democrats in the causes of their involvement over the years, with the exception that Democrats were slightly more apt to view politics as an avenue for personal or group advancement than the Republicans.

[18] Ibid., p. 85.

The political socialization patterns of Oregon legislative candidates suggest several important conclusions. First, primary groups played a crucial role in political socialization, which was a prelude to the part such groups played in the recruitment process itself. The candidates grew up in highly politicized family and school environments. Nearly half recalled one or more persons active in politics in their immediate family. Two-thirds actively participated in politics when they were students. Therefore, the candidates had developed an interest in politics and had participated in politics throughout their maturation. And such participation was reinforced by their primary groups in their adult life, as we have seen, in connection with their instigation into candidacy.

Second, although candidates entered politics in diverse ways, party activity and campaign-related work were preferred channels. For about sixty percent of the Oregon candidates, party work and campaign activity were the initial modes of participation. Third, more than three-fourths of the candidates remained active because of an interest in particular issues or out of a sense of obligation to participate. Although the party or campaign work were typical first activities, interest was sustained by issues or by an abstract sense of civic obligation rather than by more mundane commitments to local parties and officials or personal advancement. Finally, the candidates of the two parties, winners or losers, had similar patterns of political socialization.

Constituency Ties

It has become a commonplace tradition in American politics that legislators are "small town boys." In the four-state study, Wahlke and his associates demonstrated that state legislators by and large are "locals" with deep roots in the community which they sought to represent in the legislature.[19] Thus, local attachment precludes newcomers or outsiders from seeking legislative careers at both the state and national levels.[20]

Anyone who aspires to legislative office must have ties to his constituency. We measured constituency ties with two criteria: the length of time a candidate had lived in the state and the length of time he resided in his district. As Table VI–4 shows, a majority of Oregon candidates had lived in the state for longer than 30 years, while only four percent had lived in Oregon for less than 10 years. Republican candidates had resided in the state somewhat longer than had the Democrats. The

[19] Ibid., pp. 488–489.
[20] An excellent analysis of the image of "local boys" in the legislature is found in LeRoy N. Rieselbach, "Congressmen as 'Small Town Boys': A Research Note," *Midwest Journal of Political Science*, XIV (May, 1970), pp. 321–330.

TABLE VI–4

Constituency Ties of Candidates
(Percentages)

Constituency Ties	Total	Winners		Losers	
		Republican	Democrat	Republican	Democrat
	N = 107	N = 31	N = 20	N = 24	N = 32
Length of Residence in Oregon:					
Less than 10 Years	4%	0%	0%	8%	6%
11–20 Years	20	13	20	21	25
21–30 Years	21	20	25	17	22
31–40 Years	22	20	30	17	25
Over 40 Years	33	47	25	37	22
NA	(1)	(1)	(0)	(0)	(0)
Length of Residence in Electoral District:					
Less than 10 Years	19%	10%	10%	38%	19%
11–20 Years	30	19	35	29	39
21–30 Years	17	19	25	13	13
31–40 Years	22	26	20	17	23
Over 40 Years	12	26	10	4	6
NA	(1)	(0)	(0)	(0)	(1)

data reveals a striking difference between the winning and losing candidates. Substantially more winners had long residence in Oregon than the losing candidates. This finding is reinforced when we consider how long the candidates had lived in their local constituency. Most of the candidates had lived in their districts for a long period. Over half of the respondents had lived in their local communities for twenty years or more. As a group, the Republicans had resided in their home districts longer than the Democrats. Thus, the Republican party in Oregon seems to recruit more "local boys" than does the Democratic party.

Winning and losing candidates again showed substantial differences in length of residence in their home districts. Over sixty percent of the winners had lived in their districts at least twenty years, as compared with only thirty-seven percent of the losing candidates. Relatively long residence in the state and the district is therefore one of the keys to electoral success. Research suggests that the strong ties that bind lawmakers to their local constituencies influence the legislative process. Legislators tend to look to locally oriented opinion leaders for guidance, and place local, constituency interests above broader statewide concerns.[21] As a

[21] Ibid., p. 321.

result, the legislative process must try to accommodate many parochial interests.

SOCIAL BACKGROUND AND RECRUITMENT PATTERNS

The candidates for the state legislature were not typical of their constituents. They were better educated, earned more money, were engaged in occupations of higher status, and were more active in politics than the average citizen. Most of the candidates worked in their legislative district, had raised their families there, and had long-standing friendships and associations in the community. The candidates were a cross section of the political influentials in their communities, not of the general electorate.

Thus, individuals with long records of political participation and public service in the community become candidates. For such people, becoming a candidate is made easy by their intimate knowledge of the community. It is no surprise that those who instigate their candidacies are also involved in local politics in many ways. The candidates, and individuals like them in the constituency make up the pool of eligibles from which political influentials and officeholders of all kinds are drawn. They are members of the social circles which dominate the political affairs of the community, county, and legislative district.

The selection of candidates occurs among such circles of activists in the local community. Those who encourage the candidates, and the intensity of such encouragement indicates to us the criteria which govern selection and the strategies which instigators employ to screen candidates. The incentives that political activity in general and public office in particular offer to activists generate types of candidates, e.g., enthusiasts, reluctants. In rural constituencies, where incentives are low, candidates are selected from within local political circles. Local activists seek one of their number who will agree to run. Consequently, the rural reluctant candidates epitomize the social background, outlooks and experiences of the local groups which instigated them and to which they belong. In rural constituencies, such candidates are found among the successful farmers, ranchers, local businessmen and professionals who have lived in the community for a long time.

Similar constraints structure the selection of minority party candidates in urban one-party districts. The more ambitious, skillful and prominent figures in the community run in the majority party. The minority party leadership constitutes a small group of men and women of lower status and limited ambition who use party office for social and economic advancement. They are drawn into party circles by the small measure of prestige, influence, preferments, and in some cases, patronage that accrues to the minority party leadership. They also enjoy meeting and working with like-minded men and women.

Electoral politics poses serious problems within the minority party organization. Every two years, the minority party leadership must find candidates to run and lose for the party. If no one volunteers, the local organization drafts candidates from among its activists. In some cases, the local leadership agrees to rotate legislative candidacy among members of the group. As one minority candidate stated:

> We play Russian roulette. Two years ago, [former candidate] ran. This year it's my turn. Next election [local party leader] will be in the hot seat.

Thus, the minority parties draft candidates (hence, the conscripts) from among their elite corps of activists. Like those who initiate and support them, such candidates are of lower status, less successful, and less prominent than their counterparts on the majority party.

Enthusiasts and those who encourage them are drawn to politics by a broader range of incentives, and their interactions reflect the attractiveness of office. In the hothouse political atmosphere of the urban districts, many potential candidates come forward, some seeking help from party or interest group leaders, others soliciting support from friends and colleagues who are active in local affairs. Some enthusiasts file on their own, expecting to gather support as the campaign progresses, while others have promises of sponsorship from their party, or more often, from interest groups or associations in which they are active.[22] Only advertisers seem to run unencouraged and unsupported. They are essentially political outsiders, with less experience, fewer connections with local political leaders, and lower status than the serious contenders and their sponsors.

The social characteristics of the enthusiasts reflect the makeup of the various groups and associations that are involved in the affairs of the urban one-party constituency. The majority party candidates, for example, are usually prominent spokesmen of the principal factions within the party. They are drawn from the upper echelons of local activists and represent the most active and successful among the constituency's political leadership. Although different interests predominate in Republican and Democratic urban and rural one-party districts, the spokesmen and leadership in either type of district are middle-class or

---

[22] See Supra, Chapter V, for a discussion of the patterns of support received by the various urban enthusiasts.

upper middle-class. For example, in one-party Republican districts, candidates are drawn disproportionately from business and commercial circles, together with prominent lawyers. Democratic candidates are most often self-employed attorneys, insurance salesmen, high school or college teachers, and minor professionals. Blue-collar workers and union leaders are conspicuously underrepresented.[23]

Similarly, candidates in the urban two-party districts are often selected from among the top leadership of local groups and associations. However, competition within and between the parties occasionally forces local factions to seek candidates from outside their top echelons. In order to win against strong opposition, they attempt to coopt prominent local figures who are not identified with partisan politics. Such candidates are usually members of old and respected families, television or radio personalities, or owners of large local corporations who are reluctant to run because they have little to gain from service in the legislature. Such "notables" are wealthier, better educated, and are of higher status than those who initiate their candidacies or the other candidates who oppose them.

The background characteristics of the Oregon candidates reflected their varied recruitment patterns. For example, nearly all serious contenders were college graduates, the majority of whom enjoyed high occupational status and substantial income. Of these, the urban coopted candidates consistently ranked highest in status, followed by the rural reluctants and the urban enthusiasts (Table VI–5). By contrast, the urban minority-party candidates (conscripts) and advertisers, who had little chance to win, were either of lower status or had lower incomes than one might expect from individuals with such high educational and occupational attainments. In other words, some of the urban conscripts and advertisers were individuals of lower status than the serious contenders, while other nonserious contenders had considerable education and prestigious occupations, but were less successful and made less money than their counterparts among the serious candidates.[24] It is

---

[23] The few blue-collar workers and union leaders who actually filed in the majority party in these districts had an unusual set of occupations. Witness, for example, a fireman with a law degree who practiced law on the side, or the union business agent who worked in a factory but also owned and operated a large suburban farm.

[24] Specifically, seven of the thirteen minority candidates were of lower occupational and educational status and received commensurate incomes. Four of the minority party candidates held prestigious professional or managerial positions, had been awarded baccalaureate degrees and/or advanced degrees, but made at least $5,000/yr. less than their counterparts of the majority party side. Only two of the minority-party candidates had incomes, educational and occupational status comparable with the average candidate of the majority party.

TABLE VI–5

Socio-Economic Status and Styles of Candidacy
(N = 107)

Status Variables	*Rural Reluc- tant N = 32*	*Urban Co- opted N = 13*	*Urban Con- scripts N = 14*	*Urban Enthu- siast N = 31*	*Adver- tiser N = 17*
Education:					
Grade School or Less	0%	0%	0%	3%	0%
High School	9	8	14	6	18
College	66	23	64	61	41
Advanced or Professional					
Degree	25	69	22	29	41
Occupation:					
Higher Executive,					
Proprietors, Major					
Professionals	41%	62%	38%	32%	24%
Business Managers,					
Lesser Professionals	41	38	31	26	24
Administrative Personnel,					
Small Business Owners	12	0	23	29	35
Clerical & Technical					
Workers	6	0	8	6	0
Skilled, Blue Collar	0	0	0	6	17
Income:					
$5,000 or Less	0%	0%	8%	7%	12%
$5,001–$10,000	16	0	46	30	36
$10,001–$15,000	16	8	31	50	18
$15,001–$25,000	44	38	8	10	29
$25,001 or Over	25	54	8	3	6

no surprise that such candidates used politics as an avenue for occupational advancement.

The candidates' self-evaluations of their class, status and generational mobility show that the serious contenders were born and raised
in middle-class surroundings, while the advertisers and conscripts were
of lower middle-class or working-class origins. We asked the candidates
their social class and the status of their parents. With the responses
we received, we divided the candidates into two groups: (1) those
whose parents were middle-class and who had maintained or risen in
status; and (2) those candidates whose parents enjoyed less than
middle-class status and who had remained at the same level or achieved
middle-class status through their own efforts (Table VI–6). The data
show that all coopted candidates were of middle-class background and

TABLE VI–6

Intergenerational Mobility and Styles of Candidacy
(N = 107)

Intergenerational Mobility	*Rural Reluctant N = 32*	*Urban Co-opted N = 13*	*Urban Conscript N = 14*	*Urban Enthusiast N = 31*	*Advertiser N = 17*
Maintained or Improved Upon Middle-Class Status	81%	100%	42%	71%	53%
Lower than Middle-Class or Achieved Middle-Class Status through Own Efforts	19	0	58	29	47
	100%	100%	100%	100%	100%

had maintained or improved upon their middle-class origins. Similarly, the rural reluctants and urban enthusiasts were predominantly of middle-class backgrounds. The conscripts and advertisers were more likely to see themselves as lower middle- or working-class, or to report that they had achieved middle-class status.

The political backgrounds of the candidates also show how they first became active in politics. The advertisers and conscripts were less likely to come from families with a history of political activity than the serious contenders (Table VI–7). The first political activities of the candidates presaged their modes of entry into candidacy. For example, the minority-party candidates' first political activities more often included work in a political party or support of other minority-party candidates. The most common first activity of the advertisers was filing for the legislature, which shows little or no involvement prior to candidacy. Similarly, a significant minority of the (rural) reluctant candidates and urban coopted candidates listed running for public office as their first political activity. The remaining coopted notables and rural reluctants participated first on behalf of their parties or in support of political candidates.[25] The urban enthusiasts worked first in party and campaign activity. Nine out of ten of them had participated in some way, either

[25] In their social and economic backgrounds, the rural reluctant candidates with no prior political experience resembled the more experienced rural reluctants. The less-experienced rural reluctants were more easily persuaded to file than the experienced reluctants. Perhaps because they were less active in politics in their community explains why the less-experienced rural reluctants were more willing to run without much incentive. They were more ignorant of the advantages and disadvantages of office-seeking in their constituency. Much the same may be true of the coopted notables with little prior experience.

TABLE VI–7

Political Socialization and Styles of Candidacy
(N = 107)

Socialization Experiences	Rural Reluc- tant N = 32	Urban Co- opted N = 13	Urban Con- script N = 14	Urban Enthu- siast N = 31	Adver- tiser N = 17
Immediate Family Members Active in Politics:					
Yes	50%	46%	29%	50%	29%
No	50	54	71	50	71
First Political Activity:					
Party Work	33%	41%	42%	34%	24%
Work for Candidate	33	33	36	46	29
Filed for Office	31	26	21	10	41
Support of Issues	3	0	0	10	6
Sources of Continuing Interest in Politics:					
Party or Political Personality	3%	15%	46%	32%	12%
Issues	41	39	38	32	47
Personal or Group Advantage	6	0	0	10	24
Sense of Civic Duty	50	46	16	26	18

in support of issues, in party work, or on behalf of candidates of their choice, before they considered running for office. Thus, the enthusiasts were most likely to have had experience in politics prior to filing for the legislature.

When candidates were asked what had prompted their political interest over the years, their answers generally reflected the way they were recruited. Over eighty percent of the rural reluctant and coopted candidates cited interest in good government, civic responsibility, or political issues as the reasons for their interest in politics. Because such candidates were motivated by a sense of civic duty or commitment to issues rather than partisan politics or private advantage, it is easier to understand why they ran despite the small incentives that candidacy offered.

The urban minority-party candidates (conscripts) participated in politics because they were interested in their party or party-related issues. The advertisers stated that they were primarily interested in political issues; their desire to promote their own interests or those of particular groups and associations was secondary. But in most cases, the issues in question pertained to their occupations or group affiliations. Thus, the advertisers viewed politics in terms of their self-interests and as a means of private advancement and material benefit. The urban enthusiasts followed politics closely for many reasons, frequently mentioning the fortunes of their party or favorite candidate. Others were concerned with issues that divided the local community, while still others expressed a desire to help their local labor unions or business community; some wanted to promote good government. In the aggregate, their answers reflect the diverse incentives and concerns that lead many to participate in such urban constituencies.

Earlier, we reported that approximately six out of ten victors had resided in their constituencies for over twenty years, while only four of ten of the losers had lived in their districts for that long (see Table VI-4 above). Such data show that long residence is necessary to make the connections, build a reputation, and acquire the experience in local affairs needed to become a successful legislative candidate. Generally, the longer a candidate had resided in his constituency, the greater the chance that he would be a serious contender for office. In other words, the urban enthusiasts, coopted candidates and rural reluctants were more likely to have resided in their constituencies for over twenty years than the advertisers and conscripts (Table VI-8).

Moreover, when candidates were recruited from the dominant political circles in the community, as the rural candidates and the urban enthusiasts were, it was traditionally expected that they would have deep roots in the community. Constituency ties were less important when candidates were recruited from outside the ranks of local activists (the notables), or were drawn as self-starters from the periphery of local political circles (the advertisers), or were drafted by the minority-party leadership (the conscripts). The high status of those few coopted candidates who had recently moved into the community compensated for their relative lack of experience in local affairs. The advertisers were

TABLE VI-8

Length of Residence and Styles of Candidacy
(N = 107)

Length of Residence	*Rural Reluc- tant* N = 32	*Urban Co- opted* N = 13	*Urban Con- script* N = 14	*Urban Enthu- siast* N = 21	*Adver- tiser* N = 17
20 Years or Less	44%	54%	69%	39%	59%
Over 20 Years	56	46	31	61	41

never serious candidates, and the minority leadership was forced to accept those individuals who would agree to run, regardless of the quality of their credentials.

To summarize, each mode of recruitment produces candidates with distinct social and political credentials. The differences reflect the opportunities that spur the candidates and those around them to participate in local and legislative politics. The candidates' occupations, education, income, political socialization and ties to the community are the bases for close relations with their sponsors. The candidates who compete seriously for office are successful in their occupations, have considerable income and substantial education. These individuals are, in turn, sponsored by the successful, influential and prestigious elements of the community.

The particular characteristics of each candidate and his sponsoring coalition vary with the competitive pattern of the constituency and the obligations and dependencies that bind together the candidate and his coalition of support. The rural candidates, for example, were primarily successful ranchers, farmers, local professionals, or small town businessmen, who drew their support from most, if not all of these same elements in the local community. Recruitment occurred essentially from within a homogeneous local elite in the rural constituencies. Much the same is true of the urban enthusiasts, although their support was narrower and tied to particular interests and groups within local political circles. Here again, however, recruitment was from within the ranks of local influentials—interest groups would recruit one of their leaders to run, and individuals from the top echelon of the local party would be recruited by the local party leadership. Of the serious contenders, only the coopted candidates were drawn from the periphery of local political circles. The backgrounds of these candidates show both their higher status and their less-extensive experience in partisan politics.

The conscripts and advertisers represented the marginal elements in the local polities affairs. They were of lower or inconsistent status, had less-extensive political experience, and had lived in their constituencies a shorter time than the serious contenders. Moreover, their sponsors, if any, were on the periphery of local politics. The minority party leadership at best was on the fringe of local politics. Success in politics lay with the majority party, and the ambitious and successful sought their political fortunes in the majority party. Those with less occupational success, as well as an occasional committed ideologue, found modest influence and prestige as leaders of the minority party. The minority candidates were recruited from among this group, and their background characteristics reflected those of their sponsoring coalition. The advertisers were not genuine candidates. They were individuals of lower status and little or no political experience who sought private rather than political advancement. They ran unsponsored, and, after they lost, returned to the haze of political obscurity from whence they came.

SELECTION PROCESSES AND POLITICAL OPPORTUNITY IN OREGON

Why do legislative districts consider the same types of individuals for candidacy for public office year after year? One explanation is that in stable communities, the processes of political socialization, the channels of political activity, the issues, and the styles of politics do not change year after year. The successful politicians and officeholders of the past and present become role models that all political aspirants emulate. The opportunities and risks of political candidacy and the political career become traditions, so that candidates are drawn from a particular pool of individuals, who are either motivated or persuaded to run, and are "acceptable" in the district.

The pool of *individuals* certified for office is *not* identical in size or composition in each legislative district. Both *certification* and *selection* are determined by the ways that social and economic diversity and political competition influence "who" *survives* each *successive* phase of recruitment.

In the model outlined in Chapter II, certification was conceptualized as a phase distinct from selection to show how some citizens were more available for candidacy than others by virtue of their social status, skill, motivation and political socialization. The selection process then chooses from such a pool of the socially and politically certified. In reality, as the model in Chapter II also indicates, these two phases of recruitment (certification and selection) are reciprocal because certification, competition and selection are structured in each district. These factors determine the criteria candidates must satisfy to be elected and when these criteria will be applied. Who is selected depends in large part on who is selecting. The decisive phases of selection, whether the instigation, the primary or the general election phases, attract different groups to the selection process. These groups apply their own standards to each candidate's credentials. The more competitive selection becomes, the more such criteria become refined and specific.

In each phase, some candidates qualify and others are excluded. Thus, the characteristics of those who qualify for each stage may be compared and the selectivity of recruitment can be measured. To measure the effects of this selectivity, we constructed a scale in the following way. First, we collected biographical data on all Oregon legislators from 1958 to 1966.[26] With this data a political, social and economic profile of legislators in each district was constructed, which was then compared with the distribution of such characteristics among the electorate of the district. The comparison yielded the number of people who are effectively certified for office in the district. The ratio of this number to the size of the electorate measured how representative the legislators from each district were.

The profiles of each legislator included their religious affiliation, occupation, sex, length of residency in the constituency, membership and activity in various associations, as well as party affiliation and county of residence. Party affiliation was considered for our comparison because in both urban and rural one-party districts, only members of the majority party could be considered in the pool, while in more competitive districts, the total electorate constituted the eligible pool.[27] County of residence was added because many legislative districts in Oregon include more than one county. Such districts usually include a densely populated "core" county and several sparsely settled counties. Usually, residents of the core county are elected. However, in some districts, office rotates as if by informal agreement from one county to the next.[28] Only residents of those counties that had actually enjoyed representation were added to the pool of the certified.

We constructed similar indices of the scope of certification for all candidates and primary winners. These three scales allow us to gauge the screening of candidates that occurs during each of the three stages of the selection process, i.e., the instigation, the primary election, and the general election. The statistics from our studies indicate that the contestants in all three phases represent less than one percent of the population in some districts and that successful legislators personify many of the social and economic characteristics of their constituents.

Certification Patterns and Political Competition

The social and economic diversity of a constituency, together with its pattern of political competition determine how broadly based or restricted the recruitment process will be. The pattern of political competition defines what resources and strategies are necessary to win a

[26] The biographical data were drawn from Oregon, Secretary of State, *Oregon Blue Book* (Salem: Secretary of State, 1958–1966 editions).
[27] Factor scores derived from the partisan competition factor (Factor III) in Table III–2 were used as measures of inter-party competition.
[28] See Edwin L. Cobb, "Representation Theory and the Flotorial District: The Case of Texas," *Western Political Quarterly*, XXII (December, 1969), pp. 790–805, for an analysis of the electoral politics of "flotorial" or multi-county districts.

seat in the legislature, and thus makes it possible only for some individuals to become serious contenders. An increase in competition in a particular phase of selection or an increase in the number of phases in which candidates must compete increases the costs and risks of candidacy. These higher risks force many potential candidates, who lack the necessary qualifications, out of the field of the viable. At the same time, competition creates opportunities and incentives to participate for more individuals who do have the appropriate credentials. Thus, competition drives out individuals who cannot afford to run, and simultaneously gives incentives and opportunities to those who can afford to compete.

In each type of district, a particular balance among incentives, opportunities and costs prevails. For example, in the rural constituencies, only a few stages of recruitment are contested, which reduces the costs of candidacy. However, the incentives to run for the legislature are modest. Consequently, even with little competition and low costs of candidacy, the rural constituencies, by their very nature, restrict recruitment opportunity. By contrast, in the urban districts, competitive primaries, general elections, and the range of controversial issues stimulate greater public involvement and attract a variety of office seekers. Certification and eligibility become broader because the opportunities for notoriety attract many serious, as well as casual, candidates. Consequently, candidates enjoy broader opportunities to succeed and are drawn by a richer range of incentives where competition is greatest.

Competition also shapes the role that sponsors play in determining opportunities and incentives. Where public competition exists, candidates can choose their sponsors. Opportunity is broadened because no single group controls recruitment. Sponsors use their resources to influence the electorate. By contrast, in districts with little or no public competition, sponsors can handpick their candidates by raising the incentives and lowering the costs of candidacy. The lack of public competition makes it easier for them to control the informal screening during instigation. Sponsors can thus control the channels of entry and select the prospective legislators themselves.

When sponsors are of one group, such as ranchers or farmers, or when a small number of groups control the entry, selection criteria become specific and selectivity is increased. For example, when a small group of farmers or ranchers select one of their number as the candidate, or when party leaders control recruitment, the standards for the selection of candidates are more specific and clearly defined than when party voters or the general electorate is involved in the selection process. Consequently, when in fact candidates are "elected" during the instigation phase of recruitment, those who control that phase also severely restrict eligibility. When the decisive phases of selection are those in which the electorate participates, it becomes more difficult to control the channels of recruitment. Self-starters, political "mavericks," and other challengers can bypass the pre-primary screening of party organizations and other groups.[29]

The relationship between the scope of eligibility in each district and patterns of competition is shown in Table VI–9. At each stage of

TABLE VI–9

Patterns of Competition and Scope of Eligibility

| | Initiation Stage | | | |
	Rural One-Party District	Rural Two-Party District	Urban One-Party District	Urban Two-Party District
Mean Eligibility Score	$\overline{X} = 113.00$ (N = 8)	$\overline{X} = 164.20$ (N = 5)	$\overline{X} = 300.50$ (N = 4)	$\overline{X} = 259.25$ (N = 4)
	$F_{3.17} = 5.61$, p < .01		N = 21	

| | Primary Election Stage | | | |
	Rural One-Party District	Rural Two-Party District	Urban One-Party District	Urban Two-Party District
Mean Eligibility Score	$\overline{X} = 109.40$ (N = 10)	$\overline{X} = 164.20$ (N = 5)	$\overline{X} = 255.43$ (N = 7)	$\overline{X} = 232.13$ (N = 8)
	$F_{3.26} = 8.28$, p < .001		N = 30	

| | General Election Stage | | | |
	Rural One-Party District	Rural Two-Party District	Urban One-Party District	Urban Two-Party District
Mean Eligibility Score	$\overline{X} = 86.50$ (N = 10)	$\overline{X} = 161.43$ (N = 7)	$\overline{X} = 170.29$ (N = 7)	$\overline{X} = 184.50$ (N = 8)
	$F_{3.28} = 5.26$, p < .01		N = 32	

the selection process, the pool of eligible candidates becomes smaller in all types of districts. However, at each selection phase, the rural districts seem to restrict certification to a greater extent than the urban districts. The rural one-party districts, in which candidates do not face effective competition after they file, consistently proved most restrictive. The urban one-party districts displayed the broadest array of candidates

[29] See Table IV–1 for a tabulation of the number of candidates who file in districts with different competitive patterns.

during the first two phases of recruitment, but the urban two-party constituencies ultimately elected legislators who most epitomized the characteristics of their constituents, while the urban one-party districts ranked second in this regard.

These patterns of selectivity stem from the competitive structure of each type of district. In the rural one-party districts, candidates encounter no effective competition during the primary or general elections. The marginal restriction that did occur during these elections reflects the presence of two or three token candidates who filed for office but did not campaign.[30] Virtually the same elements of the population were represented by the candidates at instigation, after the primary, and after the general election because the field of candidates was not altered significantly by the primary or general election. In the rural two-party districts, the scope of eligibility did not change after the primary election, which shows that the primaries were not competitive in these constituencies. However, the number eligible for office remained at virtually the same level after the general election even though half of the candidates were defeated. This would indicate that the victorious candidates resembled those they defeated in occupation, religion, ethnicity, education, sex, and organizational affiliations. In such districts, competition tests the strength of factions whose members do not differ in social status and occupations. One group of ranchers may oppose another, or two factions of small-town merchants may compete in the general election, but always a farmer or small businessman is elected.

In the urban districts, the primary and general election stages successively reduced the number of candidates, and this is reflected in narrowed eligibility at each succeeding selection stage. In both types of urban districts, the primary eliminated most of the advertisers and a few minority-party candidates. In the urban one-party districts, the field remained broadly representative after the primary because the minority-party candidates were still in the race. The minority-party candidates' social characteristics contrasted with those of their majority-party opponents. For example, in the one-party Republican districts, the Republican candidates were often Protestant businessmen, corporate executives, or younger members of leading law firms. The minority-party Democrats were disproportionately Catholic educators, small businessmen, solo attorneys, and occasionally, labor leaders. These individuals,

[30] Technically, none of the three candidates filed to run for office. Instead, they won the minority nomination through a few write-in votes. Apparently these votes were unsolicited, since all three candidates did not campaign at all. They refused our request for an interview on the grounds that they were not actual candidates for office.

in combination with their opponents on the majority party, kept the field of candidates broadly representative until the general election, when the minority-party candidates were eliminated. In the urban two-party districts, there were fewer advertisers. Most aspirants were incumbents seeking reelection or serious challengers. These individuals were recruited, as we have seen, from the top leadership of a broad spectrum of groups and interests in the community. As a consequence, the field of candidates remained broadly representative through all phases of selection.

It is clear that the more the electorate participates in selection, the more open to diverse candidates become recruitment channels. At each phase, the rural one-party districts restrict eligibility more than the other constituencies in which the voters make meaningful choices during at least one phase of recruitment. Thus when a candidate can take his case directly to the voters, he can avoid the screening of group and party leaders before the primary. This forces these leaders to coalesce with such candidates or to sponsor candidates of their own who they think appeal to the broadest electorate. Thus, public competition expands effective opportunity because sponsors cannot afford to recruit candidates with limited appeal who are likely to be identified with only a few special interests. Alternatively, when the competitive structure between the political parties allows sponsors to control the channels of entry, then direct appeals to the electorate are both impossible and unnecessary, and opportunities for independents and self-starters vanish. This was the case in rural one-party districts where candidates were screened by sponsoring groups that controlled the narrow channels of entry.

Economic and Social Diversity and Political Eligibility

It appears in retrospect, that each district's pattern of political competition determines whether candidates from various walks of life will be considered or only those from an exclusive group of the citizenry. Still, it is doubtful that an increase in political competition alone broadens proportionately the criteria of eligibility. Since the level of social diversity in a district shapes political competition, it is not yet clear whether social diversity determines *both* political competition and the scope of eligibility.[31]

We should consider the differentiation among the causal relation-

---

[31] As we have seen, the social diversity of a constituency is strongly related to its competitive structure (Table III–3).

ships: diversity, competition and certification. Throughout this study, we have presented one model of the relationships among the variables of recruitment (Figure VI–1). The heavy lines indicate the expected

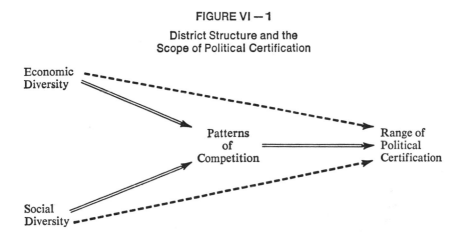

FIGURE VI — 1

District Structure and the
Scope of Political Certification

channels of influence among diversity, competition and aspects of the recruitment process (in this case, the scope of certification). The dotted lines suggest other potential avenues of influence.[32] The findings reported in Chapters III, IV and V are consistent with this model except in one instance. The expected relationships among social diversity, competition, initiation and support proved true. Economic diversity does not appear to influence either competition or recruitment interactions.[33]

However, selection refers to the *outcome* of recruitment interactions, and is therefore strongly linked to the particular patterns of social and economic differentiation and cleavages that divide a community. In other words, who is selected, regardless of the particular pattern of recruitment he experienced, relates directly to the social and economic cleavages that underlie political conflict in the community.

[32] Figure VII–1 is roughly equivalent to Figure II–1. The latter focuses on recruitment as a process and shows the patterns of interactions among and within the various phases of recruitment. The former traces the causal linkages between the structure of a constituency and the recruitment process.

[33] See Table III–4, above, for data relating economic diversity to political competition. Separate analyses showed that after controlling for political competition and social diversity, economic diversity was unrelated to instigation and support activities.

In particular, social and economic diversity shape the incentives, costs and opportunities that confront legislative candidates.

In diversified communities, social and economic cleavages generate political issues which influence some individuals to consider candidacy and thus increase the pool of those certified to run. Conversely, fewer and more homogeneous candidates are drawn into the fray when the range of cleavages is narrower. Moreover, social and economic cleavages structure the risks of candidacy. Such costs include the expense of filing (or the trouble of circulating nominating petitions), the purchase of space in the voters' pamphlet, the costs of the campaign itself, the risks of loss of income from one's regular occupation while running or serving in the legislature or on interim committees, as well as disruption of the family routine. In diverse constituencies, the successful candidate must come to grips with all these costs and risks, plus others that a highly diversified, complex constituency imposes. He must appeal to a multiplicity of interests and must adopt proper attitudes on a variety of issues. In doing so, he must satisfy the divergent interests of his supporters while striving to mold them into a unified organization capable of winning a plurality of the electorate. Such efforts increase his personal campaign costs and add risks and uncertainties.

In addition, the legislative role itself is more demanding for those who represent diversified constituencies than for their counterparts from homogeneous districts. Representatives from diverse communities must act as brokers in their constituencies *and* in the legislature. At home, the legislator must satisfy his sponsors and the coalition of interests that successfully elected him. Each group among his coalition of support expects him to champion their cause, and these expectations often conflict. The legislator must adroitly balance competing demands and yet hold fast to his sponsors. If the lawmaker is cross-pressured in his constituency, he will be cross-pressured in the legislature. The urban lawmaker must consider party policies, the leadership of the House, the committee system and seniority. He must orchestrate the competing interest within each political arena if he is to remain influential and secure in both, for his success in one shapes his fortunes in the other.

The adroit political management this orchestration requires is extremely demanding. The urban representative must reconcile his personal interests with those of his sponsors and the demands of the legislature. The lawmakers from homogeneous districts must satisfy fewer expectations and deal with fewer issues. The voters of a farm community generally agree on agricultural or conservation policy, or on tax measures relevant to farming or the forest industry. The legislator's job is to champion district interests in the competition for public resources among statewide interests.[34] Legislators from rural districts spend little time and energy on constituency politics. Without cross-pressures from home, they may follow a simple, inexpensive strategy, i.e., they can trade their votes on the issues to which their constituents are indifferent in exchange for support on the few issues of primary concern to the voters in their district.

The degree of urbanization (and social and economic diversity) also determines the minimum investment needed to run and serve in the legislature. Running for office in a city requires extensive campaign organization and electioneering. Depending upon the circumstances, candidates will campaign in different ways. They often seek to use campaign publicity to simply link their name with their party, develop a public image, familiarize the public with the issues, or inform the voters about their positions on public issues. Which objectives a candidate will pursue depends upon whether he is well known or whether he is of the majority or minority party. For example, the novice candidate must struggle for public attention. A minority-party candidate may try to project his name and his personality; he will play down his party affiliation and his stand on issues. Such strategies require extensive planning, organization, energy and money. The creation and maintenance of an organization is costly. The media are essential in urban campaigns, and television ads, spots on the radio, billboard advertising and newspaper space are expensive. Rural candidates do not need to use these campaign techniques. Everyone knows the candidate and his reputation is established and common knowledge.[35]

Social and economic diversity shape the incentives, costs and opportunities of candidacy. In socially diverse districts, the costs of running and serving are greater, but the opportunities and incentives are also greater. In homogeneous communities, selection is not choosing from a large field of aspirants so much as finding someone who can afford to

[34] Unlike their urban colleagues, the rural candidates tended to report that (1) their primary function as legislators was to serve the interests of their districts; and (2) they preferred membership in the following committees in the legislature: Agriculture, Natural Resources, Ways and Means. Urban candidates were more apt to say that they championed particular interests and sought committee assignments that would enable them to do so.

Although we have little evidence on the degree of consensus over major issues in rural areas, the interviews suggested that the politically active elements of the rural districts tended to agree on issues vital to the district's economy, although they often conflicted over local issues. See Arthur Vidich and Joseph Bensman, *Small Town in Mass Society,* Anchor Books (New York: Doubleday, 1958), passim, for similar findings.

[35] See James D. Barber, *The Lawmakers* (New Haven: Yale University Press, 1965), Chs. II and IV.

serve. Although the costs and risks of seeking and keeping office are more modest, the rewards of public life do not compensate for these costs. For these reasons it seems likely that the influence of diversity on certification is independent of each district's competitive pattern. If the data prove this to be true, then our model must be modified.

A Causal Analysis of Certification

As a first step in examining the linkages among diversity, competition and the scope of political eligibility, correlation coefficients were computed, relating social and economic diversity with eligibility at each selection stage. The results are presented in Table VI–10. For purposes of comparison, correlation ratios derived from the analyses of variance in Table VI–9 are included. Since the coefficients in Table VI–10 are zero-order correlations and correlation ratios, we cannot as yet sort out the independent effects of each recruitment parameter on the scope of certification. However, it appears that social diversity and the competitive structure of a constituency determine eligibility at each selection phase more than does the district's economic configuration. Since social diversity and patterns of competition are closely interrelated, it is difficult to say whether both exercise an independent influence on candidate certification. However, it is clear that social diversity alone, or through its relation with political competition, determines who will be included in the pool of eligibles. Moreover, the relationship between economic diversity and eligibility becomes stronger as the selection process enters into phases in which the public participates. The economy of a district influences "who" is selected to a successively greater degree as we pass from the initiation phase to the primary election with its light turnout, to the general election where more of the electorate participates. Conversely, the impact of competition seems to diminish somewhat.

TABLE VI–10

Parameters of Recruitment and Scope of Eligibility in Three Selection Stages

| | *Stages of Selection* | | |
Parameters	*Initiation*	*Primary Election*	*General Election*
Economic Diversity	.407*	.420*	.544**
Social Diversity	.765***	.497**	.547**
Competitive Pattern	.705**	.698***	.601**

* Significant at the .05 level
** Significant at the .01 level
*** Significant at the .001 level

We computed an analysis of covariance to assess the independent impact of social and economic diversity and political competition on the scope of certification in each district. This technique enabled us to compute partial coefficients describing the relationship between any two (or more) of the variables controlling for all others.[36] Separate analyses were performed for each selection stage in the recruitment process. Figure VI–2 relates diversity and competition to the composition of the pool of eligibles in each district at the instigation phase.

FIGURE VI — 2

The Determinants of Certification:
The Initiation Phase

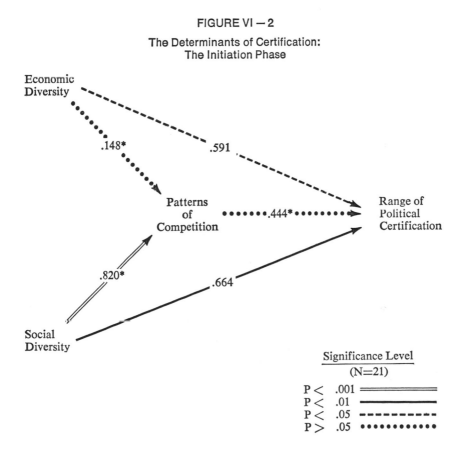

*Partial Correlation Ratios

[36] See Hubert M. Blalock, Jr., *Social Statistics* (New York: McGraw-Hill, 1960), Ch. XX.

The data show that the strong relationship between competitive patterns and eligibility (see Table VI–10) disappeared when the effects of economic and social diversity were controlled. Instead a moderately strong direct relationship prevailed between the limits of eligibility for the position of "primary candidate" and the levels of social and economic diversity. The original relationship between competition and certification apparently resulted from the strong linkage between competition and social diversity. The correlation ratio was reduced from .705 to .444. Given the small number of districts in our pre-primary sample, this is not statistically significant.[37] It is also clear that the number of cleavages in a constituency determined the diversity of candidates after the instigation phase. The initial field of candidates was broader in diverse districts.

When the recruitment process entered another phase, the primary election, the situation changed markedly (Figure VI–3). For the first time the electorate was involved in selection in some of the constituencies. At the same time, the direct impact of both social and economic diversity on who is eligible for the position of "general election candidate" disappeared. Only competition was related to the patterns of certification in each district. The competitive pattern, in turn, was determined to a large degree by social diversity. Thus, patterns of eligibility after the primary election were almost exclusively the outgrowth of primary election competition. Districts which had competitive primaries all restricted eligibility during the primary, while those without competitive primaries remained at much the same level. It was the social structure of the district which determined whether the primary would be competitive.

After the general election, the situation again changed (Figure VI–4). The indirect linkage between social diversity and certification remained strong. However, economic diversity influenced the pattern of selection that occurred in the general election as it did at initiation. The evidence shows that the number of economic cleavages in a district, its level of industrialization and urbanization strongly influenced how "representative" its legislator would be. Legislators in economically diverse districts were drawn from a broadly based pool of eligibles.

Why do legislative posts, city council seats, judgeships, school board membership and the like, remain the domain of a small segment of the population? Our data shed light on some of the ways that social, economic and political conditions in a community make political

---

[37] See Table VII–10 regarding the original relationship between competition and the scope of eligibility before controls.

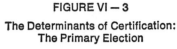

FIGURE VI — 3

The Determinants of Certification:
The Primary Election

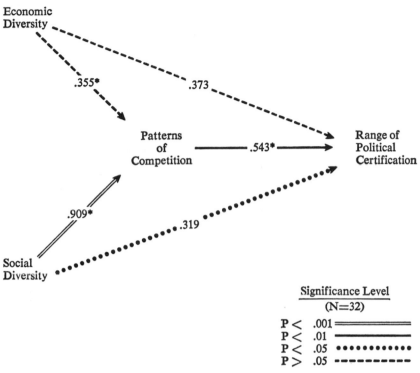

*Partial Correlation Ratios

activism the province of a minority of the citizenry. We have discovered as legislative recruitment progresses, three major factors shape the size and composition of those people who were certified at each phase of selection. These factors include: 1) initial screening; 2) the relative visibility of selection phases; and 3) economic diversity.

Initial Screening

Our data show that social and economic diversity lay the foundations of certification in a constituency. Diversity, as manifested in social differentiation, industrial development and urbanization, broadens certification, while social homogeneity, an agrarian economy and rural life

FIGURE VI — 4

The Determinants of Certification:
The General Election

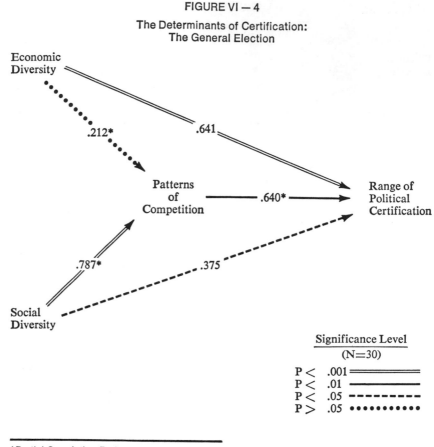

*Partial Correlation Ratios

restrict recruitment opportunities. *The social screening that occurs during the instigation phase sets the stage for the public phases of selection in the primary and general elections. During the stage of informal instigation, the majority of the population is barred from effective participation, either through choice or necessity. Social and economic diversity determine how open or closed will be the gates of political opportunity for those initially considered.*

Several reasons govern the direct linkage between social and economic diversity and the scope of certification at instigation. The level of diversity influences the incentives in the district. Each social and economic cleavage is a potential source of candidates. Similarly, the availability of political and nonpolitical inducements to run vary with the level of social and economic diversity. Moreover, the prospects for sponsors who can cushion the risks of candidacy increase as districts become diversified. Consequently, the resources of candidacy depend upon the levels of diversity. Proportionately, more people can afford to become candidates in diverse districts. At the same time, entry is less controllable in diverse constituencies. Many competing groups sponsor candidates, and seldom can one group or a coalition of groups hand-pick the legislator. When many sponsors support their own standard-bearers, selection criteria in the aggregate tend to overlap and spread out.

The Visibility of Selection Phases

As the successive selection phases of recruitment become more visible, they invite public scrutiny, and then political competition plays a greater role in determining which elements of the population will be represented in the legislative elite. As recruitment moves in phases from candidate initiation to the primary election and on to the general election each district's pattern of competition increasingly shapes eligibility and the direct impact of social diversity declines.

Patterns of competition determine how instrumental voters will be in selecting state legislators in the primary and general elections. When the party electorates and/or the general electorates are effectively disfranchised (as they are in varying degrees in all districts other than the two-party urban constituencies), candidates and sponsors can safely ignore the excluded elements. Where the competitive structure of a district has taught local party recruiters and other sponsors that they need not fear opposition in the primary or general election, they can safely select candidates who represent their own special interests. Conversely, where their party is divided by factional struggles, or the two parties are evenly balanced in strength, local activists must find standard-bearers who will appeal to party voters or the general electorate. Under such circumstances, public competition broadens certification at instigation and thereafter, because local leaders must constantly guard against the maverick or "dark horse" who may ignore their efforts to control the selection of candidates and take his case directly to the voters.

Social diversity appears to decline in importance after the instigation phase. During the primary and general elections, social diversity influences certification only through its impact on competition. Apparently, social differences such as religion, race, ethnicity, or length of residency play an important part in determining who gets into the recruitment process initially, but have only marginal effects on the pattern of issues that arise during the course of the campaign or on the incentives, resources, or selection criteria that determine the scope of eligibility during the more public phases of recruitment.[38]

Economic Diversity and Certification

Economic diversity influences candidate certification at two phases of the recruitment process: instigation and the general election. This reflects both the differences in incentives to run and the relevance of economic issues in different economic milieus.

During the instigation phase, the number of economic cleavages, plus the level of industrialization in a constituency shape the issues and perhaps the political and nonpolitical incentives that draw potential aspirants to candidacy. Since economic diversity describes the character of economic stratification in the local community, the greater the economic diversity, the larger the proportion of the population who work in secondary and tertiary industries. Such diversity increases disproportionately the middle- and upper middle-class sectors of the population. It is these people who are most likely to follow politics closely and to have the resources to participate. Thus, at instigation, the district's economic structure shapes certification by determining the number of individuals who, by virtue of their economic status or economic interests, can afford to run for office.

Economic diversity is not strongly related to eligibility after the primary election because selection, where it occurs, takes place *within* each of the two major-party coalitions. The economic milieu of the district reenters the picture after the general election. Districts with diverse economies are less restrictive after the general election than those with simpler economic configurations. This finding is somewhat misleading since little, if any, restriction occurs in the economically homogeneous constituencies after the initiation phase (see Table VI–9). In fact, the data suggest that the economically diversified constituencies successively restrict their choices to individuals who resemble the characteris-

---

[38] Unlike many other states, Oregon has had few *public* racial or religious issues in recent years, yet Catholics, for example, seldom win in any but a few predominantly Catholic districts, and there have been virtually no black legislators. However, the findings suggest that "undesirable" religious, racial and ethnic groups are excluded during the informal screening of initiation. The candidates who emerge from the initiation phase display similar racial, ethnic and religious characteristics. Consequently, there is little incentive to raise them as issues.

This situation may change if black militance increases in the Portland ghetto and on the state's college campuses. We would expect a stronger relationship between social factors and selection in the states of the East and South where racial, ethnic and religious differences are more explicitly and publicly linked to politics.

tics of their constituents as recruitment passes through its phases. The result is that economically homogeneous districts start with candidates who are drawn from a narrowly based rural elite, and these same individuals are elected to the legislature. The more diversified districts begin with a broadly representative field of candidates who are successively screened in the primary and general elections until those who succeed roughly embody the characteristics of the majority economic coalition in the constituency. Eligibility after the general election, is a good deal broader, and remains more open in the economically diverse districts than it does in the communities with simple economies where candidates are drawn from cliques of the local social and economic elite.

SUMMARY AND CONCLUSIONS

Oregon candidates, like legislators and candidates in other states, were not a microcosm of the characteristics of their constituents. The Oregon legislative candidates were predominantly male, white, native-born, middle-aged Protestants with extensive education, prestigious occupations and substantial incomes. Most had grown up in politicized environments and had been involved in their local communities for many years. Most were born in their constituencies or had resided there for the better part of their adult lives. The party nominees differed little in education, place of residence, place of birth, occupation and political socialization. However, the winners tended to be white, native-born males who had acquired their interest in politics from their primary social groups and who had resided in their constituencies for many years.

The candidates' social and political characteristics are indicative of their modes of entry into candidacy. The serious contenders (i.e. the rural reluctants, notables and urban enthusiasts) were of higher status, had more intense socialization, and deeper roots in their local communities than either the advertisers or conscripts. The serious contenders were drawn from the top levels of political circles in their local communities, and their background characteristics reflect their privileged status. The minority candidates and advertisers represented marginal elements in local affairs, as was shown by their backgrounds, and patterns of instigation and support.

The size of the pool of eligibles in each district differed according to the constituency's social and economic structure and its competitive pattern, which defined the phases at which the candidates must compete for the approval of local sponsors or the electorate. The pattern of social and economic cleavages in the local area generated the election issues (or lack thereof) and influenced the distribution of resources necessary for candidacy. Thus, the constituency's level of social and economic diversity determined how broadly representative were the candidates at the initial phase of recruitment. In the later stages, political competition and economic diversity determined the selectivity of those phases. The resulting patterns of restriction varied widely among Oregon constituencies. Some districts perennially have elected legislators who are drawn from a segment which constitutes less than 1 percent of the population of the district, while other districts have provided broader political eligibility.

CHAPTER VII

The Political Attitudes of the Defeated Candidates

WE HAVE SHOWN how a potential candidate perceives a major component of the recruitment risk—the probabilities and uncertainties of various net losses or costs of running for the state legislature. This chapter, as a result, will report the reactions of defeated candidates.

All selected candidates were interviewed at three different times: before and following the primary, and following the general election. These interviews enabled us to ascertain quite clearly how election outcomes affected attitudes of the candidates. Defeated candidates were asked how much they supported prevailing laws and practices regarding recruitment and election competition. They were also asked about their political futures and how they perceived political risk, i.e., the material and psychological net gains and losses they experienced under varying conditions of probability or uncertainty (see Appendix).

THE DEFINITIONS AND MEASURES OF KEY VARIABLES

The candidates' attitudes toward prevailing recruitment rules or norms and their intentions regarding future political activity constitute the two dependent variables. The degree of continued endorsement by the unsuccessful candidates, for the established norms of recruitment and electoral competition, shall be termed "support." This support was an indication of candidates' attitudes concerning: (a) the legal and practical requirements for getting elected, (b) their perceptions of the fairness of the election outcome, and (c) their judgments of the equity of political opportunity.[1] Responses to three interview items were cumulatively scaled and a single support scale was constructed (CR = .92).

A candidate's intention concerning continued political activity was measured by his responses to three questions: Does he or she intend to become more involved or less involved with political issues than before the election? Does the candidate intend to become more or less concerned with politics than before the election? And despite the election outcome, does the candidate intend to further pursue a political career? When a candidate gave a positive answer, a score was assigned and these scores were added, forming a simple index of speculated changes in political activity.

Political risk is a key concept in our analysis of the unsuccessful candidates. For individual candidates, recruitment *risk* consists in the chances of net losses and costs they expect, attendant upon their candidacies. We define reward and cost in terms of both material and psychological gains or losses that result directly from election activity. Clearly, the rewards are considerable when an election victory enhances the candidate's prestige, income, influence, and opportunity for career advancement. Conversely, the costs are considerable if defeat diminishes a candidate's status, prestige, income and influence. The attempt to measure the net reward-cost balance of winning and losing posed several problems. First, the candidates have different hierarchies of values and may therefore rank particular rewards and costs differently. Second, election to the state legislature does not necessarily mean a career advancement; that depends on a candidates social status before election.[2] Each candidate has particular status, skills, and resources. Therefore the reward and cost effects of an election are relative to a candidate's starting level. Finally, measuring reward-cost balance is further complicated because of complex incentives associated with public office. It was

---

[1] The support items are: (a) "In general, do you feel that the legal requirements in getting elected give each candidate the same chance of winning, or do some (candidates) have an advantage?" (b) "In general, do you feel, that the practical requirements in getting elected give each candidate the same chance of winning or do some candidates have an advantage?" (c) "In running for office in this district, do you believe that a person can succeed primarily on the basis of ability and initiative, or are other things important for success in politics?" and (d) "Is this the way it should be?"

On the concept of risk, see Milton Friedman and L. J. Savage, "The Utility Analysis of Choice Involving Risk" *Journal of Political Economy,* LVI, No. 4 (August, 1948), pp. 279–304; J. D. Hammond, *Essays in the Theory of Risk and Insurance* (Glenview: Scott Foresman, and Co., 1968); William J. Baumol, *Economic Theory and Operations Analysis* (Englewood Cliffs: Prentice-Hall, 1965), p. 550.

[2] James D. Barber, *The Lawmakers* (New Haven: Yale University Press, 1965), p. 36.

found that there were two types of incentives. One type is termed "extrinsic," defined as the gains or losses of income, occupation, prestige, influence and career opportunity. The other type is termed "intrinsic," referring to the various personal gratifications derived from political experience, such as a sense of fulfillment of civic duty or community service.

Operational measurement of reward-cost was based on a battery of questions designed to determine the effects of electoral victory and defeat on a candidate's social esteem, income, occupation, career opportunity and political influence. To be sure, some reward-costs are more important than others but for the purpose of present analysis each reward-cost item was assigned the same weight.[3] Nine such items were used and the responses to these questions were coded into positive, neutral and negative categories.[4] For example, the candidates responded to questions like: "As a consequence of the election, do you anticipate any change in your circle of close friends?" Responses are coded as positive, negative or neutral: (a) gained more friends, (b) no change, or (c) lost some friends. A summated scale of perceived reward-cost was constructed: each respondent who answered with a positive and/or negative response is assigned a score based on the arithmetic sum of his coded responses.

A candidate's defeat could also have an effect on his political aspirations. An ambitious candidate might possibly perceive the loss of the election as a serious career setback, but a less ambitious candidate would probably regard defeat as minor. Career ambition is defined as the level of office a candidate wishes to achieve. The levels of office to which candidates aspired were divided into four categories: national, state, local and "no particular ambition." Candidates' expectations about the election outcome might also affect their reactions to defeat, so we asked each candidate to assess his chances of winning at the beginning of the

---

[3] One of the authors, Chong Lim Kim, is engaged in detailed analysis of the various types of reward-cost expectations attendant upon electoral victories and defeats in order to determine their relative importance to candidates.

[4] The following terms are used to measure reward-cost: (1) As a consequence of the election, do you anticipate any change in your job? (2) As a consequence of the election, do you anticipate a change in your circle of close friends? (3) Do you anticipate a change in your income as a consequence of the election? (4) Do you feel that your esteem among members of your religion has gone up or down? (5) Do you feel that esteem among your colleagues in your occupation has gone up or down? (6) Do you feel that your esteem among your neighbors has gone up? (7) Do you feel that your esteem in your family has gone up? (8) Do you expect that your loss in the election will help or hinder your chances if you decide to run again for the House? (9) Do you feel that your political influence has increased as a consequence of the election?

electoral campaign. For instance, at the outset a candidate might describe his chance of winning as "excellent," "good," "fair," or "poor." Such differential assessment of chances of winning would presumably influence the attitudes of the defeated candidates. We expected relevant variables to affect candidates' reactions to defeat: types of district, types of election, candidates' occupations, income and education. Districts were classified as safe, competitive, or unsafe, given a candidate's party affiliation (see Chapter III). The types of election simply refer to the primary and general elections. Our assumption was that types of election and district would affect the reactions of the defeated candidates because a candidate running in a safe district, for example, and therefore relatively sure of victory, would find unexpected defeat more difficult to face than candidates in competitive or unsafe districts. In the same vein, a defeat in the primary election may be of less consequence than a defeat in the general election, and if this should be the case, we would then expect significant differences in the reactions of the primary and general election losers.

The three stratification variables, occupation, income, and education, were included, stemming from theoretical considerations. We have shown how social and economic status is related to political opportunity. Research has shown that socio-economic status determines political attitudes, activity and support. More importantly, a candidate's socio-economic status can effectively *cushion* the costs of defeat and thus influence personal perceptions of failure. An ousted politician cannot fall below the level that his skills and training ensure.[5]

In addition to the eight variables discussed above, the incumbency of a candidate would affect his attitudes toward defeat, for the adverse effects of defeat might be greater for incumbents. Out of 60 possible winners for election to the Oregon House, 45 were incumbent winners and the remaining 15 were nonincumbents. There were only five cases of defeated incumbents and all but two of them refused to be interviewed. So regrettably, we could not assess this potentially important variable.

SUPPORT AND ACTIVITY OF WINNERS AND LOSERS

Winners in both primary and general elections supported the rules governing recruitment more than did the losers. The difference between winners and losers in the primary election is less pronounced than between winners and losers in the general election, which suggested that

[5] Lester G. Seligman, "Political Leadership: Status Loss and Downward Mobility," (a paper presented at the annual meeting of the American Political Science Association, New York, 1966), p. 24.

the primary election is less critical than the general election in modifying attitudes of the candidates. This finding is reinforced when we compare the losers only (see Table VII–1). Fifty-nine percent of the losers

TABLE VII–1

Political Support of Winners and Losers
(In Percentage)

Support	Primary Election		General Election			X^2	P
	Winner N = 84* (A)	Loser N = 17 (B)	Winner N = 46 (C)	Loser N = 31 (D)			
High	64.2	58.8	65.1	25.9			
					A&B	0.72	NS
					C&D	11.75	.01
Medium	33.5	41.2	28.4	64.4			
					A&C	1.57	NS
Low	2.3	0.0	6.5	9.7	B&D	6.01	.05
Total	100.0	100.0	100.0	100.0			

* 8 cases are excluded because of the lack of information on their support.

in the primary election expressed high support, as compared to only 26 percent of the losers in the general election.

Of course, such a difference in support for the rules and norms of recruitment between the winners and losers may not result from the election itself. It is quite likely that a large percentage of the winners were strongly supportive of the recruitment rules and practices before the election. Since we asked about support during several phases of recruitment, we can resolve this issue by comparing a candidate's support over the time from the instigation to the general election. Table VII–2

TABLE VII–2

Change in Support of the General Election Winners and Losers
(In Percentage)

Support Change	Winners N = 44	Losers N = 28
Increase	22.6	11.2
No Change	63.8	44.4
Decrease	13.6	44.4
No response	(2)	(3)
Total	100.0	100.0

N includes only those interviewed twice.
$x^2 - 9.03$, p < .01.

shows that almost one-half of the losers, in contrast to only 14 percent of the losers, in contrast to only 14 percent of the winners, expressed diminished support; whereas, a significantly greater proportion of the winners increased their support for the existing rules of recruitment. Thus, the losers are less supportive of the rules than the winners, and the former are more likely than the latter to reduce their support as a result of their loss.

Regardless of the outcome of the election, only a few candidates objected to the rules for recruitment. Ten percent of the losers in the general election and none of the losers in the primary election evidenced such objections. Although winning or losing does appear to affect some changes in support, the losers do not become disenchanted with the rules of recruitment. Win or lose, the Oregon candidates generally supported the rules of recruitment.

With respect to the candidates' intentions to continue their political activity, Table VII–3 shows that the winners intended to remain more politically active than the losers. Almost 83 percent of the winners, as compared to only 39 percent of the losers, said that they would become more actively concerned with political issues after the general election than before it. Similarly, over one-half of the winners intended to discuss politics more frequently after the general election than before, while only one-third of the losers expressed the same intention. The difference in the intention of winners and losers to continue a political career was not marked, even though the winners responded more positively toward political activity than did the losers.[6]

FACTORS INFLUENCING SUPPORT AND ACTIVITY OF DEFEATED CANDIDATES

In this section we shall analyze variables which affect the political attitudes of defeated candidates (see Table VII–4). The level of political ambition of the defeated candidates is strongly associated with their intention to continue political activity.[7] The evidence suggests that the

[6] Despite defeat, many candidates were inclined to continue a political career. There are two possible explanations for it. First, a majority of defeated candidates believe that they will have a better chance of winning the next election, for they have gained at least some name familiarity in the unsuccessful campaign. Second, many defeated candidates are what Barber might call "advertisers." Their main motive for seeking office is to gain publicity through campaigns to help their private occupations (such as legal practice). Therefore, they will remain politically active as long as they obtain publicity.

[7] We have examined both cross-tabulations and between-item rank order intercorrelations. Although tau-b values tended to be smaller than Gammas reported in Table VII–4, basically the same pattern emerged.

TABLE VII–3

Expected Changes in Political Activity of
the General Election Winners and Losers
(In Percentage)

Activity	*Response*	*Winner* $N = 46$	*Loser* $N = 31$	X^2	P
1. Do you intend to spend more time thinking about politics and following issues in mass media than before the election?	More Time	82.6	38.7	14.24	.001
	No Change	15.2	48.4		
	Less Time	0.0	3.2		
	No Response	2.2	9.7		
2. Do you intend to devote more time to discussing politics with your friends and associates than before the election?	More Time	56.5	25.8	7.13	.05
	No Change	36.9	51.8		
	Less Time	4.4	12.9		
	No Response	2.2	9.7		
3. In the light of your experience in the election, do you wish to continue your political career?	Yes	58.7	48.4	3.23	NS
	Undecided	32.6	25.8		
	No	6.5	19.4		
	No Response	2.2	6.4		

ambitious losers are more likely than the less-ambitious losers to remain politically active. The candidates' expectations about the election outcome correlates negatively with support and intention to continue political activity. The losers who were optimistic about their chances of winning manifested a less supportive attitude toward the rules of recruitment

TABLE VII–4

Some Correlates of Support and Activity
(Gamma)

Variables	*Support*	*Activity*
Level of Ambition: national, state, local	.05	.75
Expectation of Election Outcome: excellent, good, poor	−.45	−.36
Type of District: safe, competitive, unsafe	−.08	−.25
Type of Election: primary, general	.41	.39
Occupation: prestige ranking	.22	.16
Income	.26	.06
Education	−.02	−.12
Reward-Cost Score	.56	.61

and were less inclined toward continued political activity than other losers who were pessimistic about their chances of winning.

The type of district in which a loser ran influenced his intention to remain politically active. The losers in relatively safe districts were less inclined to continue political activity than losers from competitive or unsafe districts. The kind of election in which a candidate contested also affected his reaction to defeat. The results of the general election affect candidates more deeply than the results of the primary election; losers in the primary election intended to remain politically active more than the losers in the general election. Defeat in the general election diminished a candidate's support for the rules of recruitment and his intention to continue political activity.

Contrary to our expectation, a candidate's education is unrelated to support either for the rules and norms of recruitment or intention for future political activity. Likewise, the occupations and incomes of candidates have little bearing on their support and intention to remain politically active. Compared to the ambition, expectation, and types of election, stratification variables seen to have little effect on the attitudes of defeated candidates.[8]

PERCEPTIONS OF REWARDS AND COSTS

The data in Table VII–4 indicate that perceived rewards and costs are strongly associated with both support for the rules and norms of recruitment and intentions of engaging in future political activity. Other factors: ambition, expectation, type of district, and type of election, have considerable impact on the attitudes of the defeated candidates. Therefore, the effects of these factors must be controlled before we make inferences about the relations between candidate's perception of reward-cost and their support of the rules of recruitment and their intentions to continue political activity.

The small number in our sample of the defeated candidates ($N = 48$) precluded the use of a conventional partialling technique. Instead, an *index formation technique* was employed to control simultaneously for political ambition, expectation about the election outcome, type of district, and type of election. The method is based on the relation

[8] One possible reason why our stratification variables turned out to be weak predictors of the attitudes is the highly homogeneous backgrounds of the candidates. For instance, 79 percent of our candidates have received college education or advanced degrees, 71 percent were engaged in prestigious occupations such as lawyers, doctors, and proprietors of large or medium-sized businesses, and finally, 66 percent earned an annual income of $15,000 or above.

of each control classification to the dependent variable. On the basis of these relationships, weights are assigned to each category in the control classification; each individual in each category receives the designated weight. These weights are summed for each individual to yield an index based on all of the controls. Finally, the index is used as a control classification in the usual sense.[9]

With the amount of perceived reward-cost as the independent variable and the level of support for the rules of recruitment as the dependent variable, an index score for each candidate was computed based on four controls (ambition, type of district, type of election, and expectation). These index scores were then dichotomized into support control groups I and II respectively. Within *each* control group the relationship between perceived reward-cost and support is examined. A similar procedure was used to construct control groups with regard to candidates' intentions of political activity.

Table VII–5 shows the relationships between the perceived reward-

TABLE VII–5

Relationships Between Reward-Cost and the Attitudes of the Defeated Candidates with Ambition, Expectation, Type of District and Election Controlled (Gamma)

Support Group I (N = 20)	.63
Support Group II (N = 28)	.53
Activity Group I (N = 21)	.65
Activity Group II (N = 27)	.60

cost and the attitudes of defeated candidates within each control group. Our data clearly indicate that the level of reward-cost perceived by the defeated candidates strongly correlates with both their support for the recruitment process and intention to continue political activity, even after controlling for the effects of level of career ambition, expectations of the election outcome, type of district, and type of election. *The evidence is clear that a candidate's expectations, experience and perception of rewards and costs significantly determines how he will react to election defeat.* If a candidate regards candidacy as highly rewarding then he is likely to support the rules of electoral competition and continue political activity after the election. Conversely, if a defeated candidate perceives candidacy as costly, he is likely to become disenchanted with the rules

[9] Sanford I. Labovitz, "Methods for Control With Small Sample Size," *American Sociological Review*, XXX (April, 1965), pp. 243–249.

of recruitment and is not likely to continue political activity. The amount of perceived reward-cost is critical in determining the extent to which defeated candidates supported recruitment norms and practices and planned continued engagement in political activity.

POLITICAL RISK: HIGH- AND LOW-RISK SYSTEMS

What difference does winning or losing an election make in terms of the reward-cost? Table VII–6 reports on the reward-cost as perceived by the winning and losing candidates, showing that the losing candidates in both primary and general elections perceived significantly smaller rewards than did the winning candidates. Thus, the winners and losers were rewarded differently. It is, however, important to note that most candidates, regardless of the election outcome, benefit from the election. Among the losers, 82 percent of the candidates in the primary and 81 percent of the candidates in the general election reported some rewards. Clearly, electoral competition in Oregon is not a winner-take-all contest. *Despite electoral defeat, a predominant majority of the defeated candidates gained in social esteem and in political influence, enhanced their private occupations, and furthered their political careers.*

The relatively small difference perceived by the winning and losing candidates makes Oregon a low-risk system. Such a system bestows modest rewards on the victors and exacts minimal losses from the defeated. By contrast, a high-risk recruitment system confers high rewards in status, wealth, and influence on the winners and inflicts severe deprivations on the losers. For example, many new Asian and African

TABLE VII–6

Perceived Reward-Cost as a Result of Winning and Losing
(In Percentage)

Amount of Reward-Cost	Primary Election		General Election			X^2	P
	Winner $N = 92$ (A)	*Loser* $N = 17$ (B)	*Winner* $N = 46$ (C)	*Loser* $N = 31$ (D)			
Large Reward	10.9	17.6	30.5	6.4			
Moderate Reward	33.7	17.6	36.9	38.7	A&B	19.16	.001
Little or No					C&D	14.09	.01
Reward	55.4	47.2	32.6	35.6	A&C	10.19	.01
Some Cost	0.0	17.6	0.0	19.3	B&D	3.27	NS
Large Cost	0.0	0.0	0.0	0.0			
Total	100.0	100.0	100.0	100.0			

States appear to be high-risk systems. The potential rewards for political victors are immensely great, for political positions traditionally confer high social prestige and give control over access to wealth. The rungs of the ladder for upward social mobility are made up of political offices.[10] The cost of political defeat in many of these foreign nations is devastating, for political competition tends to be warlike and often results in total victory or total defeat. Various factors account for such warlike competition. Among them are the deep cleavages between elites concerning the system goals and the methods of their implementation, a set of mutually reinforcing antagonisms that run along ethnic, tribal, religious, or regional lines, and widespread antigovernmental reflex which Shils has called an "oppositional syndrome."[11] Moreover, the dominance of a single authoritarian party in many new foreign nations discourages the development of a legitimate role for political opposition and thereby increases the potential cost of being a member of the counter-elite.[12]

The high cost of political defeat in some of these new states may also be attributed to the fact that many politicians have only limited occupational skills. They tend to be "professional" politicians in the sense that they have no occupation other than politics. Therefore, as Apter has put it, "for them to go out of office is, in effect, to be unemployed."[13] And sometimes going out of office means going into exile as well. Because of the great rewards associated with political victory and the severe deprivations inflicted by defeat, political contest in these new systems tends to be less constrained by the accepted rules of the game than in low-risk systems.

Yet, we need not overemphasize the contrast between our findings of low risk in Oregon and political recruitment among new nations. Comparative studies of recruitment risk will likely show how variable are the hazards of recruitment in other American states. Recruitment risk would be higher in states where deep social and economic cleavages and the relative rewards of political influence are ample and intensify

[10] See Lester G. Seligman, "Political Parties and the Recruitment of Political Leadership," in Lewis J. Edinger, ed., *Political Leadership in Industrialized Societies,* pp. 304–306; "Political Risk and Legislative Behavior in Non-Western Countries," in R. Boynton and C. L. Kim, *Legislators in Non-Western Countries* (Sage, 1974).

[11] Edward Shils, "The Intellectuals in the Political Development of the New States," in Jason L. Finkle and Richard W. Gable, eds., *Political Development and Social Change* (New York: Wiley, 1966), pp. 353–355.

[12] David E. Apter, *The Politics of Modernization* (Chicago: University of Chicago Press, 1965), pp. 179–222; and Ruth Schachter, "Single-Party Systems in West Africa," *American Political Science Review,* LV (June, 1961), pp. 294–307.

[13] David E. Apter, "Some Reflections on the Role of a Political Opposition in New Nations," in his *Some Conceptual Approaches to the Study of Modernization* (Englewood Cliffs, N.J.: Prentice-Hall, 1968), p. 73.

the contest for public offices. Indeed, the openness of channels to public offices varies with net balance of rewards and costs.

PATTERNS OF COMPETITION, STYLES OF CANDIDACY, AND PERCEPTION OF REWARD-COST

The candidates confront different political risk, for they run in electoral districts with different socio-economic characteristics. The number and configuration of social cleavages in a district also interact to produce a distinct pattern of competition. In Oregon we have discovered four such patterns: rural one-party districts, rural two-party districts, urban one-party districts, and urban two-party districts.[14] Each pattern reflects a distinct political milieu in which specific types of candidates and incentives predominate. Candidates' perceptions of rewards and costs therefore vary, depending upon the particular pattern of competition which characterize their districts. For instance, candidates in a rural one-party district perceive greater costs or smaller rewards than do the candidates in a rural two-party district, because there are few incentives for candidacy in a rural one-party district. Similarly, candidates running in an urban one-party district might perceive smaller rewards than those in an urban two-party district, due to different incentives operating for candidacy.

In Tables VII–7 and VII–8, we compare the candidates' perceptions of rewards and costs as they vary with different patterns of competition in the districts. In both primary and general elections the candidates perceived divergent rewards and costs, indicating that different political milieus in which they sought office create different incentives. Among the candidates in the primary election, those running in rural one-party districts expected smaller rewards or greater costs than did those running in rural two-party districts. Among the urban candidates, those in urban two-party districts are more likely to expect greater rewards or smaller costs than were the candidates in urban one-party districts. A similar pattern emerges when we examine the perceptions of the candidates in the general election. Those running in rural two-party districts were more likely to perceive large rewards than their counterparts in the rural one-party districts. However, there are marked differences between the candidates in the two types of urban districts. A higher proportion of those in urban two-party districts perceived large rewards than did their counterparts in the urban one-party districts.

A candidate's perception of rewards and costs is at once both an

---

[14] We have discussed the four patterns of political competition in Chapter IV.

TABLE VII–7

Patterns of Competition and Perceived Reward-Risk;
the Primary Election (N = 109)
(In Percentage)

Reward-Cost	Rural One-Party (N = 18)	Rural Two-Party (N = 17)	Urban One-Party (N = 39)	Urban Two-Party (N = 35)
Large Reward	0	30	8	14
Some Reward	45	30	23	34
Little/No Reward	45	41	67	52
Some Cost	11	0	2	0
Total	100	100	100	100

$X^2 = 17.2$, P < .05

TABLE VII–8

Patterns of Competition and Perceived Reward-Risk;
the General Election (N = 71)

Reward-Cost	Rural One-Party (N = 14)	Rural Two-Party (N = 13)	Urban One-Party (N = 22)	Urban Two-Party (N = 22)
Large Reward	14	16	9	46
Moderate Reward	36	41	37	27
Little/No Reward	43	31	50	27
Some Cost	7	13	4	0
Total	100	100	100	100

$X^2 = 16.2$, P < .10

objective and subjective matter. Each legislative district offers different objective incentives to candidacy. These objective incentives are rooted in the socio-economic and political structure of a district. Another factor is the subjective one—motivation for candidacy. In Oregon, we found that some were weakly motivated candidates who needed strong urging before they decided to file. Some other candidates were the "enthusiasts" who found office-seeking so richly rewarding that they needed little encouragement to run.[15] On the basis of a detailed analysis of the candidates' orientations we established earlier five distinct styles of candidacy: the reluctants, the coopted candidates, the conscripts, the urban enthusiasts, and the advertisers.[16]

[15] For a full discussion of the styles of candidacy, see Chapter IV.
[16] Different characteristics of rural reluctants, coopted candidates, minority candidates, urban enthusiasts, and advertisers are discussed in detail in Chapter IV.

Although each style of candidacy represents a different motivational basis for office-seeking, the rural reluctants, the coopted candidates, and conscripts share one characteristic: they filed only after their sponsors had appealed to their sense of civic duty, party loyalty, or their commitment to a political cause. Thus, they were the "reluctants" who perceived little rewards in candidacy. By contrast, the urban enthusiasts and the advertisers expected to profit directly from running. Because of the differences in motivation, candidates had different stakes in the election outcome.

As Tables VII–9 and VII–10 show, highly motivated candidates tended to perceive greater rewards than less-motivated ones. Among

TABLE VII–9

Styles of Candidacy and Perceived Reward-Cost,
Primary Election (N = 107)
(In Percentage)

Reward-Cost	Rural Reluctants (N = 34)	Coopted Candidates (N = 13)	Minority Candidates (N = 13)	Urban Enthusiasts (N = 30)	Advertisers (N = 17)
Large Reward	15	0	8	3	35
Moderate Reward	32	31	23	33	30
Little/No Reward	47	61	69	64	35
Some Cost	6	8	0	0	0
Total	100	100	100	100	100

$X^2 = 18.3, P < .10$

TABLE VII–10

Styles of Candidacy and Perceived Reward-Cost,
General Election (N = 71)
(In Percentage)

Reward-Cost	Rural Reluctants (N = 26)	Coopted Candidates (N = 10)	Minority Candidates (N = 9)	Urban Enthusiasts (N = 26)	Advertisers*
Large Reward	16	20	0	39	
Moderate Reward	35	20	22	42	
Little/No Reward	35	60	68	19	
Some Cost	14	0	10	0	
Total	100	100	100	100	

$X^2 = 18.9, P < .05$

* Note: There were no advertisers in the post-election sample. Most were defeated in the primary and the others refused to be interviewed after the general election.

the candidates in the primary election, the advertisers, more than any other group, perceived greater rewards. Many of the advertisers were young, aspiring attorneys. They participated in the election not because they were serious contenders but because they could exploit the campaign for the publicity that would help their private occupations. Typically, the advertisers organized a minimal campaign and quickly bowed out, avoiding the prospect of a costly campaign in the general election. Win or lose, the advertisers therefore have most to gain in the primary election.

Among the candidates in the general election, the difference between the enthusiasts and the others was more pronounced; the enthusiasts were at least twice as likely to perceive considerable reward. Like the coopted candidates, none of them perceived costs attendant upon their candidacy. Evidently, the highly motivated candidates such as the urban enthusiasts and the advertisers perceived larger rewards in their candidacy than did the others. Thus, evidence leads to the conclusion that both incentives and motivation determine a candidate's perception of rewards and costs.

SUMMARY AND CONCLUSIONS

The defeated candidates in both the primary and the general election support the rules and norms of recruitment less than do the winning candidates. The defeated candidates are less enthusiastic about continuing political activity than the winning candidates. Despite such differences between the winners and losers, only a few of them give little support for the rules of recruitment and electoral competition. In fact, the difference in support is not between high and low support but between *high* and *medium* support. This suggests that among losers, beliefs in the democratic rules of electoral competition remain unshaken.

Defeat in the primary election affected the attitudes of candidates less than defeat in the general election. Defeat in the primary election did not discourage candidates from continuing political activity, whereas in some instances defeat in the general election did. Similarly, the candidates defeated in the primary election endorsed the rules of recruitment more strongly than the candidates defeated in the general election. Where the parties were competitive and the general elections were closely contested, the outcome of the general election affected the attitudes of candidates more than did the outcome of the primary elections.

The political ambitions of candidates, their expectations about election outcomes, the competitiveness of the district, and the type of election in which they ran determined their post-election attitudes.

Despite defeat, the ambitious candidates were more inclined to continue political activity after the election than those who had little or no ambition. A candidate's expectation of victory also influenced his attitudes toward the rules of recruitment and his inclination toward continued political activity. Those who were optimistic about their chances of winning before the election reacted to defeat by reducing their support for the rules of recruitment and their inclination toward continued political activity, while others who were pessimistic did not. Our data also show that the type of district in which a candidate is defeated is related to his post-election attitudes. For example, candidates defeated in safe districts were less inclined to engage in political activity than those defeated in competitive districts.

The most important finding is the role of recruitment risk, i.e., expectations about the probabilities of net losses. The losing candidates who perceived high rewards expressed greater support for the rules of recruitment and were more inclined to remain politically active than those who perceived low rewards. The relationship holds even when the effects of career ambition, expectation about the election outcome, types of district and election are accounted for. Thus political risk is a critical variable which determines the reactions of candidates to defeat.

Our analysis of the perceptions of rewards and costs revealed that (1) the winners in both the primary and the general elections benefit more than the losers in terms of occupation, social prestige, influence, and career opportunity, as we can easily expect; but (2) a preponderant number of the losers also gain considerable rewards. The winners do not take all of the rewards and the losers do not lose too much. This makes political competition in Oregon a "low-risk system."

The findings discussed above indicate the important role of political risk in the recruitment process. The perceptions of risk determine who will seek office, and how he will seek it. Moreover, the perceptions of risk determine the way candidates react to defeat. If they perceive high risk they might react to defeat by withdrawing their support for the basic rules of political competition. At times, they might be so disenchanted that they would turn against the system, and widespread disenchantment might well result in fewer candidates, public cynicism and violations of electoral norms. The incidence of fraudulence and violence in elections in many countries, where recruitment risks are high, attests to this fact.

CHAPTER VIII

Conclusion: The Intricacies of Passage

WOODROW WILSON ONCE described recruitment in the following words: "candidacy must precede election, and the shoals of candidacy can be passed only by a light boat which carries little freight and can be turned readily about to suit the intricacies of passage."[1] We have found that the "shoals of candidacy" of state legislators in Oregon follow four patterns: (1) competitive recruitment, (2) majoritarian recruitment, (3) rural oligarchy and (4) rural competition. The variations in recruitment opportunity, risk and the selection process in these distinct patterns determine styles of candidacy, mechanisms of selection and the decisive phases of recruitment. We shall summarize these four patterns, the role of sponsors, the political risk and their implications for representation and legislative decision-making. We shall then consider how the recruitment of state legislators in Oregon creates a role culture among them and the relationship of that culture to the political culture of the state.

FOUR PATTERNS OF RECRUITMENT

Each legislative district is a particular recruitment milieu. The district's social, economic, and political characteristics determine whether a broad or narrow stratum of the electorate will be considered for candidacy, which phases of selection will prove decisive, and how much risk candidates will incur in running for office. Fundamental in determining the parameters of opportunity, risk and selection in a legislative

[1] Woodrow Wilson, *Congressional Government* (Boston: Houghton, Mifflin, 1925).

district is the social diversity of the electorate because it determines the extent to which inter-party and intra-party competition will prevail. The extent of each kind of competition will determine which phases of selection will prove decisive in determining the winning candidate. The expectation that a particular phase will be decisive in turn will determine the kinds of interactions among candidates and their sponsors.

The initial phase of recruitment, when individuals decide whether or not to become candidates, tests the entry barriers to recruitment opportunity. During that phase, factors which emerge from the social and economic diversity of a district exert greater influence than the degree of competition between political parties. During the initial phase only a few activists, the primary groups of potential candidates and/or leaders of interest groups, parties and party factions participate. However, the degree of party competition does not determine which one of these instigators of candidates will predominate.

In theory, when candidates compete for political office, they should give expression to the issues which divide a community. The proponents of the direct primary believed and hoped that competition would give representation to conflicting views within parties and make candidates more representative of party voters. In one-party states, where direct primaries originated, it was hoped that competition among candidates within the same party might substitute for the absence of competition between parties in the general elections.

But in reality, the primaries do not conform to their legal design but work in the way they were intended *only* under special social, economic and political conditions. In most legislative districts in Oregon, neither the primary nor the general elections are competitive. Oregon is not unique among the states in this respect. In 1948, approximately 45 percent of the legislative primaries in Ohio were not contested.[2] The figure for Pennsylvania in 1958 was 66.2 percent.[3] In the nation as a whole, between 1946 and 1963, only 25 states had a competitive two-party system.[4] The figure is based on party strength in the state legislatures and electoral outcomes of statewide and congressional elections. In Oregon, the parties are divided evenly, more or less, in the legislature; yet a majority of the legislators are elected in one-party districts.

In states which use the direct primary in many legislative districts, neither the general election nor the primary election is contested. Yet, the primary system presupposes at least competition within political

[2] V. O. Key, Jr., *American State Politics* (New York: Knopf, 1956), p. 178.
[3] Frank J. Sorauf, *Party and Representation*, p. 111.
[4] Austin Ranney, "Parties in State Politics," in Herbert Jacob and Kenneth N. Vines, eds., *Politics in the American States* (Boston: Little, Brown, 1965), p. 65.

parties if not between them. When the social cleavages which generate such competition are lacking, the procedures of the electoral system become only the legal shadows and the informal processes become the political substance in the four types of legislative districts.

The Competitive Pattern

DECISIVE SELECTION STAGES: INITIATION, THE PRIMARY AND THE GENERAL ELECTION. One particular setting fits the conditions assumed by a direct primary system: an urban constituency with a highly diverse electorate and numerous crosscutting social cleavages. If the political parties in the district are balanced in strength and the principal social cleavages run parallel to the lines which divide the parties, then the general election will be competitive. If social cleavages overlap, then many candidates will compete during the initial phases of recruitment within *each* party.

Oregon's urban two-party districts fit such a model. In urban, socially diverse districts, heavy competition prevails in both the primary and general elections. However, the terms diversity and competition characterize inadequately the complexity of such districts. Urban-competitive constituencies are densely populated. In some cases the state legislator represents over 100,000 people. The legislator knows only a small proportion of the voters and is a somewhat remote figure. The mass media are an important link between the incumbent and his constituents, and during the campaign the candidates must rely on heavy advertising to reach the public. The impersonal atmosphere makes it difficult to stimulate voter interest, and consequently voter turnout, especially in the primary election, is low. Yet, the socially diverse district generates many competing interest groups which the candidates must mobilize during the election campaigns. Issues are carefully chosen and exploited with an eye to the opinion polls. The ability to activate voters through groups and associations is the key to success for the candidate and his sponsors.

Such urban two-party constituencies produce a distinctive pattern of recruitment. Here, political activists and the politically ambitious find strong incentives to become a candidate because an urban constituency is a springboard to higher political office. The rewards, both material and social, of seeking and holding office are considerable. In an urban area the livelihood of an attorney, a realtor, or an insurance agent depends upon his public visibility and social prominence. Interpersonal skills are essential in such occupations and a large network of contacts brings success, which can be gained through campaigning for office. Many enter an urban primary contest with little or no desire to win. To finish a respectable third or second fulfills their expectations and aspirations. To become better known to the public is their goal; therefore, losing is "winning" for these so-called candidates.

Yet, not all candidates seek the advertisement, which campaigning for office in order to enhance their occupational status provides. The incentives for candidacy are sufficient in urban two-party districts to attract a diverse group of candidates. Some are drawn into the contest in order to advocate particular issues; others to advance the cause of their party; and still others are attracted by the political and nonpolitical rewards of candidacy. Still others run for all the reasons mentioned above.

The diversity in objectives of candidates is equally true of their sponsors. Party leaders and interest groups seek standard bearers from among civic leaders, religious leaders, news broadcasters, members of "old" families, famous athletes, and other prominent persons. The strategy of seeking the notables creates some risks for sponsors. Prominent individuals have little to gain by running for office and therefore must be coaxed to run. Since they are secure in their status, sponsors cannot control them as easily as candidates who are agents. With the coopted notables, sponsors sacrifice some influence in exchange for better chances of victory at the polls. Urban two-party districts had many such coopted candidates.

The incentives which diversify the field of candidates determine patterns of support throughout the primary and general election campaigns. The casual candidates file, solicit a modicum of support, stage a respectable, though uninspired campaign, and after defeat in the primary election withdraw gracefully. The serious contenders attract greater support. The incumbents enjoy established support, which gives them an enormous edge. The already prominent coopted candidate is sponsored most frequently because he stands the best chance as a challenger. The ample support he receives (or is promised) also reassures this reluctant notable candidate and persuades the candidate to run.

Compared to the other district types, the urban two-party districts provide the broadest recruitment opportunity. The selection process filtered the candidates in each phase, and as a result the legislative candidates were more representative of the electorate than in other districts. The primary election filtered out all the casual candidates, who were "going along for the ride," and a few of the serious candidates. The eventual winners in the general election stem from backgrounds which make them personify the various political, social and economic character of these diversified districts.

Thus, the social and political conditions in urban-competitive districts fulfill the historical expectations and purposes of the direct primary. One other urban district resembles the competitive one in many ways, but deviates enough to produce a different pattern of recruitment.

The Majoritarian Pattern

THE DECISIVE SELECTION STAGES: INSTIGATION AND THE PRIMARY ELECTION. A second recruitment pattern unfolds in an urban district where social cleavages divide the electorate into two parties, unequal in strength. One party clearly dominates and some candidates compete for a place in that dominant party. However, factional differences are important, and many candidates remain loyal to their respective parties. In the dominant party, the initiation and primary election phases of recruitment are competitive, but within the minority party only one candidate enters. In fact, party officials must solicit candidates to fill slots on the party ticket.

In the urban one-party districts, the instigation phase of recruitment and the primary election phase within the majority party (two phases which do not arouse much public interest) are the decisive selection stages. The low visibility of legislators compared with the contestants for other elective offices dampens interest in the legislative primary. In these urban one-party districts, city politics gets much of the coverage in the local media. Local issues fight for attention with the contest for the state legislature. Statewide contests for U.S. Senate and congressional elections, both of which revolve primarily around national issues, also compete for public notice. The certainty of the outcome of the legislative contest in urban one-party districts also reduces public interest.

Many voters in urban one-party districts are indifferent or apathetic toward the state legislative contests. In these districts, few sponsors approach candidates and urge them to run. Even during the competitive primary election campaign in the dominant party, only a few candidates receive substantial support. Incumbents are fully supported. The initiation of candidates and the primary election elicit little attention from the "man on the street."

It is evident that the public shows greater interest in the general election campaign in urban one-party districts. Almost all the candidates, by the time they advance to the general election, have acquired interest-group sponsorship and nominal-party sponsorship. However, even during the general election when voter interest is at its peak, the campaign is kept very low key. Compared with other districts, the minority candidates receive modest support because neither candidate believes his efforts will alter the election outcome. The minority party candidates felt the support they received was some psychological compensation for their certain defeat. Incumbents received support from interest groups as a reward for services they had rendered in the legislature.

Analysis of urban one-party districts suggests that when competition occurs only in the least-visible stages of recruitment, then incumbents enjoy an overwhelming advantage. Challengers within the majority party who take popular stands on issues present a better image, conduct a more intensive and skillful campaign, and often do well in debates with incumbents. Rarely can a challenger find an issue so meaningful to voters and threatening to an opponent, the incumbent. So, the challengers almost invariably are beaten in the primary if their opponents are the incumbents. The challengers may conduct well-organized campaigns, but few voters are listening.

The incumbents whose names are familiar to the voters have an enormous advantage when the voters are not angry and the issue differences do not take hold. When voters examine the names on the ballot, they often choose a familiar one. Name-familiarity is hard to acquire in these one-party districts. Sometimes an unknown person with a well-known name, like Kennedy or Johnson, gets many votes. When voters are not interested, the challenger finds it hard to achieve the name-familiarity that the incumbent enjoys. Nevertheless, the one-party urban district is fertile ground for the entrepreneurial, publicity-seeking candidate. He can run and gain some notoriety at little expense, secure in the knowledge that he cannot win. In each district, nearly as many self-promoted certain losers contested during the primary campaign as the combined total of minority candidates and serious contenders.

Among all legislative constituencies in Oregon, urban one-party districts provided abundant recruitment opportunity. But opportunity for whom? Often it was only for the "advertisers" competing in the majority party, who were easily eliminated in the primary. The victorious candidates in the general election were somewhat less socially and economically representative of the voters in their constituencies than the victors in urban-competitive constituencies.

The Oligarchical Pattern

INSTIGATION AS THE DECISIVE SELECTION STAGE. Recruitment processes in rural districts contrast sharply with the ones just described. Social cleavages in rural one-party districts crosscut each other, which reduces the level of political conflict. In such districts candidates usually run unopposed, or face only token opposition. A small circle of farmers, small businessmen, and local professionals controls recruitment. All the members of this circle of high social status, long-time residents in the community, are close friends. The legislators and sponsors all belong to this exclusive social stratum.

In Chapter III, we pointed out that the population in the rural one-party districts includes many transients, who move into the district, remain for five years or less, and then move on. During the time such transients reside in the community, they do not participate in politics.

In rural one-party districts, politics, like village gossip, is communicated by word of mouth. Each voter is on a first-name basis with nearly all the permanent residents in the district. Political conflict could threaten such close relationships. When a candidate seriously challenges the incumbent, the challenge arouses personal animosities that pit cliques against cliques, thus upsetting the whole community. In communities with an oppressive consensus, challengers threaten established relationships and are therefore frowned upon. Cleavages are suppressed and mavericks and "troublemakers" are snubbed or ostracized. Informal, behind-the-scenes negotiation is the customary method for "managing" conflict.

In such a milieu, few individuals come forward as candidates because the incentives to run for office are so meager. For example, successful candidates for the state legislature cannot aspire to higher office because a sparsely populated rural constituency cannot serve as a springboard to statewide office. At most, a candidate from a rural one-party district might be able to advance to the state senate. The nonpolitical incentives to candidacy are likewise meager. For example, a successful farmer has little to gain by serving in the legislature. He does not wish to live in the state capitol, nor incur the expense this entails. Similarly, lawyers or realtors who might consider running have little need for political prominence in a community where they already enjoy high social status. In this pastoral district, the costs of candidacy and legislative service far outweigh the benefits and so it is difficult to find someone willing to run. Once a candidate is found and is elected, he serves many terms because no one is eager to replace him. The pool of aspirants remains small at all times.

The candidate for the state legislature is a consensus candidate. The primary and general elections are merely rituals. Candidates file, secure a little publicity, attend a few meetings, go to a few county fairs, and little more. They tell the voters they will defend the interests of their small constituency against opposing interests in the legislature. On election day turnout musters the voters who wish to show their loyalties to the predetermined winner.

State legislators are not important in the politics (or lack of politics) in such districts. Issues are limited also because the single party insulates the district from issues that divide the parties in the nation. In such socially homogeneous districts, only issues that mobilize the district solidarity against opposing interests become important. Farming is the principal occupation, and urban-sponsored measures that disadvantage the farmer evoke greatest animosity. The legislator is the voice of his constituents on farm issues, assisted by the Grange or the Farm Bureau. Such interest groups are so active and influential, they obscure the legislator's role.

The patterns of instigation and support in such districts are easily explainable. Even though candidates face no opposition in the primary or general elections, they receive a good deal of support anyway. Even though the winner is determined during the initiation phase, the primary and general elections are mere ceremonies. Support is promised to those induced to run to reassure the candidates when they waver. The candidate's sponsors are just demonstrating their loyalty to him. The two phases of selection, instigation and support, taken together give symbolic expression to an unrequited political consensus.

Rural Two-Partyism: A Small House Divided

INSTIGATION AND THE GENERAL ELECTION AS DECISIVE SELECTION STAGES. The fourth pattern is exhibited in a rural, socially homogeneous district similar to the one described above. Two phases, initiation and the general election, are the critical ones. But the primary election is not contested. Political conflict in the district is not conducive to diversified competition in the primary and general election, but enough to allow the public airing of both sides of at least one issue. Sometimes the few cleavages are reinforced and differences become sufficiently intense so that they become public issues, and then attract rival candidates for office. Competition in such districts is often based on local issues. Elections are neither tests of liberal or conservative persuasions nor identifications with the Republican or Democratic parties. No ideological rationale explains how the mix of groups divides the population aligned with each candidate. Such is the profile of a rural two-party district.

An outside observer would regard the issues in these districts as especially parochial. For example, in one district exclusively Protestant, issues arose over the differences between two Protestant denominations. In another legislative district that incorporated more than one county, the voters of the two counties competed for dominance. In another district, the leaders of the Grange disagreed with leaders of the Farm Bureau, and two fraternal organizations, the Elks and Moose Lodges, opposed each other. Such conflicts were cumulative so that merchants who were members of the Chamber of Commerce and the Elks fought against the local ranchers who belonged to the Grange and the Moose Lodges. The cleavages in rural two-party districts derive from specific economic or social differences; the conflict is intense and bitter because the stakes in status are high.

Candidacy is risky in this setting. The material costs of the campaign are not as important as the threatened losses from engaging in an open face-to-face conflict. Much more is at stake than the choice of the state legislator. The election is a test of strength between opposing factions. At first glance it would seem that finding candidates in such districts would be more difficult than in rural one-party districts. The political inducements to run are no greater than in one-party districts. Name-familiarity and advertising are not eagerly sought in rural settings. Open conflict means that, if anything, the risks of running and serving are greater. However, even here candidacy brings some rewards. Candidacy means becoming a "champion" of one faction, win or lose. Victory brings great prestige, not so much because the successful candidate becomes a state legislator, but because he becomes a leading spokesman for his faction.

Thus, both the costs and benefits of running and serving are considerable. The persuasiveness of sponsors during instigation and support phases lessens the costs of candidacy. Candidates in rural competitive constituencies consistently received the greatest encouragement and assistance. During the initial stages of recruitment most candidates reported that their primary groups were their principal sponsors, which sustained their candidacy during the uncontested phases of recruitment.

As the general election approached, the battle lines became more sharply defined. Candidates' perceptions of the conflict changed. When interviewed during the initiation and the primary election, they were concerned with whether or not sponsors were close friends, family, or acquaintances whom they esteemed highly. Encouragement and help from those close to them meant more to candidates than how substantial it was. Most candidates interviewed stated that they would rather be supported by primary groups than by other sponsors.

During the general election campaign the contest was defined in terms of friends and enemies. Labels were given to the social circles that enlisted on each side of the conflict. These labels were the names of organizations, such as the Grange or the Chamber of Commerce, in districts where the conflict divided agricultural and business interests. Candidates classified sponsors in ways that reflected their changing perception of the conflict. Early in the process, a campaign contributor might have been called a friend first and a member of the Grange second.

These priorities were reversed during the general election campaign. A "friend" during the initiation became a "representative of the Grange" during the general election. This shows how social relationships are disrupted in such a proto-gemeinschaft. Political conflict restructured social relationships.

In sum, we found that only if candidates received a great display of support would candidates run in rural two-party districts. Yet, in such districts sponsors line up on opposite sides and battle more intensely than in urban competitive districts. As a result, the range of certification is broadened, although not to the extent found in urban districts; the costs of candidacy increase and necessitate extensive sponsorship.

The Role of Economic Diversity

The economic diversity of a district does not affect either its social diversity or the decisive selection stages, and therefore was not a factor in the four patterns of recruitment. Economic diversity becomes significant only where economic issues are relevant to selection. If a district contains some industry, then economic issues are more likely to affect recruitment. Unlike many other states, Oregon's industry is not concentrated in large urban areas. Factories and mills of the lumber industry often are located close to the sources of raw materials. Lumber, paper and plywood mills are scattered throughout the sparsely settled Coastal, Southern, Central and Eastern regions of the state, as well as the more populous Willamette Valley. Consequently, little relationship exists between the social homogeneity of a district and the proportion of its population that is employed in industry.

As we can see, only in rare instances are legislators chosen competitively. Indeed, in most instances, the primary election decides the winner and the general elections are rituals.

Four Recruitment Patterns and Types of Candidates

From Machiavelli's *Prince* to Harold Lasswell's *Political Personality,* the politician has been described as the compulsive power-seeker, driven to self-manipulation and the manipulation of others in pursuit of political power. We hasten to add that we did not study the personalities of our respondents, but it seemed to us that the candidates we interviewed did not fit this stereotype. None appeared single-mindedly devoted to seeking power, or driven by inordinate political ambition. Nor did any of the candidates resemble some other American political types. No one seemed a budding "boss," a strident demagogue or a self-dramatizing "ham." We encountered no David Harums, Billy Sundays, Joe McCarthys or Huey Longs. Perhaps we should not have expected them since Oregon politics throughout its history has only rarely had such demagogic types.

Many of the candidates seemed hesitant about seeking office and some others were reluctant office seekers. At this starting level of a political career, the political aspirations of candidates were modest, and only a few could see themselves devoting their lives to politics. The incumbent state legislators seemed self-assured, but not enthusiastic about their positions. Among those seeking office for the first time, many seemed more naive than ambitious. They lacked sophisticated knowledge about the campaigns that lay ahead, and knew even less about the demands of legislative office. Understandably, few of the new candidates realized the demands made upon a state legislator today. They also had exaggerated expectations about the influence they might exert once they were in office. Apparently, ambition and political sophistication grow with success or experience, or both. The appetite, as the expression goes, "comes with the eating."

Candidates exhibited so wide a range of talents and temperament that the question arises—What talents are required to run for the state legislature in Oregon? The state legislator's role is ambiguous and non-technical, and no specific skills or level of performance are mandatory. Some of the candidates were articulate, others reticent; some thought like organizers; some seemed manipulative; few were contemplative, and all seemed sensible if not imaginative when they talked about politics. Above all, the serious candidates seemed to us to be saying to the electorate: 'Elect me because I am one of you and can give expression to your values and interests.' The urban candidates were occupational types, lawyers, insurance men; the rural candidates were less stereotyped, more independent and more individualistic.

The greater the incentive to candidacy in a district, the larger the number of candidates will be. As said before, many of these are casual candidates who do not expect to win and get their rewards from the campaign itself, not from winning or losing the election. Low recruitment risk in the contest for the state legislature attracts many candidates who seek publicity and prominence. Such self-promoters are not the only kind; there are the martyrs, the candidates of the minority party who, certain they will lose, find defeat a confirmation of the virtue of their cause.

High incentive also attracts serious candidates of two types: the advocates and the spokesmen. The advocates are concerned with issues. They are concerned individuals who have been politically active throughout their adult years. The advocates are true politicians; the public life is their calling. Politics has intrinsic meaning to them. They enjoy the activity and are devoted to public purposes.

The spokesmen become candidates because they have a strong sense of civic duty. They are prominent in the community because of their occupational success and community service. They cannot resist the persuasion of important sponsors. They are enmeshed in a social relationship in which obligations and favors are exchanged. Indeed, the candidate's success is attributable to his unusual acumen in such exchanges. When they are called upon to run, they cannot refuse without rejecting those friends and supporters to whom they owe their social status.

Essentially, candidates are differentiated according to how much sponsorship they need to make them run. The self-starters require the least support and, therefore, seem the most strongly motivated. Those who receive more extensive sponsorship can be, and often are, less motivated. In the absence of direct data on motivation, our observations are plausible inferences, drawn from data on sponsorship, perceived risk and realized costs and benefits. The motivation of self-starters has little to do with anything intrinsic to politics. In contrast, the serious candidates, with a wider circle of support, acquire a political identity as special interest representatives. Ironically, the self-starters may be, therefore, the least "political" of the group.

The table that follows presents a typology of candidates according to their (1) perception of district incentives, (2) motivation, and (3) relations with their sponsors.

The findings lead us to conclude that on the aggregate level the personal attributes of the candidates do not explain their success or failure. More compelling are diversity of the district, party competitiveness, and the selection process which explain the various types of candidacy. Only in the rare instances when particular contests are close do the personal attributes of the candidates make a difference, but only after the character of the district and process have already filtered the admissable and effective candidates. The role of sponsors, primary groups, political parties, and interest groups, is noteworthy. The part they play shows how much candidacy relies on some collective support. These collective sponsorships exhibit great variety.

PRIMARY GROUPS, POLITICAL PARTIES, INTEREST GROUPS AND OTHER SPONSORS

Primary Groups

Primary groups play an important part in the candidate's decision to file in all four types of district. In each instance, the potential candidate's initial consideration of the decision to file begins with his pri-

TABLE VIII–1

Styles of Candidacy and Their Determinants: Incentives, Motivations, and Relations with Sponsors

Styles of Candidacy	Perceived Level of District Incentives		Motivation	Goals and Incentives	Relation with Sponsors		District
	Political	*Non-political*	*Desire to Run*	*Goals*	*Mechanisms of Instigation*	*Intensity of Instigation*	
The Serious Candidates							
Advocates (Enthusiasts)	High	Moderate to High	High	Advocate issues; foster political careers; enhance private occupation and prestige	Self-starting; agency or bureaucratic ascent	Low	C, M
Notables (Reluctants)	Low to Moderate	Low	Low to Moderate	Serve district and/or interests of sponsors; perform civic duty	Cooptation	High to Moderate	C, O HD
The Casual Candidates							
Entrepreneurs (advertisers)	Low	High	High	Enhance private occupation and prestige	Self-starting	Low	C, M
Martyrs	Low to Moderate	Low to Moderate	Low to Moderate	To serve as spokesmen for party or other sponsors; give symbolic opposition to dominant party or faction	Conscription	High to Moderate	M, O

KEY:
M—Majoritarian
HD—Rural Competitive
O—Rural Oligarchy
C—Competitive

mary group. The change in role from political activist to candidate even though it is for the part-time position as state legislator, can be a dramatic one for the candidate as well as for his family. Running for office imposes hardships and psychological strains; therefore, a person can make the decision to run more easily when those closest to him reinforce his decision. Without their encouragement and active assistance, many potential candidates will refuse to run or will approach the campaign with debilitating doubts.

The importance of primary groups in this instance supports the extensive research that shows that an individual's primary groups generate and sanction the norms which govern decision-making.[5] In Prewitt's study of the recruitment of city councilmen, he observed that: "Political choices are no less influenced by primary groups than other types of choices. . . . In tracing the experiences which led from their general interest in politics to their political activities, to their candidacy for office, two-thirds of the councilmen cite the importance of small, informal groups of friends or acquaintances."[6] We found that candidates who have active primary group support perceive high benefits and low costs or low risks in candidacy. Conversely, those candidates who received little support from their primary groups perceived fewer benefits and higher costs or higher risk. Primary group support, because it comes from those who matter most to the candidate, strengthens the candidate's capacity to sustain risks.

Candidates whose primary groups were the initial link in a chain of support that included interest groups and party factions were more successful than those candidates whose primary groups did not link them to such associations. Hence, in some instances, the primary group determines how much other groups will support a candidate. The primary group is a nucleus from which concentric circles of support may develop.

Primary groups are often contrasted with formal organizations. Yet, often a candidate's primary group becomes organized into a small scale organization, and the smallness of the group is not disadvantageous. For example, in a legislative district made up of small communities, a campaign organization consisting of a candidate's family and his close friends is all the "organization" he needs. A large campaign organization would neither be possible nor necessary. A few conscientious people working efficiently and harmoniously, can do all the necessary mailing, phoning, and solicitation of votes. In a small constituency, the candi-

[5] Sidney Verba, *Small Groups and Political Behavior.*
[6] Kenneth Prewitt, *The Recruitment of Political Leaders* (Indianapolis, Ind.: Bobbs-Merrill, 1970), p. 111.

date's family and a circle of friends, reaching out to people informally and directly, have the ability to conduct a successful campaign.

Political Parties

Among the variety of groups and individuals that sponsor legislative candidates (primary groups, interest groups, civic associations, political party leaders, factional leaders, and legislative leaders), political parties are neither the most important, nor are they even first among equals. To be sure, the direct primary prevents a political party from officially endorsing particular candidates. Yet, even sub rosa, party leaders do not exercise much influence in instigating candidates, except in the case of the minority party in the districts with one dominant party.

The categories used in organizational analysis of political parties do not fit the structure of Oregon parties.[7] How then shall we characterize the part that political parties play in recruitment? Nonhierarchical, fragmented organizations staffed with sporadically active volunteers and some steadfast activists often elected to their precinct posts because they received a few write-in votes. How does one characterize such an organization? Even after the primaries have designated the official party nominee, he or she usually campaigns independently of the party. The boundaries between party association and nonparty association are difficult to demarcate, so that one party becomes almost indistinguishable from the others. Political parties are at once legal entities, reference groups for symbolic identification, and partial organizations used now and then when groups need to coalesce for electoral purposes.

A distinction is often drawn between strong and weak political parties, according to their degree of organizational complexity, cohesiveness and effectiveness in mobilizing the electorate. Urban political machines are called "strong" organizations while the loosely knit, informal associations usually found in small communities and rural areas are regarded as weak parties. The distinction is misleading because it overlooks the functional test of adequacy of diverse organizations in different settings. The informal circles which substitute for party organizations in small communities are "strong" organizations judged by their capacity to handle party tasks in such milieus. Yet, such "organizations" would prove woefully ineffective in a large metropolis. In a large metropolis where population is quite dense and diverse and the economy is complex, the corollary is true only if political parties are so organized that they can mediate among a mass electorate and various associations and organizations. Small political groups alone could not perform such electoral tasks.

[7] William Wright, ed., *A Comparative Study of Party Organization.*

Interest Groups

Time and again, the candidates referred to interest groups and their importance in the recruitment process, which we explain in several ways. Where the direct primary and other influences have fragmented political parties, interest groups become more salient. It is not true that Oregon has *more* interest groups or *stronger* interest groups, such quantitative and qualitative terms are irrelevant and, in a comparative sense, confusing. In a state with a simple economy, whose electorate is relatively homogeneous in ethnic and religious backgrounds, then it is expected that only social- and economic-interest cleavages will become salient, and other divisions unlikely, if not impossible.

In Oregon, interest groups perform many of the functions that political parties do in other states. The variety of organized interests embraces the economic, welfare, and ideological concerns of the citizenry. They sponsor candidates for elective office, present public policies before the legislature and executive agencies. Both interest groups and political parties are loosely knit organizations. In these respects, the parties and interest groups are not dissimilar.

The fuzziness of the boundaries between parties and interest groups derives from the particular antiparty traditions in Oregon. Antiparty movements played a significant role in the development of the political culture of Oregon. The state pioneered in the adoption of the direct primary, the initiative, referendum and recall. All such reforms were designed to give direct expression to the popular will and to counter organized elites in political parties, the legislature and business. The special antiparty bias in Oregon has persisted since its beginnings in the decade before World War I. In some other states during the same period, mayors of large metropolitan areas, who were strong leaders, built political machines, and dynamic governors created legions of patronage employees to staff a state party apparatus. This was not the case in Oregon. Portland retains the commission form of government which diffuses authority, and the governor of Oregon has neither a cabinet of his appointees nor other patronage that might enable him to become a legislative leader, a strong executive, or leader of his party. The antiparty, antiexecutive tradition removed two influences that might have challenged the pre-eminence of interest groups.

Thus, recruitment sponsorship in Oregon is a network of primary groups, interest groups and party factions. The loose, freewheeling character of political life makes it necessary for most candidates, especially the urban ones, to rely on their own resources. Candidates must construct their campaign organizations, for the electorate frowns upon elaborate party organization. It is believed widely in Oregon that electorate politics should be open and individualistic, a view which figures significantly in the risks of recruitment.

RECRUITMENT AND RISK

Candidates for the state legislature in Oregon face little risk because the outcome is uncertain in only a few elections. Only a few candidates are in doubt as to whether they will win or lose. Furthermore, those who do lose suffer minor deprivations, if they suffer any at all. Indeed, in some instances electoral defeat has some advantages. It is not surprising then that few losers become disaffected with the prevailing process of nominating and electing candidates. The losers support the nominating and electoral process no less than the winners; their defeat does not diminish their desire to continue political activity.

The small losses that the defeated candidate incurs also stem from the way the public views the political contest. The losers do not suffer shame or public embarrassment. The absence of a sharp ideological contest and the low intensity of most campaigns contribute a gamelike aura to politics. Small losses are also the result of the low level of prestige and status attached to the office of state legislator. The income and privileges associated with the position are also modest. Losing an election to the state legislature is somewhat analogous to falling from a lower rung of a ladder; the bruises are not serious, painful, nor lasting.

Further, in politics, victory and defeat are relative terms. Elections are won by small margins, large margins, or by landslides. In each case the loser receives a different percentage of votes, but has he given up more if he is roundly defeated than when he loses by a narrow margin? That depends on the expectations of candidates and the public that have been learned from past history. For example, in a district that one party has dominated with a consistent margin of 65 percent, when the losing party secures 40 percent of the vote, then their adherents will interpret it as a victory. The defeated candidate who has made a stronger showing than was expected will be regarded as a "winner." Conversely, the winning candidate will be regarded as a loser. The defeated candidate may be considered a "strong" candidate with a promising political future. Victory and defeat are always relative to the expectations of performance of the party, the candidate, and the voters. Thus, neither the number nor the percentage of votes in an electoral defeat predicts the loser's attitudes toward that defeat. For most candidates, the loss of an election does not alter their political attitudes towards the system or diminish their zest for political activity.

Losing the primary or the general election has different consequences which affect candidates' strategies. The most common kind of primary election losers are candidates of the majority party who, against heavy odds, are attempting to unseat the incumbent. Commonly, challenger-candidates of the majority party are the entrepreneurial self-starters who are "running to lose" but seek the prominence that a campaign provides. Such losers bask in the sunlight of their new-found celebrity status. The contacts they have made and the prominence gained make an electoral loss a personal gain. The losers in the general election fall into several types: sacrificial challengers of the minority party and the losers in the close contests in urban competitive and rural two-party districts. As we have illustrated, nearly all such losers gain enough in notoriety, community standing, or business contacts to compensate for their electoral losses.

Low recruitment or entry risk has several salutory consequences for legislative recruitment. Low risk encourages the eligibles in the pool, lowers the intensity of political competition, makes political recruitment an avenue to social mobility, and tempers the prestige and status of state legislators. Low risk lowers the threshold of political opportunity because political activists are more easily persuaded to run if the uncertainty is reduced and losses, if any, are modest. When the losses are so few, new positions which serve as cushions are unnecessary, which is another disincentive for elaborate party organization. Candidates who lose on their first attempt may try again without loss of face.

Low risk also keeps the minority parties alive. Even if or because its candidates are certain of defeat, the party and its candidates can afford to keep trying. Indeed, under conditions of low risk, the "underdog" challenger enjoys some special advantages. The role of the underdog gives him latitude to attack his opponent, who then has the responsibility of explaining a record in office which is usually marred with compromises and unfulfilled promises. Moreover, the voters who regularly support the minority party regard the party's defeat as an outcome which substantiates their view that the oligarchs of the majority party control politics. The confirmation of one's political outlooks may be more comforting than the victory of one's candidate.

Low recruitment risk makes politics more inviting to the ordinary man who lacks political ambition or outstanding talent. When ordinary men become candidates, they make the public feel that the legislative office is close to them. The public is less suspicious of officials and candidates who are beginning their political careers; they seem neither too remote from the public nor too superior to them.

RECRUITMENT AND LEGISLATIVE BEHAVIOR

Each pattern of recruitment influences legislative decision-making through two principal factors: (1) the social representativeness of legislative candidates and (2) their political socialization. We did not observe the legislative behavior of the successful candidates whom we interviewed, but our observations of the Oregon legislature and those of other states makes us suggest some direct and indirect effects of recruitment on legislative decision-making.

We have illustrated that the social characteristics of candidates are not explainable as an entity separate from the selection process. The question of "who" will be selected is part and parcel of "how" they were chosen. The selection process in each type of district determines who will be considered available and who will be selected. For example, the rural oligarchical pattern allows only a few people, a preselected elite, to be considered for candidacy. The rural competitive districts and urban one-party districts also restrict the pool of the certified, but nevertheless consider a broader segment of the political activists. In general, the more competitive the district, the more diversified are those considered for candidacy.

The selection process is biased to favor those who typify the characteristics esteemed by the majority of the voters in the district. Thus, the lawyers in the urban district, the successful farmers in the rural district possess qualities that are looked up to in their respective communities. The social and economic status of the successful candidates represents the approved values in that district as well as the approved methods of social achievement. Candidates are chosen not alone for what they are but "who" they are, as personifications of the values, folkways, and the enduring historical memories in that district. The successful candidates are at home with the political syntax and styles of their constituency. No outsider or Johnny-come-lately would have a chance to win legislative office. The district constitutes not only the candidate's roots, but also his political destiny.

The social background of legislators comes into play in the legislature in various ways. Thus, Pierce on the powerful Ways and Means Committee of the Oregon House of Representatives observed that, "the efficiency standards used by committee members come, for the most part, from their practical experience as managers of insurance companies, farms, or real estate businesses."[8] The experience that legislators

[8] Lawrence C. Pierce, Richard G. Frey, and S. Scott Pengelly, *The Freshman Legislator* (Eugene, Ore.: American Political Science Association and the Department of Political Science of the University of Oregon, 1972), p. 70.

have acquired is applied routinely to the myriad items considered in reviewing budget requests.

The social background of legislators may make them respond selectively. Their occupational background is often related to major economic interests in their constituencies. Often, occupational groups seek out one of their members and sponsor his candidacy. Thus, a legislator's concerns and his social background are often closely related.

The social representativeness of legislators is not synonymous with their responsiveness. How a legislator translates the interests of his constituency is mediated, in part, by his relationship with his sponsors and the extent to which they are representative of the districts. The legislator's responsiveness is engendered by the socialization of his selection experience. Another factor that affects a legislator's responsiveness is the extent to which he is dependent on his sponsors for his reelection and career advancement.

The Selection Process and Role Socialization

From beginning to end, the selection process socializes the candidates in various ways. First and foremost, the mechanisms of candidacy generate particular role styles which we have labeled the advocates, the notables, the agents, and the martyrs. These styles are a combined result of two factors: the eagerness of the candidates to seek office and the degree to which a candidate is obligated to his sponsors. Among these, only candidates with the first three role styles become successful. Such role styles shape the orientations of candidates toward their legislative roles.

Parenthetically, only in rare instances did a person become a candidate through bureaucratic ascent. The absence of elaborate party organizations in Oregon made that kind of promotion to candidacy exceptional. Nor did we find evidence of bureaucratic advancement to candidacy through interest groups or other organizations. The infrequency of bureaucratic ascent reflects the entrepreneurial way in which most individuals became candidates and entry of most activists into candidacy from their private positions rather than party office.

The selection process is a learning experience through which a candidate acquires a political style, develops political skills, cements identifications with issues and crystallizes obligations to various groups. The candidate learns to what extent the support of his sponsors is sufficient to ensure his election or reelection. In simple rural areas, the major interests of the constituency and those espoused by the principal sponsors are identical. A candidate doesn't have to discover the dominant issues.

He must learn nuances of policy that relate to the implementations of policies and how specific aspects of agricultural policy, for example, will affect particular individuals and groups.

Each of the four district types and their corresponding recruitment patterns gives rise to predispositions in the decision-making behavior of legislators. Studies by Snowiss and Fiellin[9] have shown how recruitment affects the orientations and policy predispositions of congressmen. We contend that sponsorship determines in large part the legislator's policy preferences. Thus the legislator who is appointed by a handful of men in the rural oligarchical pattern is thereby committed to their dominant interests. However, on legislative issues that do not directly affect his sponsors, the legislator will follow predispositions that flow from his background, political socialization, and bargaining with his legislative colleagues. In the latter instance, the legislator trades his votes on some policies for the sake of support for policies close to his sponsors' interests.

In the urban one-party districts, where victory in the primary has ensured victory in the general election, the candidate has a sponsorship pattern that obligates him to maintain, for his own sake, the coalition of the majority party. The candidate's victory in the primary, if he were a challenger, meant that he had to battle rival sponsors and candidates and thus threaten the consensus of the majority party. In such a case, when he becomes a legislator he will serve as a broker for his winning coalition.

This candidate contrasts with the urban candidate who faced contests in all phases of his campaign. This legislator emerges as a broker of many interests, a logroller par excellence. A significant cross section of the interests of his district have a place in his sponsorship coalition. The notables or advocates so typical in such districts are more independent of any one sponsor than is the agent. He needs a broad coalition to finance and organize his campaign.

Election campaigns for the state legislature in Oregon retain a traditional character. The political technician and professional consultant have not permeated the state legislative campaigns. Except for the urban areas, polling is hardly used at all. No candidates running for the State legislature used public relations experts or "image makers," and no candidates used professional campaign managers or sophisticated campaign techniques. Political campaigning, at this level, retains its

[9] Leo M. Snowiss, "Congressional Recruitment and Representation," *American Political Science Review*, LX (September, 1966), pp. 627–639; Alan Fiellin, "Recruitment and Legislative Role Conceptions: A Conceptual Scheme and a Case Study," *Western Political Quarterly*, XX (June, 1967), pp. 271–287.

traditional folkishness. Candidates have to meet people face to face, so they go to supermarkets, factory parking lots, county fairs, and any other place people gather. They rely on friends and neighbors to spread the word about their qualities. The candidates learn that the many bills that come before the State legislature are largely invisible to the public. They also learn that state taxes are uppermost in the minds of their constituents; other issues are secondary. In this kind of campaign, the term "interests" loses its insidious meaning. The people who rely on wheat farming care about wheat farming; the dairymen care about the price of dairy products in the market. These are not special interests; they are just the bread-and-butter concerns of many citizens of the district. Only in the context of the legislature do they become "interests," defined and represented by legislators and lobbyists who compete for the limited state budget, which the law requires to be balanced.

Intra-party factionalism and interest cleavages are more important than regional cleavages or the division between Democrats and Republicans in the State legislature. Francis's study of Oregon legislators showed that they regarded factional conflict and interest group pressures as more salient in the legislature than partisan and regional conflict.[10] In their study of lobbying in four states (Utah, Massachusetts, North Carolina and Oregon), Ziegler and Baer concluded that interest groups had greater influence on the legislative process in Oregon and Utah than in Massachusetts and North Carolina.[11]

Factionalism arises because the party organization has no way of constraining it. Factionalism erupts without inhibition because candidates either build their own coalition or act as agents of coalitions. Factionalism also emerges when the party lacks the personnel or institutional leadership to restrain the autonomy of sponsors and candidates. Generational differences among leaders, rivalrous camps of ambitious candidates or liberal-conservative splits (deriving from the national level of the parties) further the cause of factionalism. Legislative district recruitment and campaigns are often insulated from statewide campaigns, which also reinforces the autonomy and separatism of factions.

The importance of interest groups in the Oregon legislature is consonant with the active role they play as sponsors of candidates. The major lobbies are three: the Associated Oregon Industries (AOI), an aggregate of major businesses and industries, and the AFL-CIO lobby which pulls together most labor unions. Government and social services, which include local governments, education and health lobbies, make up

---

[10] Wayne L. Francis, *Legislative Issues in the Fifty States* (Chicago: Rand McNally), p. 45.
[11] Ziegler and Baer, *Lobbying,* p. 103.

the third major group.[12] Ziegler and Baer also found that in Oregon legislators worked more closely with lobbyists than in any of three other states they studied. Oregon legislators were more favorably disposed toward lobbyists and often solicited their assistance. Lobbyists played an active role in initiating legislation, planning the strategy of its enactment and in persuading other legislators to support it. Oregon legislators acknowledge the influence of lobbyists.[13]

[12] This tabulation shows the proportionate distribution of lobbies in 1971. We have no reason to think that the figures were substantially different in the year of our study or before. (Source: Pierce, Frey, and Pengelly, *The Freshman Legislator,* p. 15.)

Professional & Labor	19%	
Professional Associations		8%
Employee–Labor Groups		11
Business & Industry	58%	
Insurance & Banking		12
Misc. Business Associations		10
Agriculture & Farm Products		8
Travel & Recreation		7
Utilities		4
Misc. Businesses		10
Lumber & Paper		3
Construction		2
Gas & Oil		2
Other Business Services		1
Government & Social Services	23%	
Local Governments		4
Citizen & Charitable Groups		12
Health		2
Education		4

[13] The following table illustrates the comparative influence of lobbyists in the Oregon legislature.

Percentage of Legislators and Lobbyists
Interacting for "Influence" Services*

	Influencing Other Legislators	Mobilizing Public Support	Participating in Planning Strategy	(N)
Massachusetts				
Legislators	11%	17	17	(244)
Lobbyists	22%	38	36	(175)
North Carolina				
Legislators	25%	27	39	(164)
Lobbyists	51%	65	73	(132)
Oregon				
Legislators	53%	32	65	(84)
Lobbyists	55%	46	64	(193)
Utah				
Legislators	46%	45	42	(70)
Lobbyists	68%	65	73	(134)

*Percentages of respondents who "frequently" or occasionally request (or are requested to perform) a service.
Source: Ziegler and Baer, *Lobbying,* p. 103.

Interest cleavages in the legislature mirror the importance of party faction and interest groups in the recruitment process. In other words, the principal actors in the recruitment process are also the principal actors in the legislative process. The muted importance of partisan cleavages contrasts sharply with states where party cohesion in the legislature reflects the active role that party organizations play in the recruitment of candidates.

Given such congruence between recruitment and legislative cleavage in Oregon, what is the role of the individual legislator? We emphasize the legislator's relations with his recruitment sponsors because they are important to the legislator's future career. In general, a legislator's influence varies with his seniority. Yet, few first-term legislators will move up or on to other public offices. A study of the sixty legislators elected to the lower house in 1961 showed that only 28 percent, or seventeen members, went on to other public offices, including the State Senate, statewide offices, the U.S. Congress or important municipal or county offices.[14] Thus, the prospects for advancement from the State House of Representatives are not very great. The first-term legislator must rely on the sponsorship coalition that elected him because they might well be responsible for his reelection, or his defeat, should he not perform as expected.

The rookie legislator usually finds the first session a great disappointment. There is usually some shock when the rookie discovers that the first-term legislator has little influence. Optimistic and enthusiastic, the rookie legislator is quickly overwhelmed by constraining routines, customs and the hierarchical structure. The freshman legislators must therefore devote a good deal of time to consolidate their position with both their sponsors and constituents, on whom their future influence in the legislature depends. The more vulnerable the rookie and the more powerless he feels, the more concerned he will be with strengthening his position with his sponsors and bolstering their influence as lobbyists or with lobbyists. In sum, the pattern of recruitment is congruent with the faction and lobby-oriented legislature. Recruitment processes train interest-brokers, whose background and selection experience induce such an orientation to legislative tasks.

THE ELITE ROLE-CULTURE AND THE POLITICAL CULTURE

Observing recruitment processes for the first time and during one election made it seem to us at times as if the recruitment of state legis-

[14] Pierce, Frey, and Pengelly, *The Freshman Legislator*, p. 34.

lators were occurring for the first time. We realize however that we were observing a regular process that had considerable historical continuity. The patterns of interaction we detected had been going on for some time because the social and economic cleavages and their translation into politics were deeply rooted and structured in each of the four types of districts. The political opportunities, risks and sponsorship patterns characteristic of each district type were well established. The legislators chosen by the recruitment process are socialized in special ways and produce a characteristic elite role-culture.

We have called that elite role-culture a *citizen legislature* in contrast to a *professional* state legislature. Such a role-culture arises from four factors: (1) the continuity of social background of legislators within districts and collectively among all districts, (2) the legislator's orientation toward representing particular interests which makes for a bargaining disposition in legislative decision-making, (3) the legislators position as a part-time job, with modest salaries, and little expectation of political advancement, all of which closes the social distance between the legislators and the electorate, and (4) the legislature operates with high degree of consensus and bipartisan bargaining. We shall elaborate on this elite role-culture and compare it with the political culture of the state.

Considerable continuity exists in the composition of the legislative elite. The same occupations—farmers, businessmen, and professionals—that produced Oregon legislators in the past continue to do so today. Legislators are today, as they have been, members of the middle class of Oregon's many medium-sized and small towns—a class which is especially salient in Oregon because the state has less extreme wealth and poverty than most states.[15] Almost all legislators are college-educated and are ethnically homogeneous. Those who represent Portland, the largest metropolitan area, do not differ too much in character from those elected from other parts of the state. Therefore, there is a high degree of cultural affinity among the Oregon legislators.

Members of the legislative elite may be regarded as amateur politicians. Their social status, occupational background and their transitory role in the legislature have not produced a sense of professionalism. The proportion of legislators who have had prior governmental experience is substantially less in Oregon than in Utah, Massachusetts, or North Carolina.[16] Legislators do not enter the legislature either as policy experts or as technicians. They acquire expertness as a result of service on

---

[15] Supra, Ch. III, Oregon Politics: The Eve of the Campaign.
[16] Ziegler and Baer, *Lobbying*, p. 13.

committees and their interaction with lobbyists. The legislature is closer in spirit to a citizens assembly of popularly elected public leaders.

The attitudes political elites have toward the need to solve conflicts by compromise rather than combat are an important component of an elite role-culture. As Daalder states: "Such attitudes are deeply rooted in the political culture ... traditional leadership styles ... the traumatic memory of past conflicts ... a realistic sense of what can be reached through political action and what not, the presence of substantial or imaginary common interests, the extent to which party leaders are more tolerant than their followers and are yet able to carry them along—all are important."[17]

A strong disposition prevails to settle conflicts by compromise among Oregon legislators. With few exceptions, Oregon legislators are not ideologists, nor do they interact along ideological or partisan lines. The interactions among lobbyists and legislators are fluid. The impression that is created is that of a club for interaction and exchange, made possible by a high degree of agreement about the rules of the game and a sense of affinity.

The elite culture is a result of a process of recruitment which chooses, in most cases, representatives of particular interests. The brokers and agents outnumber the advocates. The logrolling of specific legislation and the appropriation processes are the consequences of interest-oriented legislators. The legislature deals with specifics—it parcels out particular benefits and particular costs in exchange for other benefits and costs for its members.

Oregon politics presents a strange contradiction. Despite the even strength of the parties in the state, the issues of state politics do not intensify the cleavages between the parties. For this reason, Oregon voters are notorious ticket-splitters, because voters fail to see party differences between interest-oriented legislators. Observing the important Ways and Means Committee, an experienced newspaper reporter recently stated: "The Republicans attack the Republican Governor's budget just about as often as the Democrats do."[18] Bipartisanship seems to permeate every aspect of Ways and Means Committee work because there is general agreement on how to approach budget decisions and that the personal values dominant in these decisions are not easily attributed to one party or the other.[19] Partisan politics for many years has been identified

---

[17] Hans Daalder, "Parties, Elites, and Political Developments in Western Europe," in Joseph LaPolombara and Myron Weiner, eds., *Political Parties and Political Development* (Princeton: Princeton University Press, 1966), p. 69.
[18] Cited in Pierce, Frey, and Pengelly, *The Freshman Legislator*, p. 45.
[19] Daniel Elazar, *American Federalism: A View From the States* (New York: Crowell, 1966), pp. 96–99.

with national office—the Presidency, the U.S. Senate, and the lower house of Congress—more than with state office and far more than with legislative and county offices. The parties oppose each other on national issues rather than on state issues.

When the parties are viewed in relation to national issues, the cleavages between the parties then become more evident. The Democratic party of Oregon, whose revival is a product of the New Deal and especially the Fair Deal, has remained faithful to the New and Fair Deal heritage. Throughout the fifties, Oregon Democrats ardently supported Adlai Stevenson. In the presidential primary of 1960, they preferred Hubert Humphrey to John Kennedy, because the former was regarded as more liberal. For the same reason, in 1968, Eugene McCarthy defeated Robert Kennedy in the Oregon Democratic presidential primary. And in the 1972 primary Oregon Democrats favored McGovern overwhelmingly over Humphrey and Jackson.

Since the end of World War II, the Republican party in Oregon has been primarily oriented toward the anti-isolationist, liberal, eastern wing of the Republican party. That party has divided between an isolationist, conservative wing and the aforementioned liberal wing. Republican factionalism has been less virulent than that of the Democratic party and the liberal wing has generally been dominant. Despite factionalism, both parties share in their adherence to a common political culture.

Daniel Elazar has suggested that American states may be classified into three political cultures: the individualistic, traditional and moralistic. He has characterized Oregon as a moralistic political culture. Such a culture stresses the commonwealth conception of government in which politics is a means for coming to grips with issues and public concerns. The commonwealth concept of politics is ideally a matter of concern to every citizen, not just for those who are professionally committed to political careers. In the moralistic culture, the politicians are expected to give overriding concern to serving the community rather than their loyalties to individuals, groups or political parties. There is more amateur participation than in the other political cultures. There is also less corruption in government and less tolerance of those actions which are considered corrupt.[20]

A political culture may be assessed at a particular moment but it is the product of historical continuity. Such continuity is particularly true in Oregon, a state whose growth from an agrarian to a moderately industrialized economy has left intact a dominant ethos of populism and suspicion of political elites, and a desire to preserve Oregon as an Arcadia in the United States.

[20] Ibid., pp. 96–99.

Oregon's political culture is a tradition, an ethos transmitted through generations by its political leadership. Like the north central states (Iowa, the Dakotas, Minnesota, Michigan, and Wisconsin) with which Oregon shares considerable cultural and historical affinity, Oregon's political culture was stamped by the settlement of Anglo-Saxons and northern Europeans from New England, the border states, and the Midwest. Three political movements left a deep impress on Oregon's development: Populism, Progressivism, and the New Deal–Fair Deal. Populism gave rise to Oregon's vigorous farm organizations and its heritage of opposition to industrial corporate power—the banks, railroads and private utility companies. Progressivism in Oregon brought the adoption of the direct primary but added also the initiative, referendum, and recall and institutionalized suspicion of the legislative elite and professional politicians. Progressivism also gave impetus to the public power movement which forged a farmer-labor alliance in the state until that issue expired in the 1960's. Finally, the New Deal and Fair Deal activated organized labor and revived the Democratic party, giving it a liberal character.

In all respects but one, Oregon fits Elazar's characterization of the moralistic political culture. Oregon legislators owe loyalty to the interests they represent, and serve as their brokers. Yet, they are deeply committed to an underlying loyalty as Oregonians, and share a common heritage. They serve the community as brokers of those with stakes in the community as a whole. The underlying consensus is prior to the interests in their claims.

To be sure, the term political culture has its ambiguities. It distorts the varieties and differences, not only of the present but also those that are being transformed and reformed. Our delineation of Oregon's political culture stems from our study and the actual experience of living there for some time.

The amateur brokers who are the state legislators and who work so closely with the lobbyists are committed to certain common values of the state as a whole. They are as follows: the preservation of Oregon's view of itself as pristine and uncorrupted. The desire of Oregon's leadership is not to allow the state to become like Southern California, which they regard as an anomic rabble, nor like the eastern states which they regard as money-grubbing and corrupt. Oregonians see their state as a haven of respectability and rectitude, a self-image they define more clearly by what they despise rather than by what they affirm. Oregon is an "ideology," a way of life bound up with maintaining an impression of civic consensus, and the maintenance of Oregon's distinctiveness, which is not for export. Oregon does not seek to exercise leadership among the other states. Oregon's leaders hold that they maintain inviolate a life-style that the rest of the United States, who they feel is obsessed with industrialization and growth, discarded some time ago.

Brokerage politics requires certain tacit agreements on values so that only "interests" need to be reconciled. Then, bargaining can come into play as the principal technique of reconciliation. In that light, Oregon's legislators, their role-culture, and the larger political culture are consistent.

As a type of democracy, Oregon is distinguishable from the larger and more highly industrialized and ethnically diverse states of the United States, whose social structure is divided more sharply both horizontally and vertically by status and ethnicity. When we extend this difference beyond the United States, then it seems that Oregon has some affinity with the Scandinavian countries as a type of democracy. The latter are characterized by a high degree of cultural homogeneity, the extensive organization of interests, and a belief in compromise as a method for the reconciliation of political differences. The Scandinavian democracies are also based on a deeply rooted social stratification and the suppression of latent conflicts, which erupt with surprise, as recent elections in Sweden, Norway and Denmark illustrate. As the Scandinavian systems are differentiated from such ethnically divided countries as the Netherlands and Belgium, which Lijphart has called consociational Democracies, so is Oregon distinguishable from many larger states in the United States.

Democracies of this type rest on a durable historical consensus, one manifestation of which is the recruitment of elected legislators who reflect the social and political structure.[21] We have tried to show that the recruitment of one segment of the political elite in Oregon exhibits various degrees and kinds of restrictiveness and "openness" that derive from the continuities of social and political structure in the various legislative districts.

[21] See Harry Eckstein, *Division and Cohesion in Democracy* (Princeton: Princeton University Press, 1966); Arend Lijphart, "Typologies of Democratic Systems," *Comparative Political Studies,* I (April, 1968), pp. 3–44. See also Val R. Lorwin, "Belgium: Religion, Class, Language and National Politics," found in Robert Dahl, ed., *Political Opposition in Western Democracies* (New Haven: Yale University Press, 1966), pp. 147–187; Val R. Lorwin, "Segmented Pluralism: Ideological Cleavage and Political Cohesion in the Smaller Democracies" *Comparative Politics,* LXXIII (January, 1971), pp. 141–177; Arend Lijphart, "Consociational Democracy" *World Politics,* XXI (January, 1969), pp. 207–225.

APPENDIX A

METHODOLOGY

THE SAMPLE AND SAMPLING PROCEDURES

Information concerning the interactions of recruitment, social and political background data, candidate perceptions, beliefs, and evaluations regarding their recruitment experiences, and reports of the consequences of involvement in campaigning were collected during three structured interviews with candidates for the lower house of the Oregon Legislature during the 1966 campaign. Respondents first were interviewed immediately prior to the primary election. Sixty-eight interviews were completed during this first wave. After the primary, 109 primary winners and losers were interviewed. Again after the general election, interviews were completed with 78 general election winners and losers. Considerations of cost forced us to adopt different sampling techniques for each panel of candidates. The interviewing was conducted between March and December, 1966.

The First Wave

All primary candidates in 14 of Oregon's 28 legislative districts were included in the preprimary panel. The interviews spanned the two months prior to the primary election on May 24, 1966. The districts were selected according to three criteria: (1) geographic region of the state, (2) level of urbanization, and (3) level of inter-party competition.

GEOGRAPHIC REGION OF THE STATE. The districts were selected to represent all relevant geographic regions of the state. Candidates from the Portland metropolitan area, the Willamette valley, coastal areas, Southern Oregon, East and Central Oregon were interviewed.

LEVEL OF URBANIZATION. We divided the districts evenly between those with a relatively large urban population and more rural areas.[1] All the major metropolitan areas of the Willamette valley were included as

[1] The measure of population used was the percent of the population residing in cities and towns of 2,500 or more residents. The districts were dichotomized at the median into "urban" and "rural" categories.

were districts representing each of the other, more rural regions of the state.

LEVEL OF INTER-PARTY COMPETITION. Districts were also chosen according to their level of inter-party competition. Approximately one-third of the districts sampled were competitive, while the remaining two-thirds were divided equally between those dominated by the Republican party and safe Democratic districts. Inter-party competition was measured for sampling purposes by tabulating general election outcomes over a four-election period (1958–1964) and the registration balance between the parties in the two elections immediately prior to 1966.[2]

This procedure yielded a sample of fourteen districts which gave balanced representation to region, urbanization, and party competition. In all, the first panel included 86 candidates; sixty-eight were successfully interviewed for a completion rate of approximately 80 percent.

The Second Wave

All candidates selected in the preprimary sample were included in the postprimary wave of interviews. In addition, the respondent list was expanded to include all primary *winners* in the remaining 14 legislative districts. The second wave, therefore, included the universe of primary winners and some primary losers from the original 14 districts. With the additional districts, the sample increased from 68 to 126 respondents. During the summer months following the primary election, 109 of the 126 respondents were interviewed, a completion rate of 87 percent.

The Third Wave

We intended to re-interview all general election candidates, winners and losers alike, after the November 8, 1966 general election. Our interviewers met with 78 of the 112 general election candidates, a success rate of 70 percent. The 78 respondents included 46 of the 60 general election winners and 32 of 52 losers.

THE INTERVIEW SCHEDULES

During the course of the three panels of interviews, four different interview schedules were used. We interviewed all respondents in the second and third waves using common, structured interview schedules. In the second panel, however, we were meeting some respondents for the first time, while others had been included in the first wave sample. This forced us to develop separate interview schedules for respondents from

---

[2] Registration figures were not available for the 1958 and 1960 elections.

the original 14 districts and for candidates from the rest of the districts not included in the preprimary panel. The differences between these two interview schedules were minimal; every effort was made to maximize the comparability of the data collected from the two groups.

The interview schedules elicited three types of information: (1) general background data such as occupation, income, education, subjective social class, age, sex, and parent's education and occupation, as well as prior political experience, party affiliation, organizational memberships and attendance, etc.; (2) data on the process of recruitment, including measures of the interaction patterns surrounding the initiation phase and sponsorship during the primary and general election campaigns; in addition, we asked candidates to tell us their perceptions of the importance of these interactions to their decision to run, their chances in the election, and their short and long range political goals; and (3) information about candidates' evaluations and perceptions of their election experiences and the effects of winning or losing on their political career goals, their regular occupation, income prestige, political influence and social relationships with friends and colleagues.

Each interview lasted approximately two hours. Over the three waves, up to six hours were spent with each candidate. The interview schedules were pretested on a sample of candidates for local office. The interviewers were primarily graduate students in political science at the University of Oregon. Each interviewer was schooled intensively for nearly four months before he commenced his interviews. The training included the theory which guided the study and the special problems and techniques of interviewing legislative candidates. Appendix B contains excerpts from the interview schedules relevant to this study.

INDEX AND SCALE CONSTRUCTION

Social Diversity, Economic Diversity, and Inter-Party Competition Factor Scores

PROCEDURE. Measures of median family income, percent of the work force engaged in industrial pursuits, median years of schooling attained, density and size of the population, religious affiliation, length of residence, geographic mobility, median age, intra- and inter-party competition were submitted to factor analysis and factor scores derived from the resulting economic diversity, social diversity and inter-party competition factors. The factor scores rank each of Oregon's legislative districts according to each of the three factors. An oblimin rotation using the biquartimin simplicity was employed to seek a simple structure solution.

RESULTS. Table 1 shows the rank of Oregon's representative districts on the three factors.

Intra-Party Competition Index

PROCEDURE. The measure of intra-party or primary competition was developed as follows: the number of candidates who filed in the primary in each of the representative districts were tallied for the 1958, 1960, 1962 and 1964 elections. This figure was divided by the number of primary election positions in the district times the number of elections. If, for example, a district elects one legislator, there are two primary positions at stake, one for each party's nominee. Over the course of the four elections, eight primary nominations were contested. If four candidates file in each election, the district's primary competitive score is 2.00.

$$\text{Intra-Party Competition Index} = \frac{\text{Number of primary candidates}}{\text{Number of primary positions}}$$
$$\times \text{Number of elections}$$

RESULTS. Table 2 gives the ranking of districts according to their degree of intra-party competition.

Classification of Patterns of Political Competition

PROCEDURE. The classification of representative districts into four patterns of political competition was developed by first dichotomizing the inter- and intra-party competition indices at their medians and then cross-tabulating them. This procedure yielded four groups of districts with competitive patterns we have labeled urban one-party, urban two-party, rural one-party, and rural two-party, in recognition of the close relationship between competitive patterns and population density. Urban one-party districts have little or no inter-party competition, but extensive intra-party competition. Urban two-party districts have competitive primary and general elections; rural two-party districts have competition only in the general election, and rural one-party districts have noncompetitive primary and general elections.

RESULTS. Table 3 shows the breakdown of Oregon's representative districts according to pattern of competition.

Indices of Perceived Personal Campaign Benefits and Costs

PROCEDURE. During each interview candidates were asked a number of questions whose responses could be interpreted as representing a cost or a benefit which accrues to candidacy or service in the State legis-

APPENDIX A–TABLE 1

Ranking of Oregon's Representative Districts According to Economic Diversity, Social Diversity, and Inter-Party Competition

Economic Diversity		Social Diversity		Inter-Party Competition	
District	*Factor Score*	*District*	*Factor Score*	*District*	*Factor Score*
Multnomah, North	323	Multnomah, West	432	Gilliam, Morrow, Sherman	314
Multnomah, At Large	320	Multnomah, At Large	430	Umatilla, Wheeler	313
Multnomah, East	318	Multnomah, South	406	Lane	313
Multnomah, South	318	Multnomah, East	402	Yamhill	294
Multnomah, East Central	314	Multnomah, East Central	399	Benton, Lane	292
Multnomah, West	314	Multnomah, North	378	Hood River, Wasco	289
Washington	269	Columbia	313	Tillamook	272
Benton	254	Lincoln	300	Coos	255
Benton, Lane	250	Hood River, Wasco	298	Baker, Grant	251
Clackamas	239	Tillamook	292	Jackson	229
Lane	227	Josephine	274	Linn	227
Marion	221	Clackamas	263	Clackamas	225
Jackson	203	Linn	260	Coos, Curry	216
Klamath	197	Marion	255	Marion	203
Klamath, Lake	174	Clatsop	237	Lincoln	178
Umatilla	167	Polk	235	Douglas	170
Gilliam, Morrow, Sherman		Douglas	228	Multnomah, At Large	159
Umatilla, Wheeler	160	Baker, Grant	226	Klamath, Lake	123
Clatsop	156	Jackson	200	Multnomah, East Central	119
Coos	141	Coos	198	Crook, Deschutes, Jefferson	116
Hood River, Wasco	129	Crook, Deschutes, Jefferson	195	Washington	110

APPENDIX A–TABLE 1 (Continued)

Economic Diversity		Social Diversity		Inter-Party Competition	
District	Factor Score	District	Factor Score	District	Factor Score
Coos, Curry	121	Gilliam, Morrow, Sherman, Umatilla, Wheeler	188	Umatilla	109
Union, Wallowa	111	Lane	188	Klamath	82
Crook, Deschutes, Jefferson	108	Umatilla	186	Multnomah, East	78
Polk	97	Coos, Curry	175	Polk	76
Yamhill	87	Harney, Malheur	171	Multnomah, South	70
Linn	69	Washington	166	Harney, Malheur	57
Douglas	67	Benton, Lane	146	Union, Wallowa	57
Baker, Grant	66	Klamath, Lake	146	Multnomah, West	46
Tillamook	47	Union, Wallowa	143	Multnomah, North	33
Josephine	38	Klamath	109	Clatsop	24
Harney, Malheur	37	Yamhill	22	Columbia	23
Lincoln	35	Benton	1	Benton	8
Columbia	1			Josephine	1

APPENDIX A–TABLE 2

Ranking of Oregon's Representative Districts
According to Intra-Party Competition

District	Intra-Party Competition Score
Multnomah, West Subdistrict	3.25
Multnomah, County At Large	2.82
Multnomah, South City Subdistrict	2.42
Multnomah, East County Subdistrict	2.17
Columbia	2.00
Josephine	2.00
Multnomah, East Central City Subdistrict	2.00
Multnomah, North City Subdistrict	2.00
Clackamas	1.93
Coos	1.75
Lincoln	1.75
Linn	1.75
Tillamook	1.75
Marion	1.62
Lane	1.60
Benton, Lane	1.50
Douglas	1.38
Hood River, Wasco	1.25
Klamath, Lake	1.25
Polk	1.25
Yamhill	1.25
Washington	1.17
Jackson	1.10
Baker Grant	1.00
Clatsop	1.00
Coos, Curry	1.00
Crook, Deschutes, Jefferson	1.00
Gilliam, Morrow, Sherman, Umatilla, Wheeler	1.00
Gilliam, Morrow, Sherman, Umatilla, Wheeler	1.00
Union, Wallowa	1.00
Benton	.75
Harney, Malheur	.75
Klamath	.75
Umatilla	.50

lature. There were 207 such items which were suitable for use (characteristic items are presented in Appendix B). Some respondents could not legitimately be expected to respond to certain items; therefore, the maximum number of benefits and costs that it was possible for a candidate to report varied with each individual. Each individual's score was converted so that it represented a position on a single interval scale for

APPENDIX A–TABLE 3

Classification of Oregon's Representative Districts According to Patterns of Political Competition

Primary: Noncompetitive *General:* Noncompetitive (*Rural One-Party Districts*)	*Primary:* Noncompetitive *General:* Competitive (*Rural Two-Party Districts*)	*Primary:* Competitive *General:* Noncompetitive (*Urban One-Party Districts*)	*Primary:* Competitive *General:* Competitive (*Urban Two-Party Districts*)
1. Benton	1. Baker, Grant	1. Columbia	1. Clackamas
2. Clatsop	2. Benton, Lane	2. Josephine	2. Coos
3. Crook Deschutes, Jefferson	3. Coos, Curry	3. Multnomah, East Cent.	3. Lane
4. Harney, Malheur	4. Douglas	4. Multnomah, East City	4. Lincoln
5. Klamath	5. Gilliam, Morrow, Sherman, Umatilla, Wheeler	5. Multnomah, North City	5. Linn
6. Klamath, Lake	6. Hood River, Wasco	6. Multnomah, South City	6. Marion
7. Polk	7. Jackson	7. Multnomah, West	7. Multnomah, At Large
8. Umatilla	8. Yamhill		8. Tillamook
9. Union, Wallowa			
10. Washington			

benefits and another one for costs. The formula for this computation was:

$$\frac{\text{Maximum Score Possible}}{\text{Respondent Maximum Possible}} \times \text{Each Respondent's Actual Score} = \text{Index for Each Respondent}$$

RESULTS. All perceived benefits and costs constitute an index for each dimension. The benefits scores range from 8.2 to 60.5, while the costs scores range from 3.3 to 51.0. For purposes of analysis in contingency tables, each set of scores was dichotomized into "high" and "low" categories.

A factor analysis of the cost index, the benefits index, and the minimum possible for each, resulted in two factors: one on which everything except costs loaded, and one consisting of the cost index only. Subsequent factor analyses using numerous additional variables still produced similar results: the costs index appeared on a separate factor. This suggests that the benefits score for each respondent is related to the number of questions that was asked of him, while the costs score is not related to the benefits score nor to the number of questions asked. One inference which might be drawn from this is that we were able to tap a salient dimension with our questions regarding costs, while we did not do so with the benefits. Another possibility is that the benefits dimension is considerably more vast in that particular political system and our questions failed to test the upper limits of this particular area. There seem to be some indications, in our analysis to date, that these are indeed separate dimensions, rather than costs being merely the negative aspect of benefits.

Scope of Political Eligibility Index

PROCEDURE. The scope of political eligibility index is a measure of the proportion of the adult population of a district which is effectively certified to run for legislative office by virtue of their sharing social, economic and political characteristics in common with individuals who have successfully become candidates in the past. From biographical data on legislators and legislative candidates we constructed social, political and economic background profiles of individuals who successfully became candidates from each district (i.e., those who were primary election candidates), on those who won the primary (i.e., general election candidates), and on general winners (i.e., those who successfully became legislators). The three profiles were compared with census breakdowns of each district to determine the number of adults who are effectively eligible for each phase of the recruitment process. The legislative profiles included occupation, religious affiliation, party identification, sex, length of residence, education, organizational membership, and county of residence.[3] We computed the percentage of the adult population which shared each characteristic, summed the percentages for all background characteristics, and then divided by the number of background characteristics. This procedure yields the average percent eligible, where each background factor is given equal weight.

Scope of effective eligibility =

$$\frac{\sum\limits_{i=1}^{N} \text{(percent eligible by characteristic)}}{N}$$

where: N = the number of background characteristics.

The components of the index were weighted equally because data indicating the separate impact of each were unavailable. Without such data, we cannot tell, for example, if it is Catholics or blue-collar workers who are being excluded from office in districts where most blue-collar workers are Catholic. By giving each background factor a weight, irrespective of its actual political impact on eligibility, our estimate of the number of effectively eligible citizens in a district is systematically biased downward. However, this bias is more than compensated because the number of effectively eligible citizens as determined by each component of the indices were added together without regard for overlap among the categories. Thus, the number of eligible Catholics was added to the number of eligible blue-collar workers without adjusting for the number of Catholics who have blue-collar occupations. Data simply were not available on the degree of overlap.

This last procedure systematically overestimates the number of effectively eligible citizens in a district. Even by this conservative measure, a substantial number of Oregon's legislative districts appear to be highly restrictive. In several instances, less than one percent of a district's adult population is effectively eligible for legislative office.

RESULTS. Table 4 gives the effective eligibility score of each district after filing, after the primary, and again after the general election. Districts are ranked according to their scores after the general election. Missing entries indicate where comprehensive information was not available to construct candidate background profiles.

[3] See Chapter VI for a detailed discussion of each of these measures.

APPENDIX A–TABLE 4

Size of the Pool of Citizens Who Are Effectively Eligible to
Run for Office, By Phase of Recruitment (As a Percent
of the Adult Population of the District)[4]

District	Initiation	Primary	General
Clackamas	....	42.7	42.1
Multnomah, East County Subdistrict	....	54.1	36.9
Multnomah, North City Subdistrict	54.7	48.1	32.7
Multnomah, County At Large	....	37.6	32.4
Gilliam, Morrow, Sherman, Umatilla Wheeler	32.5	32.5	31.9
Multnomah, East Central City Subdistrict	....	41.0	31.3
Lane	54.4	39.9	31.0
Multnomah, West Subdistrict	61.1	43.6	30.1
Jackson	....	40.7	29.1
Crook, Deschutes, Jefferson	30.0	30.0	28.3
Linn	35.7	35.7	27.0
Hood River, Wasco	....	....	25.7
Benton, Lane	26.7	26.7	25.3
Marion	41.0	33.4	22.1
Multnomah, South City Subdistrict	....	24.3	21.4
Klamath	21.3	21.3	21.3
Tillamook	....	26.3	20.9
Douglas	24.6	24.6	20.7
Washington	....	21.7	19.1
Baker, Grant	20.3	20.3	18.7
Lincoln	....	32.7	18.3
Coos	17.0	17.0	17.0
Umatilla	15.3	15.3	15.3
Union, Wallawa	11.4	11.4	11.4
Klamath, Lake	12.1	12.1	11.3
Columbia	32.3	20.7	10.1
Coos, Curry	13.1	13.1	10.0
Harney, Malheur	22.7	22.7	9.4
Clatsop	....	8.9	8.9
Josephine	23.6	23.6	8.0
Polk	16.1	12.7	5.4
Benton	.1	.1	.1

[4] Yamhill county does not appear in this table because background data were unavailable on the candidates. Both candidates refused to be interviewed.

Support for the Democratic Rules of Competition Scale

PROCEDURE. The scale is designed to measure a candidate's degree of support for the norms of recruitment and electoral competition. The scale was constructed from responses to the following interview items:

In general, do you feel that the legal requirements in getting elected in the general election give each candidate the same chance of winning, or do some candidates have an advantage?

In general, do you feel that the practical requirements in getting elected in the general election give each candidate the same chance of winning, or do some candidates have an advantage?

In running for office in this district, do you believe that a person can succeed primarily on the basis of ability and initiative, or are other things important for success in politics? Is this the way it should be?

RESULTS. Responses to these three questions were cumulatively scored to form a Guttman scale. The scale scores range from zero to three points and the distribution of scores is as follows:

	Frequencies:	
	Primary Election	General Election
Scale Score:	Candidates	Candidates
0	8	0
1	2	6
2	35	33
3	64	38
Totals	109	77

Index of Perceived Reward-Cost

PROCEDURE. This index measures the extent to which a candidate perceives rewards or costs as a result of his election outcome. It is constructed from responses to the following nine interview questions:

As a consequence of the election, do you anticipate any change in your job?

As a consequence of the election, do you anticipate any change in your circle of close friends?

Do you anticipate a change in your income as a consequence of the election?

Do you feel that your esteem among members of your religion has gone up or down?

Do you feel that your esteem among your colleagues in your occupation has gone up or down?

Do you feel that your esteem among your neighbors has gone up or down?

Do you feel that your esteem in your family has gone up or down?

Do you expect that your loss (or victory) in the election will help or hinder your chances if you decide to run again for the House?

Do you feel that your political influence has increased or decreased as a result of the election outcome?

Responses to these items were recoded into a simple postive/negative dichotomy, e.g., helped my job or hindered my job, gained more friends or lost some friends, enhanced my esteem or damaged my esteem. Each candidate who mentioned positive and/or negative responses was assigned a score derived from the arithmetic sum of his recoded responses. The scores range between +9 and −9.

RESULTS. For the purpose of analysis, five levels of perceived reward-cost were established on the basis of these scores. The distribution of the respondents is as follows:

APPENDIX A–TABLE 5

Amount of Perceived Reward-Cost	*Scale Scores*	*Frequencies*	
		Primary Election Candidates	General Election Candidates
Large Reward	+5 or above	13	16
Moderate Reward	+2, +3, +4	34	29
Little or No Reward	+1, 0	59	26
Some Cost	−1, −2, −3	3	6
Large Cost	−4 or smaller	0	0
Totals		109	77

APPENDIX B

SAMPLE QUESTIONNAIRE ITEMS

Respondent No. _____

Interviewer No. _____

(To be filled prior to interview)

District #_____   Position #_____

Sex: M   F

Party Affiliation: Rep. _____   Dem. _____   Indep. _____

Race: Cauc. _____   Neg. _____   Orient. _____   Ind. _____

Date: _____

Introduction (Read):

    This interview is part of a research project on Oregon politics being conducted by the Political Science Department of the University of Oregon. As part of this project, candidates of both parties are being asked questions concerning certain characteristics of their districts, the primary election, their campaigns, their feelings about politics in general, and their political plans in light of the primary results.

    The information received is held in strictest confidence. No names will be used in the results of the study. If any of these results are published, they will appear only in scientific journals or books.

    Each candidate who participates will receive copies of the results of the study as soon as they are available. The interview itself lasts no more than 90 minutes.

(Read)   First, I'd like to ask some general background questions.

001 What is your age?
    ( ) 0. NR   ( ) 4. 46–55
    ( ) 1. 25 or younger   ( ) 5. 56–65
    ( ) 2. 26–35   ( ) 6. 66 or older
    ( ) 3. 36–45

002 Where are you now residing?   (Read list below)
    ( ) 0. NR   ( ) 4. Rural, non-farm
    ( ) 1. City   ( ) 5. Farm
    ( ) 2. Suburb   ( ) 6. Other (specify)
    ( ) 3. Small town

003 Where did you spend the major part of the first twenty years of your life?
    ( ) 0. NR   ( ) 4. Farm
    ( ) 1. City or suburb ( ) 5. Other (specify)
    ( ) 2. Small town
    ( ) 3. Rural, non-farm

004 Where were you born?
    ( ) 0. NR
    ( ) 1. Oregon
    ( ) 2. Washington
    ( ) 3. California
    ( ) 4. Other western states
    ( ) 5. Midwestern states
    ( ) 6. Eastern states
    ( ) 7. Southern states
    ( ) 8. Other country (specify)

005 (If "8" on 004)   How long have you lived in this country?
    ( ) 0. NR
    ( ) 1. 0–2 yrs.
    ( ) 2. 3–5 yrs.
    ( ) 3. 6–10 yrs.
    ( ) 4. 11–20 yrs.
    ( ) 5. 21–30 yrs.
    ( ) 6. 31–40 yrs.
    ( ) 7. 41 yrs. or more
    ( ) 8. Not applicable

006 How long have you lived in this state?
    ( ) 0. NR
    ( ) 1. 0–2 yrs.
    ( ) 2. 3–5 yrs.

( ) 3. 6–10 yrs.
( ) 4. 11–20 yrs.
( ) 5. 21–30 yrs.
( ) 6. 31–40 yrs.
( ) 7. 41 yrs. or more

007 How long have you lived in this district?
( ) 0. NR
( ) 1. 0–2 yrs.
( ) 2. 3–5 yrs.
( ) 3. 6–10 yrs.
( ) 4. 11–20 yrs.
( ) 5. 21–30 yrs.
( ) 6. 31–40 yrs.
( ) 7. 41 yrs. or more

008 What is the highest grade of school you have completed?
( ) 0. NR
( ) 1. Some grade school
( ) 2. Completed grade school
( ) 3. Some high school
( ) 4. Completed high school
( ) 5. Some college
( ) 6. Completed college
( ) 7. Advanced or professional degree
( ) 8. Other (trade school, business college, etc.) (specify)

009 (Ask only if attended college)   For what field did you study while in college?
( ) 0. NR
( ) 1. Professional (specify)
( ) 2. Technical (specify)
( ) 3. Social sciences (specify)
( ) 4. Arts and letters (specify)
( ) 5. Business
( ) 6. Military
( ) 7. Agriculture
( ) 8. Other (specify)
( ) 9. Not applicable

010 What is your usual occupation?
( ) 0. NR
( ) 1. Lawyer
( ) 2. Other professional

( ) 3. Small business
( ) 4. Executive—managerial
( ) 5. Other white-collar
( ) 6. Blue-collar—skilled
( ) 7. Blue-collar—unskilled
( ) 8. Farm
( ) 9. Not applicable

011 What was your father's regular occupation or job? (Specify occupation *and* check appropriate category)

( ) 0. NR
( ) 1. Lawyer
( ) 2. Other professional
( ) 3. Small business
( ) 4. Executive—managerial
( ) 5. Other white-collar
( ) 6. Blue-collar—skilled
( ) 7. Blue-collar—unskilled
( ) 8. Farm
( ) 9. Other (specify)

012 What was the highest grade of school your father completed?
( ) 0. NR
( ) 1. Some grade school
( ) 2. Completed grade school
( ) 3. Some high school
( ) 4. Completed high school
( ) 5. Some college
( ) 6. Completed college
( ) 7. Advanced or professional degree
( ) 8. Other (trade school, business college, etc.) (specify)

013 Within which of the following income categories does your normal gross income fall?
( ) 0. NR
( ) 1. Under $3,000
( ) 2. $3,001–$5,000
( ) 3. $5,001–$8,000
( ) 4. $8,001–$10,000 (CARD)
( ) 5. $10,001–$15,000
( ) 6. $15,001–$25,000
( ) 7. $25,000 or more

014 If you were to place yourself in a social class, which of the following would best suit your current position?
( ) 0. NR   ( ) 4. Lower middle class
( ) 1. Upper class   ( ) 5. Working class
( ) 2. Upper middle class ( ) 6. Lower class
( ) 3. Middle class

015 (If responded to 014) If you were to compare your social class with your parents', would yours be higher, about the same, or lower?
( ) 0. NR
( ) 1. Higher
( ) 2. About the same
( ) 3. Lower
( ) 4. Not applicable

016 If you were to compare your standard of living with your parents', would yours be higher, about the same, or lower?
( ) 0. NR
( ) 1. Higher
( ) 2. About the same
( ) 3. Lower

017 (If "higher" on question 016) To what do you attribute this change in standard of living?
( ) 0. NR   ( ) 5. Income
( ) 1. More education   ( ) 6. General rise in
( ) 2. Work harder   standard of living
( ) 3. Better opportunities ( ) 7. Other (specify)
( ) 4. Fortuitous circumstances

018 (If "lower" on question 016) To what do you attribute this change in standard of living?
( ) 0. NR   ( ) 5. Income
( ) 1. Less education   ( ) 6. Depression
( ) 2. Not as ambitious as parent ( ) 7. Other (specify)
( ) 3. Not as many opportunities ( ) 8. Not applicable
( ) 4. Bad luck

019 Do you have a religious preference?
( ) 0. NR
( ) 1. Yes
( ) 2. No

020 (If "yes" in 019)   What is your religious preference?
   ( ) 0. NR
   ( ) 1. Episcopalian
   ( ) 2. Lutheran
   ( ) 3. Presbyterian
   ( ) 4. Jewish
   ( ) 5. Methodist
   ( ) 6. Catholic
   ( ) 7. Congregational
   ( ) 8. Other (specify)

021 (If "yes" in 019)   How often do you attend services?
   ( ) 0. NR
   ( ) 1. Regularly
   ( ) 2. Often
   ( ) 3. Seldom
   ( ) 4. Never
   ( ) 5. Not applicable

022 What is your marital status?
   ( ) 0. NR
   ( ) 1. Married
   ( ) 2. Single
   ( ) 3. Divorced
   ( ) 4. Widowed
   ( ) 5. Separated

(Read)   Now I'd like to ask you some questions concerning your earlier contacts with politics.

023 Do you remember holding any elective or appointive offices while you were a student?
   ( ) 0. NR
   ( ) 1. Yes
   ( ) 2. No
   ( ) 3. Don't remember

024 (If "yes" on 023)   Which offices? Was it while you were in grade school, high school, or college?   (List and classify in chart below)
   ( ) 0. NR   (Highest educational level attained
   ( ) 9. Not applicable   _____)

List	G.S.	H.S.	College	Prof. or Graduate
1. _____				_____
2. _____				_____
3. _____				_____
4. _____				_____

025 Do you remember when you became *interested* in politics?
( ) 0. NR
( ) 1. High school or before
( ) 2. During college
( ) 3. After college
( ) 4. Don't remember
( ) 5. Other (specify)

026 (If responded to 025) What first interested you? (Check more than one if necessary)
( ) 0. NR
( ) 1. Particular issue (specify)
( ) 2. Political figure (specify)
( ) 3. Political event or crisis (specify)
( ) 4. Partisan competition (specify)
( ) 5. Other (specify)

027 Do you remember what sort of activity you engaged in when you first entered politics? (Check more than one if necessary)
( ) 0. NR
( ) 1. Attend political meetings
( ) 2. Work for party
( ) 3. Work for candidate
( ) 4. Speak publicly for party
( ) 5. Speak publicly for candidate
( ) 6. Hold party office
( ) 7. Hold public office
( ) 8. Other (specify)
( ) 9. Not applicable

028 Was anyone particularly influential in getting you to participate in politics?
( ) 0. NR
( ) 1. Yes
( ) 2. No
( ) 3. Other (specify)

029 (If "yes" on 028)   Who was it?
    (   ) 0. NR
    (   ) 1. Close friends—peer group (specify)
    (   ) 2. Close friends—non-peer group (specify)
    (   ) 3. Family
    (   ) 4. Business associates (specify)
    (   ) 5. Political activist (specify)
    (   ) 6. Teacher (specify)
    (   ) 7. Other (specify)
    (   ) 8. Not applicable

030 Over the years, how frequently have you participated in the following kinds of activities?   (Read list)

                                   Regularly Infreq. Never NR
    1. Donate money to a particular candidate
    2. Donate money to your party
    3. Work actively for your party
    4. Work actively for a particular candidate
    5. Speak publicly for your party
    6. Speak publicly for a particular candidate
    7. Hold a party office
    8. Hold a public office

031 Since you first entered politics, what has been the main thing that has prompted your participation? Have you been interested in working for your party, for certain types of issues, for the interest of certain groups, for certain individuals, or have other things been important?
    (   ) 0. NR
    (   ) 1. Party
    (   ) 2. Issues (specify)
    (   ) 3. Individuals (specify)
    (   ) 4. Groups (specify)
    (   ) 5. Other (specify)

032 How important to you personally is a political career?
    (   ) 0. NR
    (   ) 1. Very important
    (   ) 2. Moderately important
    (   ) 3. Moderately unimportant
    (   ) 4. Very unimportant

033 Have any of your relatives or members of your immediate family ever been in politics?
   ( ) 0. NR
   ( ) 1. Yes
   ( ) 2. No

034 (If "yes" to 033)   Who?   (Check more than one, if necessary)

( ) 0. NR	( ) 5. Uncle
( ) 1. Father	( ) 6. Aunt
( ) 2. Mother	( ) 7. Grandfather
( ) 3. Spouse	( ) 8. Grandmother
( ) 4. Child	( ) 9. Not applicable

035 (If specified relative(s) in 034)   In what type of political activities did he (or she) engage?   (Check appropriate activity and specify relation who performed it)

   ( ) 0. NR   Specify relative

   ( ) 1. Donate money to candidate   _____

   ( ) 2. Donate money to party   _____
   ( ) 3. Attend party or campaign
         meeting   _____
   ( ) 4. Work actively for a party
         or candidate   _____
   ( ) 5. Speak publicly for a party
         or candidate   _____

   ( ) 6. Hold a party office   _____

   ( ) 7. Hold public office   _____

   ( ) 8. Not applicable   _____

036 (If relative held an office)   What office was it?   (Specify office and relative)
   ( ) 0. NR
   ( ) 9. Not applicable

List office	Relative	When
1.		
2.		
3.		
4.		

037 (If relative held an office)   When was (he/she) in office?
(Specify above)
( ) 0. NR
( ) 9. Not applicable

038 How many times have you run for the Oregon House of Representatives including this election?

( ) 0. NR   ( ) 3. 3
( ) 1. 1   ( ) 4. 4
( ) 2. 2   ( ) 5. 5 or more

039 (If "2" or more on 038)   When did you run?   (Check more than
one if necessary)

( ) 0. NR   ( ) 5. 1958
( ) 1. 1950 or before   ( ) 6. 1960
( ) 2. 1952   ( ) 7. 1962
( ) 3. 1954   ( ) 8. 1964
( ) 4. 1956   ( ) 9. Not applicable

040 (If "2" or more on 038)   Have you ever been elected to the Oregon
House of Representatives?
( ) 0. NR
( ) 1. Yes
( ) 2. No
( ) 3. Not applicable

041 (If "yes" to 040)   In which election years did you win?

( ) 0. NR   ( ) 5. 1958
( ) 1. 1950 or before   ( ) 6. 1960
( ) 2. 1952   ( ) 7. 1962
( ) 3. 1954   ( ) 8. 1964
( ) 4. 1956   ( ) 9. Not applicable

042 Have you ever lost a legislative election?
( ) 0. NR
( ) 1. Yes
( ) 2. No

043 (If "yes" on 042)   Did losing help or hinder your chances when
you ran again?
( ) 0. NR
( ) 1. Helped
( ) 2. Hindered
( ) 3. Neither
( ) 9. Not applicable

044 (If "helped" on question 043)   If losing helped, why?
( ) 0. NR
( ) 1. Name familiarity
( ) 2. Experience
( ) 3. Helped occupation
( ) 4. Brought public attention to issues he supported
( ) 5. Other (specify)
( ) 9. Not applicable

045 (If "hindered" on question 043)   If losing hindered, why?
( ) 0. NR
( ) 1. Branded as a "loser"
( ) 2. Poor showing at polls
( ) 3. Financial strain
( ) 4. Lost friends and acquaintances
( ) 5. Other (specify)
( ) 9. Not applicable

046 Have you ever held a public office other than a legislative seat?
( ) 0. NR
( ) 1. Yes
( ) 2. No

047 (If "yes" on question 046)   What sort of an office was it?   (Specify and check appropriate category)

Office(s):

	Elective	Appointive
National level	( ) 1	( ) 2
State level	( ) 3	( ) 4
Local level	( ) 5	( ) 6

( ) 0. NR
( ) 9. Not applicable

048 Have you ever lost an election for a public office other than a legislative seat?
( ) 0. NR
( ) 1. Yes
( ) 2. No

049 (If yes on 048)   Did losing help or hinder your chances when you ran for the legislature?
( ) 0. NR

( ) 1. Helped
( ) 2. Neither helped nor hindered
( ) 3. Hindered
( ) 9. Not applicable

050 (If "helped" on question 049)   If losing helped, why?
( ) 0. NR
( ) 1. Name familiarity
( ) 2. Experience
( ) 3. Helped occupation
( ) 4. Brought public attention to issues he supported
( ) 5. Other (specify)
( ) 6. Not applicable

051 (If "hindered" on question 049)   If losing hindered, why?
( ) 0. NR
( ) 1. Branded as a "loser"
( ) 2. Poor showing at polls
( ) 3. Financial strain
( ) 4. Lost friends and acquaintances
( ) 5. Other (specify)
( ) 6. Not applicable

062 Before you made your final decision to run for the legislature this
time, did any of the formal or informal organizations of your party
encourage you to run?
( ) 0. NR
( ) 1. Yes
( ) 2. No
( ) 3. Party encouraged candidate *not* to run
( ) 4. Don't know

065 Did any of the formal or informal organizations of your party
actually support you in the primary race?
( ) 0. NR
( ) 1. Yes
( ) 2. No

069 Before you made your final decision to run for the legislature this
time, did any organizations other than the party encourage you to
run?
( ) 0. NR
( ) 1. Yes
( ) 2. No

224

( ) 3. Other organization encouraged candidate *not* to run
( ) 4. Don't know

072 Did any organization other than the party actually support you in the primary race?
( ) 0. NR
( ) 1. Yes
( ) 2. No

076 Before you made your final decision to run for the legislature this time, did any important individuals in the district or the state encourage you to run?
( ) 0. NR
( ) 1. Yes
( ) 2. No
( ) 3. Important individuals encouraged candidate *not* to run
( ) 4. Don't know

079 Did any important individuals in the district or the state actually support you in the primary race?
( ) 0. NR
( ) 1. Yes
( ) 2. No

083 Which of the things you have mentioned was the most important in your decision to run in the primary this time?
( ) 0. NR
( ) 1. Party organizations (specify)
( ) 2. Other organizations (specify)
( ) 3. Close friends (specify)
( ) 4. Important individuals (specify)
( ) 5. Personal interests (specify)
( ) 6. Family
( ) 7. National political situation (specify)
( ) 8. Specific issues (specify)
( ) 9. Other (specify)

084 (If opposed in primary)   Whose support was most helpful in the primary race?
( ) 0. NR
( ) 1. Party organizations (specify)
( ) 2. Other organizations (specify)
( ) 3. Close friends (specify)
( ) 4. Important individuals (specify)

( ) 5. Family
( ) 9. Not applicable

109 What would you say is the natural next step, as far as political offices are concerned, for an incumbent from this district who wants to continue his political career?
( ) 0. NR
( ) 1. State Senate
( ) 2. Secretary of State
( ) 3. Local office (specify)
( ) 4. Attorney General
( ) 5. Governor
( ) 6. U.S. House of Representatives
( ) 7. U.S. Senate
( ) 8. Other (specify)

110 Realistically speaking, how far can someone starting as a legislator from this district hope to go in his political career? What is the highest political office possible?
( ) 0. NR
( ) 1. State Senate
( ) 2. Secretary of State
( ) 3. Local office (specify)
( ) 4. Attorney General
( ) 5. Governor
( ) 6. U.S. House of Representatives
( ) 7. U.S. Senate
( ) 8. Other (specify)

113 In general, do you feel that the legal requirements in getting elected in the primary give each candidate the same chance of winning, or do some candidates have an advantage? In the general election?

primary election   *general election*
( ) 0. NR   ( ) 0.
( ) 1. All candidates have equal chance   ( ) 1.
( ) 2. Some candidates have a   ( ) 2.
     moderate advantage
( ) 3. Some candidates have a   ( ) 3.
     decisive advantage

114 (If opposed in primary) Would you say that the legal requirements in getting elected in the primary put you at a disadvantage or advantage as compared with the other candidates? In the general election? (If won primary)

primary election	*general election*
( ) 0. NR	( ) 0.
( ) 1. Great advantage	( ) 1.
( ) 2. Slight advantage	( ) 2.
( ) 3. Neither advantage nor disadvantage	( ) 3.
( ) 4. Slight disadvantage	( ) 4.
( ) 5. Great disadvantage	( ) 5.
( ) 6. Unopposed in primary	( ) 6. Lost primary

115 In general, do you feel that the practical requirements in getting elected in the primary gave each candidate the same chance of winning, or do some candidates have an advantage? In the general election?

primary election	*general election*
( ) 0. NR	( ) 0.
( ) 1. All candidates have equal chance	( ) 1.
( ) 2. Some candidates have a moderate advantage	( ) 2.
( ) 3. Some candidates have a decisive advantage	( ) 3.

116 (If opposed in primary)   Would you say that the practical requirements in getting elected in the primary put you at a disadvantage or advantage as compared with the other candidates? In the general election?   (If won primary)

primary election	*general election*
( ) 0. NR	( ) 0.
( ) 1. Great advantage	( ) 1.
( ) 2. Slight advantage	( ) 2.
( ) 3. Neither advantage nor disadvantage	( ) 3.
( ) 4. Slight disadvantage	( ) 4.
( ) 5. Great disadvantage	( ) 5.
( ) 6. Unopposed in primary	( ) 6.

126 Win or lose, after the campaign do you think that it is appropriate to publicly expose any malpractices your opponents might have committed, or would it be better to let such things go and remain silent?
( ) 0. NR
( ) 1. Point out infractions
( ) 2. Remain silent
( ) 3. Other (specify)

227

127 As a consequence of the election, have you changed your membership in any groups or organizations?
( ) 0. NR
( ) 1. Yes
( ) 2. No

128 (If "yes" to 127)   How?   (Check more than one if necessary)
( ) 0. NR
( ) 1. Joined new group(s) (specify)
( ) 2. Quit participating in old group(s) (specify)
( ) 3. Other (specify)
( ) 4. Not applicable

129 (If "yes" to 127)   Why has your group membership changed?
( ) 0. NR
( ) 1. Candidate no longer has desire to participate
( ) 2. Candidate was asked to leave group
( ) 3. Candidate was asked to join group
( ) 4. Candidate actively attempted to increase group membership
( ) 5. Other (specify)
( ) 6. Not applicable

130 As a consequence of the election, has there been any change in your circle of close friends?
( ) 0. NR
( ) 1. No
( ) 2. Yes, broader—same type
( ) 3. Yes, broader—higher status
( ) 4. Yes, broader—lower status
( ) 5. Yes, narrower—same type
( ) 6. Yes, narrower—higher status
( ) 7. Yes, narrower—lower status

132 As a consequence of the election, has there been any change in your job? Have you received a promotion, changed jobs, etc.?
( ) 0. NR
( ) 1. Yes
( ) 2. No

136 Have you experienced a change in income as a consequence of the election?
( ) 0. NR
( ) 1. No

( ) 2. Yes, direct consequence

( ) 3. Yes, indirect consequence

140 Have you changed your residence as a consequence of the election?

( ) 0. NR

( ) 1. Yes

( ) 2. No

144 (If opposed in primary)   Did you expect to win or lose the primary election?

( ) 0. NR

( ) 1. Excellent chance of winning

( ) 2. Good chance of winning

( ) 3. Average chance of winning

( ) 4. Small chance of winning

( ) 5. Expected not to win

( ) 6. Unopposed in primary

147 (If opposed in general election)   Did your showing in the primary help or hinder your chances in the general election?

( ) 0. NR

( ) 1. Helped

( ) 2. No effect

( ) 3. Hindered

( ) 4. Unopposed in the general election

( ) 5. Other (specify)

148 (Primary winners only)   How do you think you will do in the general election as compared with your opponent?

( ) 0. NR

( ) 1. Excellent chance of winning

( ) 2. Good chance of winning

( ) 3. Average chance of winning

( ) 4. Small chance of winning

( ) 5. Probably will not win

( ) 6. Not applicable

( ) 7. Unopposed in general election

149 Do you wish to continue your political career (if you are defeated in the general election)?   (For winners only)

( ) 0. NR

( ) 1. Yes

( ) 2. No

( ) 3. Undecided

154 (If "yes" or "undecided" to 149)   What is the highest political office you would like to achieve in your political career?   (Specify and check appropriate category)   Office _____

			Elective	Appointive
National level	( ) 0. NR		( ) 1.	( ) 2.
State level	( ) 7. None		( ) 3.	( ) 4.
Local level	( ) 8. Not applicable		( ) 5.	( ) 6.

155 Do members of your occupation view you more favorably or less favorably as a consequence of your victory?
( ) 0. NR
( ) 1. More favorably
( ) 2. About the same
( ) 3. Less favorably
( ) 4. Don't know
( ) 5. Not applicable
( ) 6. No views on subject

159 Would you say that your overall experience in politics has helped or hindered you in your occupation?
( ) 0. NR
( ) 1. Helped greatly
( ) 2. Helped moderately
( ) 3. No effect
( ) 4. Hindered moderately
( ) 5. Hindered greatly

162 In your opinion, are there risks of any sort involved in running for the legislature?
( ) 0. NR
( ) 1. Yes
( ) 2. No

163 (If "yes" on 162)   What are the risks?   (Check more than one if necessary)
( ) 0. NR
( ) 1. Chance of defeat
( ) 2. Chance of losing money invested in campaign
( ) 3. Chance of suffering loss of status
( ) 4. Chance of setback in occupation
( ) 5. Other (specify)
( ) 6. Not applicable

174 (If opposed in primary)   What was the most important problem
   you faced in the primary campaign?
   ( ) 0. NR
   ( ) 1. Lack of political experience
   ( ) 2. Gaining support of party
   ( ) 3. Gaining support of groups
   ( ) 4. Lack of finances
   ( ) 5. Gaining name familiarity
   ( ) 6. Other (specify)
   ( ) 7. Not applicable

178 (If opposed in primary)   What are the major reasons why you won
   the primary election?
   ( ) 0. NR
   ( ) 9. Not applicable
   self: ( ) 1. Personal characteristics (specify)
            ( ) 2. Tactical moves by candidate (specify)
            ( ) 3. Candidate's religion
            ( ) 4. Candidate's social class
            ( ) 5. Candidate's background
            ( ) 6. Age
            ( ) 7. Sex
            ( ) 8. Family
            ( ) 9. Marital status
            ( ) 10. Other (specify)
   other: ( ) 11. Characteristics of other candidates (abilities, etc.)
                   (specify)
            ( ) 12. Tactics of other candidates (smear campaigns,
                   etc.) (specify)
            ( ) 13. Well organized or enthusiastic supporters
            ( ) 14. Composition of district (specify)
            ( ) 15. Strong party support
            ( ) 16. Issues (specify)
            ( ) 17. Adequate (or better) finances
            ( ) 18. National political circumstances (Vietnam, etc.)
            ( ) 19. Attribute of system (good turnout, well-informed
                   voter, etc.)
            ( ) 20. Fate or luck
            ( ) 21. Other (specify)

Respondent No. _____   Respondent Name _____

Interviewer No. _____

(To be filled in prior to interview)

District #_____   Position #_____

Sex: M   F

Party Affiliation: Rep. _____   Dem. _____   Indep. _____

Race: Cauc. _____   Neg. _____   Orient. _____   Ind. _____

General Election Outcome: Won _____   Lost _____

Date: _____

Introduction Outline.   Opening Format Should Contain:
1. Your name
2. Sponsored by Dr. Seligman, Political Science, U. of O.
3. Continuation of previous studies
4. Confidential
5. Professional journals
6. Mailbacks
7. 30 minutes
8. Any questions?

(Read)   The first questions are concerned with the general election campaign.

001 If unopposed in general election: Since you were unopposed in the general election, did you conduct a campaign?
( ) 0. NR
( ) 1. Yes
( ) 2. No
( ) 9. Not applicable
        If "no" on Question 001, go on to Question 019 and check not applicable.
        If "yes" on Question 001, go on to Question 002.

002 Did any of your close friends support you in the general election race?
( ) 0. NR
( ) 1. Yes
( ) 2. No

003 (If "yes" on 002)   Which ones?   (Get positions and, if possible, names, then list and classify below)
( ) 0. NR
( ) 9. Not applicable

List:		*Type of Support*					*Importance of Support*			
Name	Position	Fin.	Advice	Manp.	Other	NR	V.I.	Imp.	U.I.	NR
1.										
2.										
3.										
4.										
5.										

Classify (place response #s from above in chart below):

	Type of Support					*Importance of Supp.*			
	Fin.	Advice	Manp.	Other	NR	V.I.	Imp.	U.I.	NR
1. Neighbor									
2. Work associate									
3. Local party leader									
4. State party leader									
5. Local office holder									
6. State office holder									
7. Local businessman									
8. Local labor leader									
9. Other									

004 (If "yes" on 002)   What kind of support did (name) give?   (Ask for each person named and check appropriate category in above chart)
( ) 9. Not applicable

005 (If "yes" on 002)   How important was (name's) support?   (Ask for each person named and check appropriate category in above chart)
( ) 9. Not applicable

006 Did any of the formal or informal organizations of your party support you in the general election campaign?
( ) 0. NR
( ) 1. Yes
( ) 2. No

007 (If "yes" on 006)   Which ones?   (Classify below)
( ) 0. NR
( ) 9. Not applicable

	Type of Support					*Importance of Supp.*			
	Fin.	Advice	Manp.	Other	NR	V.I.	Imp.	U.I.	NR
1. County cent. committee									
2. Formal state party organ. (specify)									
3. Young Repubs. or Demos.									

4. Women's partisan
   organ. (specify)
5. Local candidate
   committee (specify)
6. State candidate
   committee (specify)
7. Other (specify)

008 (If "yes" on 006)   What kind of support did (organization) give?
(Ask for each organization named and check appropriate category
in above chart)
( ) 9. Not applicable

009 (If "yes" on 006)   How important was (organization's) support?
(Ask for each organization named and check appropriate category
in above chart)
( ) 9. Not applicable

010 Did any organization other than the party support you in the general election campaign?
( ) 0. NR
( ) 1. Yes
( ) 2. No

016 (If "yes" on 014)   What kind of support did (name) give?   (Ask for
each person named and check appropriate category in above chart)
( ) 9. Not applicable

017 (If "yes" on 014)   How important was (name's) support?   (Ask for
each person named and check appropriate category in above chart)
( ) 9. Not applicable

018 (If opposed in general election)   Of all your supporters, which
individual or group's support was most helpful in the general election campaign?
( ) 0. NR
( ) 1. Party organization's (specify)
( ) 2. Other organization's (specify)
( ) 3. Close friend's (specify)
( ) 4. Important individual's (specify)
( ) 5. Family's
( ) 6. Mass media's (specify)
( ) 9. Not applicable

(Read)   Now I would like to ask you some general questions about your
feelings concerning politics in Oregon, based on your experience in this campaign.

019 As a practical matter, do you feel that everyone in Oregon has the same chance of becoming a legislative candidate, or do some individuals or groups have an advantage? (Although we know that legally all a person must do is pay his money and file, we find that in some districts, certain types of people are at a disadvantage in becoming a candidate, because they do not have time to spend on politics. In other districts, everyone has a pretty equal chance.) What's the situation in this district?

( ) 0. NR
( ) 1. Everyone has equal chance
( ) 2. Everyone has a moderately equal chance
( ) 3. Some groups or individuals have decided advantage
( ) 4. Other (specify)

020 In general, do you feel that the legal requirements in getting elected in the general election give each candidate the same chance of winning, or do some candidates have an advantage? (Examples of legal requirements: restrictions on finances, residence, age, the position numbering system, etc.)

( ) 0. NR
( ) 1. All candidates have equal chance
( ) 2. Some candidates have a moderate advantage
( ) 3. Some candidates have a decided advantage

021 (If opposed in general election) Would you say that the legal requirements in getting elected in the general election put you at a disadvantage or advantage as compared with your opponent?

( ) 0. NR
( ) 1. Great advantage
( ) 2. Slight advantage
( ) 3. Neither advantage nor disadvantage ·
( ) 4. Slight disadvantage
( ) 5. Great disadvantage
( ) 6. Unopposed in general election

022 In general, do you feel that the practical requirements in getting elected in the general election give each candidate the same chance of winning, or do some candidates have an advantage? (Examples of practical requirements: name familiarity, financial backing, ability, contacts, prestige, etc.)

( ) 0. NR
( ) 1. All candidates have equal chance
( ) 2. Some candidates have a moderate advantage
( ) 3. Some candidates have a decided advantage

BIBLIOGRAPHY

BOOKS

Alexander, Herbert E. *Financing the 1968 Election*. Lexington, Mass.: D. C. Heath & Co., 1971.

Almond, Gabriel A., and Verba, Sidney. *The Civic Culture: Political Attitudes and Democracy in Five Nations*. Princeton: Princeton University Press, 1963.

Apter, David E. *The Politics of Modernization*. Chicago: University of Chicago Press, 1965.

Armstrong, John A. *The Soviet Bureaucratic Elite: A Case Study of the Ukrainian Apparatus*. New York: Praeger, 1959.

Baltzell, E. Digby. *The Protestant Establishment: Aristocracy and Caste in America*. New York: Random House, 1964.

Barber, Bernard, and Barber, Elinor G. *European Social Class: Stability and Change*. New York: *Macmillan,* 1965.

Barber, James D. *The Lawmakers: Recruitment and Adaptation to Legislative Life*. New Haven: Yale University Press, 1965.

Blalock, Hubert M., Jr. *Social Statistics*. New York: McGraw-Hill, 1960.

Bullitt, Stimson. *To be a Politician*. Garden City, New York: Doubleday, 1959.

Campbell, Angus; Converse, Philip E.; Miller, Warren E.; and Stokes, Donald E. *The American Voter*. New York: John Wiley & Sons, 1960.

Dahl, Robert A., ed. *Political Oppositions in Western Democracies*. New Haven: Yale University Press, 1966.

Dawson, Richard E., and Prewitt, Kenneth. *Political Socialization*. Boston: Little, Brown, 1969.

DeVine, Donald J. *The Attentive Public: Polyarchical Democracy*. Chicago: Rand McNally, 1970.

Elazar, Daniel J. *American Federalism: A View from the States*. New York: Crowell, 1966.

Eckstein, Harry. *Division and Cohesion in Democracy: A Study of Norway.* Princeton: Princeton University Press, 1966.

Epstein, Leon D. *Political Parties in Western Democracies.* New York: Praeger, 1967.

_____. *Politics in Wisconsin.* Madison: University of Wisconsin Press, 1958.

Festinger, Leon; Schachter, Stanley; and Back, Kurt. *Social Pressures in Informal Groups: A Study of Human Factors in Housing.* New York: Harper & Row, 1950.

Francis, Wayne L. *Legislative Issues in the Fifty States: A Comparative Analysis.* Chicago: Rand McNally, 1967.

Greenstein, Fred I. *The American Party System and the American People.* Englewood Cliffs, N.J.: Prentice-Hall, 1963.

_____. *Personality and Politics: Problems of Evidence, Inference, and Conceptualization.* Chicago: Markham, 1969.

Hamilton, Alexander; Madison, James; and Jay, John. *The Federalist Papers.* With an Introduction by Clinton Rossiter. Mentor Books. New York: New American Library, 1961.

Harman, Harry H. *Modern Factor Analysis.* 2d ed. Chicago: University of Chicago Press, 1967.

Hays, Samuel P. *The Response to Industrialism, 1885–1914.* Chicago: University of Chicago Press, 1957.

Hofstadter, Richard. *The Idea of a Party System: The Rise of Legitimate Opposition in the United States, 1780–1840.* Berkeley: University of California Press, 1969.

Huntington, Samuel P. *Political Order in Changing Societies.* New Haven: Yale University Press, 1968.

Jewell, Malcolm E., and Patterson, Samuel C. *The Legislative Process in the United States.* New York: Random House, 1966.

Key, V. O., Jr. *American State Politics: An Introduction.* New York: Alfred A. Knopf, 1956.

_____. *Public Opinion and American Democracy.* New York: Alfred A. Knopf, 1961.

Kingdon, John W. *Candidates for Office: Beliefs and Strategies.* New York: Random House, 1966.

McCormick, Richard P. *The Second American Party System: Party Formation in the Jacksonian Era.* Chapel Hill: University of North Carolina Press, 1966.

Matthews, Donald R. *The Social Background of Political Decision-Makers.* New York: Random House, 1954.

Milbrath, Lester W. *Political Participation: How and Why Do People Get Involved in Politics?* Chicago: Rand McNally, 1965.

Oregon, Secretary of State. *Election Laws, State of Oregon, 1972–1973.* Salem, Ore.: Secretary of State, 1972.

————. *Official Abstract of Votes: General Election 1958.* Salem, Ore.: Secretary of State, 1958.

————. *Official Abstract of Votes: General Election 1962.* Salem, Ore.: Secretary of State, 1962.

————. *Official Abstract of Votes: General Election 1966.* Salem, Ore.: Secretary of State, 1966.

————. *Official Abstract of Votes: Primary Election 1958.* Salem, Ore.: Secretary of State, 1958.

————. *Official Abstract of Votes: Primary Election 1962.* Salem, Ore.: Secretary of State, 1962.

————. *Official Abstract of Votes: Primary Election 1966.* Salem, Ore.: Secretary of State, 1966.

————. *Oregon Blue Book 1957–1958.* Salem, Ore.: Secretary of State, n.d.

————. *Oregon Blue Book 1959–1960.* Salem, Ore.: Secretary of State, n.d.

————. *Oregon Blue Book 1961–1962.* Salem, Ore.: Secretary of State, n.d.

————. *Oregon Blue Book 1963–1964.* Salem, Ore.: Secretary of State, n.d.

————. *Oregon Blue Book 1965–1966.* Salem, Ore.: Secretary of State, n.d.

Palmer, Robert R. *The Age of the Democratic Revolution: A Political History of Europe and America, 1760–1800.* 2 vols. Princeton: Princeton University Press, 1969–1970.

Parry, Geraint. *Political Elites.* New York: Praeger, 1969.

Pierce, Lawrence C.; Frey, Richard G.; and Pengelly, S. Scott. *The Freshman Legislator: Problems & Opportunities. A Handbook on the Oregon Legislature.* Eugene, Ore.: American Political Science Association and Department of Political Science of the University of Oregon, 1972.

Pitkin, Hannah. *The Concept of Representation.* Berkeley: University of California Press, 1967.

Prewitt, Kenneth. *The Recruitment of Political Leaders: A Study of Citizen-Politicians.* Indianapolis, Ind.: Bobbs-Merrill, 1970.

Rush, Myron. *Political Succession in the U.S.S.R.* New York: Columbia University Press, 1965.

Schlesinger, Joseph A. *Ambition and Politics: Political Careers in the United States.* Chicago: Rand McNally, 1966.

Sorauf, Frank J. *Party and Representation: Legislative Politics in Pennsylvania.* New York: Atherton Press, 1963.

U.S. Bureau of the Census. *County and City Data Book: 1962.* Washington, D.C.: Government Printing Office, 1962.

_____. *Statistical Abstract of the United States: 1966.* Washington, D.C.: Government Printing Office, 1966.

_____. *Statistical Abstract of the United States: 1968.* Washington, D.C.: Government Printing Office, 1968.

_____. *U.S. Census of Population: 1960. Vol. I, Characteristics of the Population.* Part 39, Oregon. Washington, D.C.: Government Printing Office, 1963.

Verba, Sidney. *Small Groups and Political Behavior: A Study of Leadership.* Princeton: Princeton University Press, 1961.

Vidich, Arthur J., and Bensman, Joseph. *Small Town in Mass Society: Class, Power and Religion in a Rural Community,* Anchor Books. New York: Doubleday, 1958.

Wahlke, John C.; Eulau, Heinz; Buchanan, William; and Ferguson, LeRoy C. *The Legislative System: Explorations in Legislative Behavior.* New York: John Wiley & Sons, 1962.

Wilson, Woodrow. *Congressional Government: A Study in American Politics.* Boston: Houghton, Mifflin, 1925.

Wylie, Laurence W. *Village in the Vaucluse.* Cambridge: Harvard University Press, 1957.

Zeigler, Harmon, and Baer, Michael A. *Lobbying: Interaction and Influence in American State Legislatures.* Belmont, Cal.: Wadsworth, 1969.

ARTICLES, CHAPTERS, AND MONOGRAPHS

Apter, David E. "Some Reflections on the Role of a Political Opposition in New Nations," in David E. Apter, *Some Conceptual Approaches to the Study of Modernization.* Englewood Cliffs, N.J.: Prentice-Hall, 1968, pp. 72–87.

Browning, Rufus P., and Jacob, Herbert. "Power Motivation and the Political Personality." *Public Opinion Quarterly,* XXVIII (Spring, 1964), 75–90.

Cobb, Edwin L. "Representation Theory and the Flotorial District: The Case of Texas." *Western Political Quarterly,* XXII (December, 1969), 790–805.

Converse, Philip E. "The Nature of Belief Systems in Mass Publics," in David E. Apter (ed.) *Ideology and Discontent.* New York: The Free Press of Glencoe, 1964, pp. 206–261.

Daalder, Hans. "Parties, Elites, and Political Developments in Western Europe," in Joseph LaPolombara and Myron Weiner (eds.) *Political Parties and Political Development.* Princeton: Princeton University Press, 1966, pp. 43–77.

Dawson, Richard E., and Robinson, James A. "Inter-Party Competition, Economic Variables, and Welfare Policies in the American States." *Journal of Politics,* XXV (May, 1963), 265–289.

Dye, Thomas R. "Income Inequality and American State Politics." *American Political Science Review,* LXIII (March, 1969), 157–162.

Edinger, Lewis J., and Searing, Donald D. "Social Background in Elite Analysis: A Methodological Inquiry." *American Political Science Review,* LXI (June, 1967), 428–445.

Eulau, Heinz, and Koff, David. "Occupational Mobility and Political Career." *Western Political Quarterly,* XV (September, 1962), 507–521.

Fiellin, Alan. "Recruitment and Legislative Role Conceptions: A Conceptual Scheme and a Case Study." *Western Political Quarterly,* XX (June, 1967), 271–287.

Hjelm, Victor, and Pisciotte, Joseph P. "Profiles and Careers of Colorado State Legislators." *Western Political Quarterly,* XXI (December, 1968), 698–722.

Kogan, Nathan, and Wallach, Michael A. "Risk-Taking as a Function of the Situation, the Person, and the Group," in *New Directions in Psychology,* III, New York: Holt, Rinehart & Winston, 1967, pp. 111–278.

Labovitz, Sanford I. "Methods for Control with Small Sample Size." *American Sociological Review,* XXX (April, 1965), 243–249.

Lasswell, Harold D. "The Selective Effect of Personality on Political Participation," in Richard Christie and Marie Jahoda (eds.) *Studies in the Scope and Method of "The Authoritarian Personality."* Glencoe, Ill.: Free Press of Glencoe, 1954, pp. 197–225.

Lijphart, Arend. "Typologies of Democratic Systems." *Comparative Political Studies,* I (April, 1968), 3–44.

Main, Jackson T. "Government by the People: The American Revolution and the Democratization of the Legislatures." *William and Mary Quarterly,* XXIII (July, 1966), 391–407.

Miller, Warren E., and Stokes, Donald E. "Constituency Influence in Congress." *American Political Science Review,* LVII (March, 1963), 45–56.

Patterson, Samuel C. "Inter-Generational Occupational Mobility and Legislative Voting Behavior." *Social Forces,* XLIII (October, 1964), 90–93.

————. "The Political Cultures of the American States." *Journal of Politics,* XXX (February, 1968), 187–209.

————, and Boynton, G. R. "Legislative Recruitment in a Civic Culture." *Social Science Quarterly,* L (September, 1969), 243–263.

Ranney, Austin. "Parties in State Politics," in Herbert Jacob and Kenneth N. Vines (eds.) *Politics in the American States: A Comparative Analysis.* Boston: Little, Brown & Co., 1965, pp. 61–99.

Rieselbach, LeRoy N. "Congressmen as 'Small Town Boys': A Research Note." *Midwest Journal of Political Science,* XIV (May, 1970), 321–330.

Rokkan, Stein. "The Structuring of Mass Politics in the Smaller European Democracies: A Developmental Typology," in Otto Stammer (ed.) *Party Systems, Party Organizations and the Politics of New Masses.* 3rd International Conference on Comparative Sociology, Berlin, 1968; Berlin: *Institut für Politische Wissenschaft an der Freien Universität Berlin,* 1968, pp. 26–65.

Rosenzweig, Robert M. "The Politician and the Career in Politics." *Midwest Journal of Political Science,* I (August, 1957), 163–172.

Sartori, Giovanni. "The Sociology of Parties: A Critical Review," in Otto Stammer (ed.) *Party Systems, Party Organizations and The Politics of New Masses.* 3rd International Conference on Comparative Sociology, Berlin, 1968; Berlin: *Institut für Politische Wissenschaft an der Freien Universität Berlin,* 1968, pp. 1–25.

Schachter, Ruth. "Single-Party Systems in West Africa." *American Political Science Review,* LV (June, 1961), 294–307.

Searing, Donald D. "The Comparative Study of Elite Socialization," *Comparative Political Studies,* I (January, 1969), 471–500.

Seligman, Lester G. "Political Change: Legislative Elites and Parties in Oregon." *Western Political Quarterly,* XVII (June, 1964), 177–187.

————. "Political Parties and the Recruitment of Political Leadership," in Lewis J. Edinger (ed.) *Political Leadership in Industrialized Societies.* New York: John Wiley & Sons, 1967, pp. 294–315.

————. "Political Recruitment and Party Structure: A Case Study." *American Political Science Review,* LV (March, 1961), 77–86.

————. "A Prefatory Analysis of Leadership Recruitment in Oregon." *Western Political Quarterly,* XII (March, 1959), 153–167.

————. *Recruiting Political Elites.* New York: General Learning Press, 1971.

Shils, Edward A. "The Intellectuals in the Political Development of the

New States," in Jason L. Finkle and Richard W. Gable (eds.) *Political Development and Social Change.* New York: John Wiley & Sons, 1966, pp. 338–365.

————. "Primary Groups in the American Army," in Robert K. Merton and Paul F. Lazarsfeld (eds.) *Studies in the Scope and Method of "The American Soldier."* Glencoe, Ill.: The Free Press, 1950, pp. 16–39.

Snowiss, Leo M. "Congressional Recruitment and Representation." *American Political Science Review,* LX (September, 1966), 627–639.

Walker, David B. "The Age Factor in the 1958 Congressional Elections." *Midwest Journal of Political Science,* IV (February, 1960), 1–26.

Weinbaum, Marvin G., and Judd, Dennis R. "In Search of a Mandated Congress." *Midwest Journal of Political Science,* XIV (May, 1970), 276–302.

Wright, William E. "Comparative Party Models: Rational-Efficient and Party Democracy," in William E. Wright (ed.) *A Comparative Study of Party Organization.* Columbus, Ohio: Charles E. Merrill Publishing Co., 1971, pp. 17–54.

UNPUBLISHED MATERIALS

Browning, Rufus P. "Businessmen in Politics: Motivation and Circumstance in the Rise to Power." Unpublished Ph.D. dissertation, Yale University, 1960.

Harrington, M. "The Populist Movement in Oregon." Unpublished Master's thesis, University of Oregon, 1935.

Hofferbert, Richard I. "Elite Influence in Policy Formation: A Model for Comparative Inquiry." Paper presented at the annual meeting of the American Political Science Association, Washington, D.C., 1968.

Jones, Judson. "Expectations of Political Opportunity." Unpublished seminar paper, University of Oregon.

Kim, Chong Lim. "Attitudinal Effects of Legislative Recruitment: The Case of Japanese Assemblymen." Paper presented at the annual meeting of the American Political Science Association, Los Angeles, 1970.

Pike, A. H., Jr. "Jonathan Bourne, Jr., Progressive." Unpublished Ph.D. dissertation, University of Oregon, 1957.

Poulton, H. "The Progressive Movement in Oregon." Unpublished Master's thesis, University of Oregon, 1949.

Rummel, Rudolph J. "Understanding Factor Analysis," The Dimensionality of Nations, Project No. 7. Honolulu: University of Hawaii, n.d. (Mimeographed.)

Seligman, Lester G. "Political Leadership: Status Loss and Downward Political Mobility." Paper presented at the annual meeting of the American Political Science Association, New York, 1966.

Wilson, Darryl. "A Study of Political Aspiration in the Oregon Legislature." Unpublished Master's thesis, University of Oregon, 1960.

SELECTED BIBLIOGRAPHY OF ELITE RECRUITMENT

FROM WHAT
Formal and Effective Political Opportunity Structure: Social Status, Education, Occupation, Political Socialization, Motivation and Political Skills.

Apter, David. *The Politics of Modernization.* Chicago: University of Chicago Press, 1967.

Aristotle. *Politics.* Edited by Ernest Barker. New York: Oxford University Press, 1946.

Baldwin, Raymond E. *Let's Go into Politics.* New York: Macmillan, 1952.

Barber, James D. (ed.). *Political Leadership in American Government.* Boston: Little Brown, 1964.

Bell, Roderick. "The Determinants of Psychological Involvement in Politics: A Causal Analysis." *Midwest Journal of Political Science,* XIII (May, 1969), 237–253.

Bendix, Reinhard, and Lipset, S. M. *Class, Status and Power.* Glencoe, Ill.: The Free Press of Glencoe, 1953.

————. "Social Stratification and Political Power." *American Political Science Review* (1952), 357–375.

Bowles, Dean B. "Local Government Participation as a Route of Recruitment to the State Legislature in California and Pennsylvania 1900–1962." *Western Political Quarterly,* XIX (September, 1966), 491–503.

Bowman, Lewis; Ippolito, Dennis; and Donaldson, William. "Incentives for the Maintenance of Grassroots Political Activities." *Midwest Journal of Political Science,* XIII (February, 1969), 126–139.

Boynton, G. R.; Patterson, Samuel C.; and Hedlund, Ronald D. "The Missing Links in Legislative Politics: Attentive Constituents." *Journal of Politics,* XXXI (August, 1969), 700–721.

Browder, Glen, and Ippolito, Dennis S. "The Suburban Party Activist:

The Case of Southern Amateurs." *Social Science Quarterly,* LIII (June, 1972), 168–175.

Browning, Rufus P. "Businessmen in Politics: Motivation and Circumstance in the Rise to Power." Unpublished Ph.D. dissertation, Yale University, 1960.

_____. "The Interaction of Personality and Political System in Decisions to Run for Office: Some Data and a Simulation Technique." *Journal of Social Issues,* XXIV (July, 1968), 93–109.

_____, and Jacob, Herbert. "Power Motivation and the Political Personality." *Public Opinion Quarterly,* XXVIII (Spring, 1964), 75–90.

Bullitt, Stimson. *To Be a Politician.* Garden City, N.Y.: Doubleday, 1959.

Bullock, Charles S., III, and Heys, Patricia L. F. "Recruitment of Women for Congress: A Research Note." *Western Political Quarterly,* XXV (September, 1972), 416–423.

Byrd, Robert O. "Characteristics of Candidates for Election in a Country Approaching Independence: The Case of Uganda." *Midwest Journal of Political Science,* VII (February, 1963), 1–27.

Canon, Bradley C. "The Impact of Formal Selection Processes on the Characteristics of Judges—Reconsidered." *Law and Society Review,* VI (May, 1972), 579–593.

Clubok, Alfred B.; Wilensky, Norman M.; and Berghorn, Forrest J. "Family Relationships, Congressional Recruitment, and Political Modernization." *Journal of Politics,* XXXI (November, 1969), 1035–1062.

Cohen, Michael. "Lawyers and Political Careers." *Law and Society Review,* III (May, 1969), 563–574.

Comer, John C. "The Ideological Consequences of Political Recruitment." Paper presented at the annual meeting of the Midwest Political Science Association, Chicago, 1973.

Connell, R. W. "Political Socialization in the American Family." *Public Opinion Quarterly* (Fall, 1972), 323–333.

Constantini, Edmond, and Craik, Kenneth H. "Women as Politicians: The Social Background, Personality, and Political Careers of Female Party Leaders." *Journal of Social Issues,* XXVIII (1972), 217–236.

"The Constitutionality of Qualifying Fees for Political Candidates." *University of Pennsylvania Law Review,* CXX (November, 1971), 109–142.

Conway, M. Margaret, and Feigert, Frank B. "Motivation, Incentive

Systems, and the Political Party Organization." *American Political Science Review,* LXII (December, 1968), 1159–1173.

Crotty, William J. "The Social Attributes of Party Organizational Activists in a Transitional System." *Western Political Quarterly,* XX (September, 1967), 669–681.

Czudnowski, Moshe M. "Legislative Recruitment under Proportional Representation in Israel: A Model and a Case Study." *Midwest Journal of Political Science,* XIV (May, 1970), 216–248.

―――――. "Sociocultural Variables and Legislative Recruitment: Some Theoretical Observations and a Case Study." *Comparative Politics,* IV (July, 1972), 561–587.

Dahl, Robert. *Who Governs?* New Haven: Yale University Press, 1961.

Davies, James C. "The Family's Role in Political Socialization." *The Annals,* 361 (1965), 10–19.

Dennis, Jack. "Major Problems of Political Socialization Research." *Midwest Journal of Political Science,* XII (1968), 85–114.

―――――. *Socialization to Politics: A Reader.* New York: Wiley & Sons, 1973.

Derge, David R. "The Lawyer as Decision-Maker in the American State Legislature." *Journal of Politics,* XXI, No. 3 (August, 1959), 408–433.

Dogan, Mattei. "Political Ascent in a Class Society: French Deputies 1870–1958," in Dwaine Marvick (ed.) *Political Decision-Makers.* New York: The Free Press of Glencoe, 1961, 57–90.

Downes, Bryan T. "Municipal Social Rank and the Characteristics of Local Political Leaders." *Midwest Journal of Political Science,* XII (November, 1968), 514–537.

Dunn, Charles DeWitt. "Recruitment Patterns among Political Party Chairmen in Different Socio-Political Environments." Paper presented at the annual meeting of the Southwestern Political Science Association, Dallas, 1974.

Edinger, Lewis J. "Political Science and Political Biography (I)." *Journal of Politics,* XXVI (May, 1964), 423–439.

―――――. "Political Science and Political Biography (II)." *Journal of Politics,* XXVI (August, 1964), 648–676.

―――――, and Searing, Donald D. "Social Background in Elite Analysis: A Methodological Inquiry." *American Political Science Review,* LXI (June, 1967), 428–445.

―――――. "Continuity and Change in the Background of German Decision-Makers." *Western Political Quarterly,* XIV (March, 1961), 17–36.

Engstrom, Richard L. "Political Ambitions and the Prosecutorial Office." *Journal of Politics,* XXXIII (February, 1971), 190–194.

Eulau, Heinz. "The Ecological Basis of Party Systems: The Case of Ohio." *Midwest Journal of Political Science,* I (August, 1957), 125–235.

————, and Sprague, John D. *Lawyers in Politics: A Study in Professional Convergence.* Indianapolis, Ind.: Bobbs-Merrill, 1964.

Farley, James A. *Behind the Ballots: The Personal History of a Politician.* New York: Harcourt, Brace, 1938.

Feld, Richard D., and Lutz, Donald S. "Recruitment to the Houston City Council." *Journal of Politics,* XXXIV (August, 1972), 924–933.

Finifter, Ada. *Alienation and the Social System.* New York: Wiley & Sons, 1972.

George, Alexander and Juliette L. *Woodrow Wilson and Colonel House.* New York: W. W. Norton, 1956.

Greenstein, Fred. "Political Socialization." *International Encyclopedia of Social Sciences.* New York: Macmillan-Free Press, 1968, 551–555.

————. *Personality and Politics.* New York: Markham, 1969.

Guttsman, W. L. "The Changing Social Structure of the British Political Elite 1886-1935." *British Journal of Sociology,* II (1951), 122–134.

Hamilton, Howard D. "Legislative Constituencies: Single-Member Districts, Multi-Member Districts, and Floterial Districts." *Western Political Quarterly,* XX (June, 1967), 321–340.

Hanna, William J. "Political Recruitment and Participation: Some Suggested Areas for Research." *Psychoanalytic Review,* LII (Winter, 1965-1966), 407–420.

Heard, Alexander. *The Costs of Democracy: Financing American Political Campaigns.* Anchor Books Edition. Garden City, New York: Doubleday, 1962.

Hirschfield, Robert S.; Swanson, Bert E.; and Blank, Blanche D. "A Profile of Political Activists in Manhattan." *Western Political Quarterly,* XV (September, 1962), 489–506.

Hjelm, Victor, and Pisciotte, Joseph P. "Profiles and Careers of Colorado State Legislators." *Western Political Quarterly,* XXI (December, 1968), 698–722.

Ippolito, Dennis S. "Motivations Reorientation and Change among Party Activists." *Journal of Politics,* XXXI (November, 1969), 1098–1101.

————. "Political Perspectives of Suburban Party Leaders." *Social Science Quarterly,* XLIX (March, 1969), 800–815.

————, and Bowman, Lewis. "Goals and Activities of Party Officials in a Suburban Community." *Western Political Quarterly,* XXII (September, 1969), 572–580.

Jacobs, Herbert. "Initial Recruitment of Elected Officials in the U.S.: A Model." *Journal of Politics,* XXIV (November, 1962), 703–716.

Janowitz, Morris. "The Systematic Analysis of Political Biography." *World Politics,* VI (April, 1954), 405–412.

————. "Social Stratification and the Comparative Analysis of Elites." *Social Forces,* XXXV (October, 1956), 81–85.

Jaros, Dean. *Socialization to Politics.* New York: Praeger, 1973.

Jennings, M. Kent, and Thomas, Norman. "Men and Women in Party Elites: Social Roles and Political Resources." *Midwest Journal of Political Science,* XII (November, 1968), 469–492.

————, and Niemi, Richard G. "Family Structure and the Transmission of Political Values." *American Political Science Review,* 66 (1968).

Jensen, Richard. "Quantitative Collective Biography: An Application to Metropolitan Elites," in R. P. Swierenga (ed.) *Quantification in American History.* New York: Atheneum, 1970, 389–405.

Key, V. O., Jr. *American State Politics: An Introduction.* New York: Alfred A. Knopf, 1956.

Kim, Chong Lim. "Socio-Economic Development and Political Democracy in Japanese Prefectures." *American Political Science Review,* LXV (March, 1971), 184–186.

King, Michael R. "The Structural Determinants of Legislative Recruitment in Oregon." Paper presented at the annual meeting of the American Political Science Association, Los Angeles, 1970.

Kogan, Nathan, and Wallach, Michael A. *Risk-Taking: A Study of Cognition and Personality.* New York: Holt, Rinehart and Winston, 1964.

Kornberg, Allan, and Thomas, N. "The Political Socialization of National Legislative Elites in the United States and Canada." *Journal of Politics,* 27 (1965), 761–775.

————, and Winsborough, Hal H. "The Recruitment of Candidates for the Canadian House of Commons." *American Political Science Review,* LXII (December, 1968), 1242–1275.

————; Smith, Joel; and Clarke, Harold. "Attributes of Ascribed Influence in Local Party Organizations in Canada and the United States." *Canadian Journal of Political Science,* V (June, 1972), 206–233.

Lane, Robert E. *Political Life: Why People Get Involved in Politics.* New York: Free Press, 1959.

————. *Political Ideology: Why the American Common Man Believes What He Does.* New York: Free Press, 1962.

Langton, Kenneth P. *Political Socialization.* New York: Oxford Press, 1969.

————. "Peer Group and School and the Political Socialization Process." *American Political Science Review,* LXI (September, 1967), 751–758.

Lasswell, Harold D. *Psychopathology and Politics,* reprinted in *The Political Writings of Harold D. Lasswell.* Glencoe, Ill.: The Free Press of Glencoe, 1951.

————. "The Selective Effect of Personality on Political Participation," in Richard Christie and Marie Jahoda (eds.) *Studies in the Scope and Method of "The Authoritarian Personality."* Glencoe, Ill.: The Free Press of Glencoe, 1954, pp. 197–225.

Legg, Keith R. "Political Recruitment and Political Crises: The Case of Greece." *Comparative Political Studies,* I (January, 1969), 527–555.

Litwin, George H. "Achievement Motivation, Expectancy of Success, and Risk-Taking Behavior," in John W. Atkinson and Norman T. Feather (eds.) *A Theory of Achievement Motivation.* New York: John Wiley & Sons, 1966, pp. 103–133.

Marcus, George E. "Psychopathology and Political Recruitment." *Journal of Politics,* XXXI (November, 1969), 913–931.

Marvick, Dwaine. "The Middlemen of Politics," in William J. Crotty (ed.). *Approaches to the Study of Party Organization.* Boston: Allyn & Bacon, 1968, pp. 341–374.

Matthews, Donald R. *The Social Background of Political Decision-Makers.* Garden City, New York: Doubleday, 1954.

————. *U.S. Senators and Their World.* Chapel Hill: University of North Carolina Press, 1960.

McConaughy, John B. "Certain Personality Factors of State Legislators in South Carolina." *American Political Science Review,* XLIV (December, 1950), 897–903.

Milbrath, Lester W. *Political Participation: How and Why Do People Get Involved in Politics?* Chicago: Rand McNally, 1965.

Mills, C. Wright. *The Power Elite.* New York: Oxford University Press, 1956.

Monsma, Stephen V. "Potential Leaders and Democratic Values." *Public Opinion Quarterly,* XXXV (Fall, 1971), 350–357.

Morgan, David R., and Kirkpatrick, Samuel A. "Policy Variations, Political Recruitment, and Suburban Social Rank: A Comparative Analysis." *Sociological Quarterly,* XI (Fall, 1970), 452–462.

Neuberger, Richard L. *Adventures in Politics: We Go to the Legislature.* New York: Oxford University Press, 1954.

Nimmo, Dan. (ed.). *Legislative Recruitment in Texas: The Case of Harris County.* Houston, Texas: Public Affairs Research Center, University of Houston, 1967.

Parker, John D. "Classification of Candidates' Motivations for First Seeking Office." *Journal of Politics,* XXXIV (February, 1972), 268–271.

Patterson, Samuel C. "Characteristics of Party Leaders." *Western Political Quarterly,* XVI (June, 1963), 332–352.

————, and Boynton, G. R. "Legislative Recruitment in a Civic Culture." *Social Science Quarterly,* L (September, 1969), 243–263.

"Political Socialization." Entire issue. *Harvard Educational Review,* 38 (Summer, 1968).

Prewitt, Kenneth. "From the Many are Chosen the Few." *American Behavioral Scientist,* XIII (November-December, 1969), 169–187.

————. "Political Socialization and Leadership Selection." *Annals of the American Academy of Political and Social Science,* CCCLXI (September, 1965), 96–111.

————, and Eulau, Heinz. "Social Bias in Leadership Selection, Political Recruitment, and Electoral Context." *Journal of Politics,* XXXIII (May, 1971), 293–315.

————; Eulau, Heinz; and Zisk, Betty. "Political Socialization and Political Roles." *Public Opinion Quarterly,* XXX (Winter, 1966–1967), 569–582.

————, and Dawson, R. *Political Socialization.* Boston: Little Brown, 1969.

Ray, David. "Membership Stability in Three State Legislatures: 1893–1969." *American Political Science Review,* LXVIII (March, 1974), 106–112.

Rieselbach, LeRoy N. "Congressmen as 'Small Town Boys': A Research Note." *Midwest Journal of Political Science,* XIV (May, 1970), 321–330.

Rokkan, Stein. "The Structuring of Mass Politics in the Smaller European Democracies: A Development Typology," in Otto Stammer (ed.) *Party Systems, Party Organizations and the Politics of New Masses.* 3rd International Conference on Comparative Sociology, Berlin, 1968; Berlin: *Institut für Politische Wissenschaft an der Freien Universität Berlin,* 1968, 26–65.

Rosenzweig, Robert M. "The Politician and the Career in Politics." *Midwest Journal of Political Science,* I (August, 1957), 163–172.

Ruchelman, Leonard. "A Profile of New York State Legislators." *Western Political Quarterly,* XX (September, 1967), 625–638.

Salisbury, Robert. "The Urban Party Organization Member." *Public Opinion Quarterly,* XXIX (Winter, 1965), 550–564.

Salamon, Lester A. "Leadership and Modernization: The Emerging

Black Political Elite in the American South." *Journal of Politics,* XXXV (August, 1973), 615–646.

Sartori, Giovanni. "The Sociology of Parties: A Critical Review," in Otto Stammer (ed.) *Party Systems, Party Organizations and the Politics of New Masses.* 3rd International Conference on Comparative Sociology, Berlin, 1968; Berlin: Institut für Politische Wissenshaft an der Freien Universität Berlin, 1968, 1–25.

Schlesinger, Joseph A. "Lawyers and American Politics: A Clarified View." *Midwest Journal of Political Science,* I (May, 1957), 26–39.

――――. "The Structure of Competition for Office in the American States." *Behavioral Science,* V (July, 1960), 197–210.

Searing, Donald D. "The Comparative Study of Elite Socialization." *Comparative Political Studies,* I (January, 1969), 471–500.

Seligman, Lester G. "Political Leadership: Status Loss and Downward Political Mobility." Paper presented at the annual meeting of the American Political Science Association, New York, 1966.

Shils, Edward A. "The Intellectuals in the Political Development of the New States," in Jason L. Finkle and Richard W. Gable (eds.) *Political Development and Social Change.* New York: John Wiley & Sons, 1966, pp. 338–365.

Smith, Roland E. "Political Recruitment and Political Risk in an Oregon Election." Paper presented at the annual meeting of the American Political Science Association, Los Angeles, 1970.

Tullock, Gordon. "Entry Barriers in Politics." *American Economic Review,* LV (May, 1965), 458–466.

Wells, Richard S. "The Legal Profession and Politics." *Midwest Journal of Political Science,* VIII (May, 1964), 166–190.

Wences, Rosalio. "Electoral Participation and the Occupational Composition of Cabinets and Parliament." *American Journal of Sociology,* LXXV (September, 1969), 181–192.

Werner, Emmy E. "Women in Congress: 1917–1964." *Western Political Quarterly,* XIX (March, 1966), 16–30.

――――. "Women in the State Legislatures." *Western Political Quarterly,* XXI (March, 1968), 40–50.

Westby, David L., and Braungart, Richard G. "Class and Politics in the Family Backgrounds of Student Political Activists." *American Sociological Review,* XXXI (October, 1966), 690–692.

Wiggins, Charles W., and Turk, William L. "State Party Chairmen: A Profile." *Western Political Quarterly,* XXIII (June, 1970), 321–332.

Wilkinson, Rupert. *Gentlemanly Power: British Leadership and the Public School Tradition. A Comparative Study in the Making of Rulers.* London: Oxford University Press, 1964.

Wilson, Darryl. "A Study of Political Aspiration in the Oregon Legislature." Unpublished Master's thesis, University of Oregon, 1960.

BY WHOM (Sponsors): Political Parties, Interest Groups, Subcultures, Primary Groups.

Berle, Adolf A., Jr. "Elected Judges–Or Appointed?" in Robert G. Sicigliano (ed.) *The Courts: A Reader in the Judicial Process.* Boston: Little Brown, 1962, 97–103.

Bowman, Lewis, and Boynton, G. R. "Coalition as Party in a One-Party Southern Area: A Theoretical and Case Analysis." *Midwest Journal of Political Science,* VIII (August, 1964), 277–297.

————, and Boynton, G. R. "Recruitment Patterns among Local Party Officials: A Model and Some Preliminary Findings in Selected Locales." *American Political Science Review,* LX (September, 1966), 667–676.

Burns, James MacGregor. *The Deadlock of Democracy: Four-Party Politics in America.* Spectrum Books. Englewood Cliffs, N.J.: Prentice-Hall, 1963.

Cornwell, Elmer E. "Bosses, Machines and Ethnic Groups." *Annals of the American Academy of Political and Social Science,* CCCLIII (May, 1964), 27–39.

Costikyan, Edward N. *Behind Closed Doors: Politics in the Public Interest.* New York: Harcourt, Brace and World, 1966.

Cutright, Phillips, and Rossi, Peter H. "Party Organization in Primary Elections." *American Journal of Sociology,* LXIV (November, 1958), 262–269.

Cotter, Cornelius, and Hennessy, Bernard C. *Politics Without Power: The National Party Committees.* New York: Atherton Press, 1964.

Duverger, Maurice. *Political Parties.* London: Methuen & Co. Ltd., 1954.

Epstein, Leon D. "British Mass Parties in Comparison with American Parties." *Political Science Quarterly,* LXXI (March, 1956), 97–125.

Hennessy, Bernard. "On the Study of Party Organization," in William J. Crotty (ed.) *Approaches to the Study of Party Organization.* Boston: Allyn & Bacon, 1968, 1–44.

Hunt, A. Lee, and Pendley, Robert E. "Community Gatekeepers: An Examination of Political Recruiters." *Midwest Journal of Political Science,* XVI (August, 1972), 411–438.

Key, V. O. "The Direct Primary and Party Structure: A Study of State Legislative Nominations." *American Political Science Review,* XLVIII (March, 1954), 1–26.

Lazarsfeld, Paul F., and Katz, Elihu. *Personal Influence.* Glencoe, Ill.: The Free Press of Glencoe, 1955.

Leuthold, David A. *Electioneering in a Democracy: Campaigns for Congress.* New York: John Wiley & Sons, 1968.

Marvick, Dwaine, and Nixon, Charles. "Recruitment Contrasts in Rival Campaign Groups," in Dwaine Marvick (ed.) *Political Decision-Makers.* Glencoe, Ill.: The Free Press of Glencoe, 1961, 193–217.

Munger, Frank, and Blackhurst, James. "Factionalism in the National Conventions, 1940–1964: An Analysis of Ideological Consistency in State Delegation Voting." *Journal of Politics,* XXVII (May, 1965), 375–394.

Ranney, Austin. "Candidate Selection and Party Cohesion in Britain and the United States," in William J. Crotty (ed.) *Approaches to the Study of Party Organization.* Boston: Allyn & Bacon, 1968, 139–157.

————. "Turnout and Representation in Presidential Primary Elections." *American Political Science Review,* LXVI (March, 1972), 21–37.

————. "Parties in State Politics," in Herbert Jacob and Kenneth N. Vines (eds.) *Politics in the American States: A Comparative Analysis.* Boston: Little Brown, 1965, 61–99.

Seligman, Lester G. "Party Roles and Political Recruitment." *Western Political Quarterly,* XI (June, 1958), 359–361.

————. "Political Recruitment and Party Structure: A Case Study." *American Political Science Review,* LV (March, 1961), 77–86.

Snowiss, Leo M. "Congressional Recruitment and Representation." *American Political Science Review,* LX (September, 1966), 627–639.

Verba, Sidney. "Organizational Membership and Democratic Consensus." *Journal of Politics,* XXVII (August, 1965), 467–497.

Voorhees, Theodore. "The Stake of the Profession in Judicial Selection." *Judicature,* LIII (October, 1969), 146–150.

Watson, Richard A., and Downing, Rondal G. *The Politics of the Bench and Bar: Judicial Selection under the Missouri Nonpartisan Court Plan.* New York: John Wiley & Sons, 1969.

————; Downing, Rondal G.; and Spiegel, Frederick C. "Bar Politics,

Judicial Selection and the Representation of Social Interests."
American Political Science Review, LXI (March, 1967), 54–71.

Watts, Thomas M. "Application of the Attribution Model to the Study of
Political Recruitment: County Elective Offices," in William J.
Crotty (ed.) *Approaches to the Study of Party Organization.* Boston: Allyn & Bacon, 1968, 307–339.

Wellhofer, E. Spencer, and Hennessey, Timothy M. "Political Party Development: Institutionalization, Leadership Recruitment, and Behavior." *American Journal of Political Science,* XVIII (February,
1974), 135–165.

Williams, Oliver P., and Adrian, Charles R. *Four Cities: A Study in
Comparative Policy-Making.* Philadelphia: University of Pennsylvania Press, 1963.

Wright, William E. "Comparative Party Models: Rational-Efficient and
Party Democracy," in William E. Wright (ed.) *A Comparative
Study of Party Organization.* Columbus, Ohio: Charles E. Merrill,
1971, 17–54.

WHAT CRITERIA: Ascription—Age, Family, Social Status, Race, Nationality, Group Affiliation. Achievement—Skill in Organizing, Communicating, Bargaining, Policy Expertise. Historical Studies that Trace Criteria and Socio-Political Change.

Bradley, Donald S., and Zald, Mayer N. "From Commercial Elite to Political Administrator: The Recruitment of the Mayors of Chicago."
American Journal of Sociology, LXXI (September, 1965), 153–
167.

Burling, Robbins. *The Passage of Power.* New York: Academic Press,
1974.

Burnham, Walter Dean. *Critical Elections and the Mainsprings of American Politics.* New York: W. W. Norton, 1970.

Daniel, Johnnie. "Negro Political Behavior and Community Political and
Socioeconomic Structural Factors." *Social Forces,* XLVII (March,
1969), 274–280.

Getter, Russell, and Cigler, Allan J. "A Test of Political Ethos: Environment, Recruitment Culture, and Policy Preferences in Wisconsin
Counties." Paper presented at the annual meeting of the Southwest
Political Science Association, Dallas, 1973.

Heclo, Hugh. "Presidential and Prime Ministerial Selection," in Donald

R. Matthews (ed.) *Perspectives on Presidential Selection.* Washington, D.C.: The Brookings Institution, 1973, 19–48.

Judah, Charles, and Smith, George W. *The Unchosen.* New York: Coward-McCann, 1962.

Main, Jackson T. "Government By the People: The American Revolution and the Democratization of the Legislatures." *William and Mary Quarterly,* XXIII (July, 1966), 391–407.

McCormick, Richard P. *The Second American Party System: Party Formation in the Jacksonian Era.* Chapel Hill: University of North Carolina Press, 1966.

Patterson, Samuel C. "The Political Cultures of the American States." *Journal of Politics,* XXX (February, 1968), 187–209.

Polsby, Nelson W. "Decision-Making at the National Conventions." *Western Political Quarterly,* XIII (September, 1960), 609–617.

————, and Wildavsky, Aaron B. *Presidential Elections: Strategies of American Electoral Politics.* 2nd ed. New York: Charles Scribner's Sons, 1968.

Pomper, Gerald M. "Factionalism in the 1968 National Conventions: An Extension of Research Findings." *Journal of Politics,* XXXIII (August, 1971), 826–830.

Preston, James D. "Identification of Community Leaders." *Sociology and Social Research,* LIII (January, 1969), 204–216.

Rosenblum, Victor G. "Politics and the Judiciary," in James Fesler (ed.) *The Fifty States and Their Local Governments.* New York: Alfred A. Knopf, 1967, 417–430.

Scammon, Richard M., and Wattenberg, Ben J. *The Real Majority: An Extraordinary Examination of the American Electorate.* New York: Coward-McCann, 1970.

Seligman, Lester G. "Political Change: Legislative Elites and Parties in Oregon." *Western Political Quarterly,* XVII (June, 1964), 177–187.

————, and King, Michael R. "Continuities and Discontinuities in the Recruitment of the U.S. Congress, 1870–1970." Paper presented at the annual meeting of the International Political Science Association, Munich, 1970.

Sundquist, James L. *Dynamics of the Party System: Alignment and Realignment of Political Parties in the United States.* Washington, D.C.: The Brookings Institution, 1973.

Walker, David B. "The Age Factor in the 1958 Congressional Elections." *Midwest Journal of Political Science,* IV (February, 1960), 1–26.

Weisberg, Herbert F., and Rusk, Jerrold. "Dimensions of Candidate Evaluation." *American Political Science Review,* LXIV (December, 1970), 1167–1185.

HOW (Selection Mechanisms): Sponsors and Candidates— Cooptation, Conscription, Agency, Bureaucratic Ascent, Self-Recruitment. Electoral Systems and Electoral Competition.

Crotty, William J. "The Party Organization and Its Activities," in William J. Crotty (ed.) *Approaches to the Study of Party Organization.* Boston: Allyn & Bacon, 1968, 247–306.

Danelski, David J. *A Supreme Court Justice Is Appointed.* New York: Random House, 1964.

David, Paul T.; Goldman, Ralph M.; and Bain, Richard C. *The Politics of National Party Conventions.* Washington, D.C.: The Brookings Institution, 1960.

Gilbert, Charles, and Clagne, Christopher. "Electoral Competition and Electoral Systems in Large Cities." *Journal of Politics,* XXIV (May, 1962), 323–349.

Grumm, John G. "Theories of Electoral Systems." *Midwest Journal of Political Science,* II (August, 1958), 357–376.

Harding, Ray M. "The Case for Partisan Election of Judges." *American Bar Association Journal,* LV (December, 1969), 1162–1164.

Hawley, Willis D. *Nonpartisan Elections and the Case for Party Politics.* New York: John Wiley & Sons, 1973.

Jacob, Herbert. "The Effect of Institutional Differences in the Recruitment Process: The Case of State Judges." *Journal of Public Law,* XII (1964), 104–119.

Johnson, Donald Bruce, and Gibson, James R. "The Divisive Primary Revisited–A Case in Iowa." *Department of Political Science, University of Iowa.* The Laboratory for Political Research. Report 42. August, 1971.

Kent, Frank R. *The Great Games of Politics.* Garden City, New York: Doubleday, Doran, 1936.

Keller, Suzenne. *Beyond the Ruling Class.* New York: Random House, 1963.

Lee, Eugene. *The Politics of Nonpartisanship: A California City Election.* Berkeley and Los Angeles: University of California Press, 1960.

Rush, Myron. *Political Succession in the U.S.S.R.* New York: Columbia University Press, 1965.

Turner, Julius. "Primary Elections as the Alternative to Party Competition in 'Safe Districts.' " *Journal of Politics,* XV (May, 1953), 197–210.

Wellhofer, Spencer E. "Dimensions of Party Development: A Study of Organizational Dynamics." *Journal of Politics,* XXXIV (February, 1972), 153–183.

TO WHAT: Specific Political Roles, the Political Career.

Atkins, Burton M., and Baer, Michael A. "The Effect of Recruitment upon Metropolitan Voting Cohesion in the House of Representatives: A Research Note." *Journal of Politics,* XXXII (February, 1970), 177–180.

Bell, Wendell; Hill, Richard J.; and Wright, Charles R. *Public Leadership.* San Francisco: Chandler, 1961.

Black, Gordon S. "A Theory of Political Ambition: Career Choices and the Role of Structural Alternatives." *American Political Science Review,* LXVI (March, 1972), 144–159.

Bowman, Lewis, and Boynton, G. R. "Activities and Role Definitions of Grassroots Party Officials." *Journal of Politics,* XXVIII (February, 1966), 121–143.

Buck, Phillip W. *Amateurs and Professionals in British Politics, 1918–1959.* Chicago: University of Chicago Press, 1963.

Derge, David R. "The Lawyer as Decision-Maker in the American State Legislature." *Journal of Politics,* XXI (August, 1959), 408–433.

Davidson, Roger H. *The Role of the Congressman.* New York: Pegasus, 1969.

Eulau, Heinz; Buchanan, William; Ferguson, LeRoy C.; and Wahlke, John C. "Career Perspectives of American State Legislators," in Dwaine Marvick (ed.) *Political Decision-Makers.* Glencoe, Ill.: The Free Press of Glencoe, 1961, 218–263.

————, and Koff, David. "Occupational Mobility and Political Career." *Western Political Quarterly,* XV (September, 1962), 507–521.

Fiellin, Alan. "Recruitment and Legislative Role Conceptions: A Conceptual Scheme and a Case Study." *Western Political Quarterly,* XX (June, 1967), 271–287.

Fischel, Jeff. "Ambition and the Political Vocation: Congressional Challengers in American Politics." *Journal of Politics,* XXXIII (February, 1971), 25–56.

————. "Party, Ideology, and the Congressional Challenger." *American Political Science Review,* LXIII (December, 1969), 1213–1232.

Hain, Paul L. "Age, Ambitions, and Political Careers: The Middle-Age Crisis." *Western Political Quarterly,* XXVII (June, 1974), 265–274.

Hofferbert, Richard I. "Elite Influence in Policy Formation: A Model for Comparative Inquiry." Paper presented at the annual meeting of the American Political Science Association, Washington, D.C., 1968.

Huckshorn, Robert J., and Spencer, Robert C. *The Politics of Defeat.* Amherst: University of Massachusetts, 1971.

Jones, Bryan D. "Competitiveness, Role Orientations and Legislative Responsiveness." *Journal of Politics,* XXXV (November, 1973), 924–947.

Kessler, James B. "Running for State Political Office," in Cornelius P. Cotter (ed.) *Practical Politics in the United States.* Boston: Allyn & Bacon, 1969, 119–141.

Kim, Chong Lim. "Attitudinal Effects of Legislative Recruitment: The Case of Japanese Assemblymen." Paper presented at the annual meeting of the American Political Science Association, Los Angeles, 1970.

————. "Political Attitudes of Defeated Candidates in an American State Election." *American Political Science Review,* LXIV (September, 1970), 879–887.

————. "Some Effects of Political Status Loss: A Comparative Approach." Iowa City: The Laboratory for Political Research, The University of Iowa, 1968.

————. "Toward a Theory of Individual and Systemic Effects of Political Status Loss." *Journal of Developing Areas,* V (January, 1971), 193–205.

— ——, and Racheter, Donald P. "Candidates' Perception of Voter Competence: A Comparison of Winning and Losing Candidates." *American Political Science Review,* LXVII (September, 1973), 906–913.

Kingdon, John W. "Politicians' Beliefs About Voters." *American Political Science Review,* LXI (March, 1967), 137–145.

Kornberg, Allan. *Canadian Legislative Behavior.* New York: Holt, Rinehart and Winston, 1967.

————. *Legislatures in Comparative Perspective.* New York: D. McKay, 1973.

Lockard, Duane. "The State Legislator," in Alexander Heard (ed.) *State Legislatures in American Politics.* Spectrum Books, 1966, 98–125.

Mazrui, Ali. "Political Superannuation and the Trans-Class Man." *International Journal of Comparative Sociology,* IX (March, 1968), 81–96.

Mezey, Michael L. "Ambition Theory and the Office of Congressmen." *Journal of Politics,* XXXII (August, 1970), 563–579.

Mitchell, William C. "The Ambivalent Social Status of the American Politician." *Western Political Quarterly,* XII (September, 1959), 683–698.

————. "Occupational Role Strains: The American Elective Public Official." *Administrative Science Quarterly,* III (September, 1958), 210–228.

Mulford, Charles L.; Klonglan, Gerald E.; Beal, George M.; and Bohlen, Joe M. "Selectivity, Socialization and Role Performance." *Sociology and Social Research,* LIII (October, 1968), 68–77.

Oleszek, Walter. "Age and Political Careers." *Public Opinion Quarterly,* XXXIII (1969), 100–102.

Patterson, Samuel C. "Inter-Generational Occupational Mobility and Legislative Voting Behavior." *Social Forces,* XLIII (October, 1964), 90–93.

Prewitt, Kenneth. "Political Ambitions, Volunteerism and Electoral Accountability." *American Political Science Review,* LXIV (March, 1970), 5–17.

————, and Nowlin, William. "Political Ambitions and the Behavior of Incumbent Politicians." *Western Political Quarterly,* XXII (June, 1969), 298–308.

Ruchelman, Leonard. *Political Careers: Recruitment Through the Legislature.* Rutherford, N.J.: Fairleigh Dickenson University Press, 1970.

Rustow, Dankwart A. "Succession in the Twentieth Century." *Journal of International Affairs,* XVIII, No. 1 (1964), 104–106. See entire issue.

Schlesinger, Joseph A. *Ambition and Politics: Political Careers in the United States.* Chicago: Rand McNally, 1966.

————. "Political Careers and Party Leadership," in Lewis J. Edinger (ed.) *Political Leadership in Industrialized Societies.* New York: John Wiley & Sons, 1967, 266–293.

Soule, John W. "Future Political Ambitions and the Behavior of Incumbent State Legislators." *Midwest Journal of Political Science,* XIII (August, 1969), 439–454.

Swinerton, E. Nelson. "Ambition and American State Executives." *Midwest Journal of Political Science,* XII (November, 1968), 538–549.

"The Parliamentary Profession." *International Social Science Journal,* Pt. 1, 13, 4 (1961).

Tugwell, Rexford G. *How They Became President: Thirty-Five Ways to the White House.* New York: Simon and Schuster, 1964.

Ulmer, Sidney S. "Public Office in the Social Background of Supreme Court Justices." *American Journal of Economics and Sociology,* XXI (January, 1962), 57–68.

Theory of Political Recruitment and Related Works on Leadership and Political Elites.

Alford, Robert R. *Party and Society: The Anglo-American Democracies.* Chicago: Rand McNally, 1963.

Almond, Gabriel A., and Powell, G. Bingham. *Comparative Politics: A Developmental Approach.* Boston: Little Brown, 1966.

Bachrach, Peter. *The Theory of Democratic Elitism: A Critique.* Boston: Little Brown, 1967.

Baltzell, E. Digby. *The Protestant Establishment: Aristocracy and Caste in America.* New York: Random House, 1964.

Barber, James D. *The Lawmakers: Recruitment and Adaptation to Legislative Life.* New Haven: Yale University Press, 1965.

Beck, Carl, and McKechnie, J. Thomas. *Political Elites: A Select Computerized Bibliography.* Cambridge, Mass.: M.I.T. Press, 1968.

Bottomore, T. B. *Elites and Society.* New York: Basic Books, 1964.

Browning, Rufus P. "Hypotheses about Political Recruitment: A Partially Data-Based Computer Simulation," in William D. Coplin (ed.) *Simulation in the Study of Politics.* Chicago: Markham, 1968, 303–325.

Crotty, William (ed.). *Approaches to the Study of Party Organization.* Boston: Allyn & Bacon, 1968.

Daalder, Hans. "Parties, Elites, and Political Developments in Western Europe," in Joseph LaPolombara and Myron Weiner (eds.) *Political Parties ana Political Development.* Princeton: Princeton University Press, 1966, 43–77.

Dahl, Robert A. (ed.). *Political Oppositions in Western Democracies.* New Haven: Yale University Press, 1966.

————. "A Critique of the Ruling Elite Model." *American Political Science Review,* LII (June, 1958), 463–469.

Dallinger, Frederick W. *Nominations for Elective Office in the United States.* Cambridge, Mass.: Harvard University Press, 1897.

Duverger, Maurice. *Political Parties.* London: Methuen & Co., 1954.

Edinger, Lewis J. (ed.). *Political Leadership in Industrialized Societies.* New York: John Wiley & Sons, 1967.

Eldersveld, Samuel J. *Political Parties: A Behavioral Analysis.* Chicago: Rand McNally, 1964.

Epstein, Leon D. *Politics in Wisconsin.* Madison: University of Wisconsin Press, 1958.

Fischel, Jeff. "Parties, Candidates and Recruitment: West Germany and the United States." Unpublished Ph.D. dissertation, UCLA, 1969.

————. *Party and Opposition: Congressional Challengers in American Politics.* New York: David McKay, 1973.

Frey, Frederick W. *The Turkish Political Elite.* Cambridge, Mass.: M.I.T. Press, 1965.

Huckshorn, Robert J., and Spencer, Robert C. *The Politics of Defeat: Campaigning for Congress.* Cambridge, Mass.: University of Massachusetts Press, 1971.

International Conference on Comparative Sociology, 3rd, Berlin, 1968. *Party Systems, Party Organizations and the Politics of New Masses.* Otto Stammer, editor. Berlin: Institut für Politische Wissenschaft an der Freien Universität Berlin, 1968.

Janda, Kenneth. "Towards the Explication of the Concept of Leadership in Terms of the Concept of Power." *Human Relations,* 13, No. 4 (1960), 345–363.

Keller, Suzanne. *Beyond the Ruling Class.* New York: Random House, 1963.

Kingdon, John W. *Candidates for Office: Beliefs and Strategies.* New York: Random House, 1966.

Kornhauser, William. *Politics in Mass Society.* New York: Free Press, 1959.

Lasswell, Harold D. *Politics: Who Gets What, When, How.* New York: Peter Smith, 1950.

————. *Power and Personality.* New York: Viking Press, 1948.

————, and Lerner, Daniel (eds.). *World Revolutionary Elites: Studies in Coercive Ideological Movements.* Cambridge, Mass.: M.I.T. Press, 1965.

————; Lerner, Daniel; and Rothwell, C. Easton. *The Comparative Study of Elites: An Introduction and Bibliography.* Hoover Institute Studies, Series B, Elites No. 1. Stanford: Stanford University Press, 1952.

Lijphart, Arend. "Typologies of Democratic Systems." *Comparative Political Studies,* I (April, 1968), 3–44.

Marsh, Robert M. *The Mandarins: The Circulation of Elites in China, 1600–1900.* New York: Free Press of Glencoe, 1961.

Marvick, Dwaine (ed.). *Political Decision-Makers.* New York: Free Press of Glencoe, 1961.

_____. "Political Recruitment and Careers," in *International Encyclopedia of the Social Sciences,* Vol. XII. New York: Macmillan, and the Free Press, 1968, 273–282.

Merritt, Richard L. *Systematic Approaches to Comparative Politics.* Chicago: Rand McNally, 1970.

Mosca, Gaetano. *The Ruling Class.* Translated by Hannah D. Kahn. New York: McGraw-Hill, 1939.

Neubauer, Deane E. "On the Theory of Polyarchy: An Empirical Study of Democracy in Ten Countries." Unpublished Ph.D. dissertation, Yale University, 1966.

Neumann, Sigmund (ed.). *Modern Political Parties: Approaches to Comparative Politics.* Chicago: University of Chicago Press, 1956.

Parry, Geraint. *Political Elites.* New York: Praeger, 1969.

Payne, James L. "The Oligarchy Muddle." *World Politics,* XX (April, 1968), 439–453.

Pitkin, Hannah. *The Concept of Representation.* Berkeley: University of California Press, 1967.

Prewitt, Kenneth. *The Recruitment of Political Leaders: A Study of Citizen-Politicians.* Indianapolis: Bobbs-Merrill, 1970.

_____, and Eulau, Heinz. "Political Matrix and Political Representation: Prolegomenon to a New Departure from an Old Problem." *American Political Science Review,* LXIII (June, 1969), 427–441.

_____, and Stone, Allan. *The Ruling Elites: Elite Theory, Power, and American Democracy.* New York: Harper & Row, 1973.

Quandt, William B. *The Comparative Study of Political Elites.* Sage Professional Papers in Comparative Politics, Vol. I, No. 01-004. Beverly Hills: Sage Publications, 1970.

Ranney, Austin. *Pathways to Parliament.* Madison: University of Wisconsin Press, 1965.

Rokkan, Stein; Campbell, Angus; Torsvik, Per; and Valen, Henry. *Citizens, Elections, Parties: Approaches to the Comparative Study of the Processes of Development.* New York: David McKay, 1970.

Rustow, Dankwart A. "The Study of Elites: Who's Who, When, and How." *World Politics,* XVIII (July, 1966), 690–717.

Schlesinger, Joseph A. *How They Became Governor: A Study of Comparative State Politics, 1870–1950.* East Lansing: Governmental Research Bureau, Michigan State University, 1957.

_____. *Ambition and Politics: Political Careers in the United States.* Chicago: Rand McNally, 1966.

Schueller, George K. "The Politburo," in Harold D. Lasswell and Daniel Lerner (eds.) *World Revolutionary Elites: Studies in Coercive Ideological Movements.* Cambridge, Mass.: M.I.T. Press, 1965, 97–178.

Schwartz, David C. "Toward a Theory of Political Recruitment." *Western Political Quarterly,* XXII (September, 1969), 552–571.

Seligman, Lester G. "Elite Recruitment and Political Development." *Journal of Politics,* XXVI (August, 1964), 612–626.

_____. *Leadership in a New Nation: Political Development in Israel.* New York: Atherton Press, 1964.

_____. "Leadership: Political Aspects." *International Encyclopedia of the Social Sciences.* New York: Macmillan, 1968, 107–113.

_____. "Political Elites Reconsidered: Process, Consequences, and Values." *Comparative Politics,* VI (January, 1974), 299–314.

_____. "Political Parties and the Recruitment of Political Leadership," in Lewis J. Edinger (ed.) *Political Leadership in Industrialized Societies.* New York: John Wiley & Sons, 1967, 294–315.

_____. "A Prefatory Analysis of Leadership Recruitment in Oregon." *Western Political Quarterly,* XII (March, 1959), 153–167.

_____. *Recruiting Political Elites.* New York: General Learning Press, 1971.

_____. "Recruitment in Politics." *PROD,* I (March, 1958), 14–17.

_____. "The Study of Political Leadership." *American Political Science Review,* XLIV (December, 1950), 904–915.

Sorauf, Frank J. *Party and Representation: Legislative Politics in Pennsylvania.* New York: Atherton Press, 1963.

Sutton, Francis X. "The Problem of Fitness for Self-Government," in J. Roland Penncok (ed.) *Self-Government in Modernizing Nations.* Englewood Cliffs, N.J.: Prentice-Hall, 1964, 26–49.

Valen, Henry. "The Recruitment of Parliamentary Nominees in Norway." *Scandinavian Political Studies,* I (1966), 121–166.

Wahlke, John C.; Eulau, Heinz; Buchanan, William; and Ferguson, LeRoy C. *The Legislative System: Explorations in Legislative Behavior.* New York: John Wiley & Sons, 1962.

Welsh, William A. "Toward Effective Typology Construction in the Study of Latin American Political Leadership." *Comparative Politics,* 3 (January, 1971), 271–280.

Zartman, T. William. "The Study of Elite Circulation: Who's on First and What's He Doing There?" *Comparative Politics,* VI (April, 1974), 465–488.

INDEX